AF608128

THE PRACTICAL UTOPIANS

THE PRACTICAL UTOPIANS

American Workers and the Cooperative Movement in the Gilded Age

Steve Leikin

WAYNE STATE UNIVERSITY PRESS
Detroit

Copyright © 2005 by Wayne State University Press,
Detroit, Michigan 48201. All rights are reserved.
No part of this book may be reproduced without formal permission.

09 08 07 06 05 5 4 3 2 1

∞The paper used in this publication meets the minimum requirements of the American National Standard for Information Sciences—Permanence of Paper for Printed Library Materials, ANSI Z39.48-1984.

Library of Congress Cataloging-in-Publication Data

Leikin, Steven Bernard.
The practical utopians : American workers and the cooperative movement in the Gilded Age / Steve Leikin.
p. cm.
Originally presented as the author's thesis (doctoral)—University of California, Berkeley, 1992.
Includes bibliographical references and index.
ISBN 0-8143-3128-9 (hardcover : alk. paper)
1. Cooperation—United States—History—19th century. 2. Labor—United States—History—19th century. 3. Working class—United States—Economic conditions—19th century. 4. Labor movement—United States—History—19th century. I. Title.
HD3444.L45 2004
334'.0973'09034—dc22

2004006442

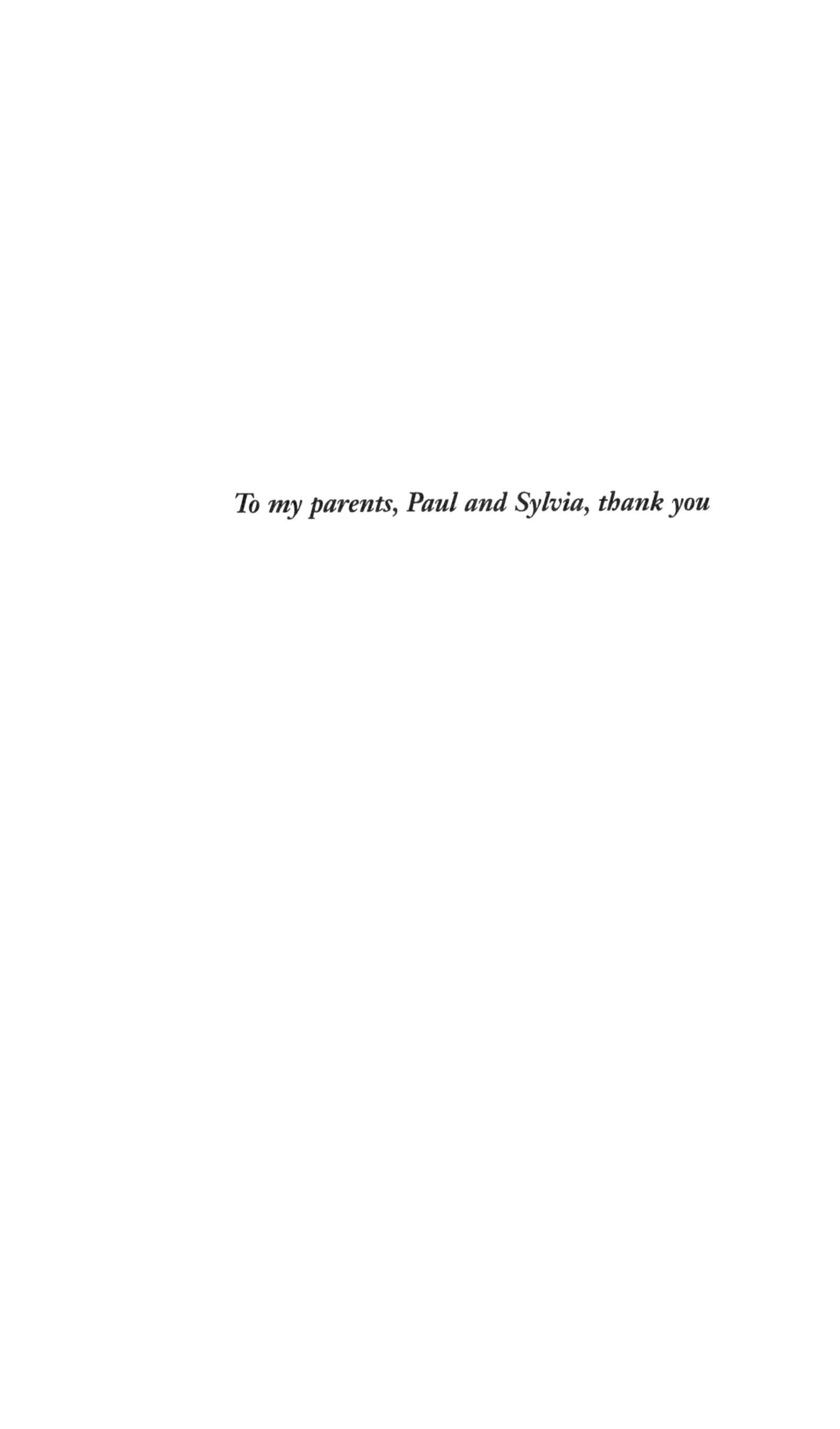

To my parents, Paul and Sylvia, thank you

Co-operation

Brothers for years we've struggled vainly
    In a hopeless up-hill fight.
But at last the clouds are breaking
    Before a gleaming light.

For there is yet one saving hope,
    One gleaming refuge left,
At which tyranny may tremble,
    And be of its power bereft.

And that's the one we've chosen,
    And embrace with willing heart,
Here under the shadow of Plymouth rock,
    We mean to make our start.

For we seek the liberty the Pilgrims sought,
    The rights they would secure,
When they first fled from tyranny,
    They could no more endure.

So we have bound ourselves together,
    Shook off all doubts and fears,
And invested the little savings
    Of bygone better years.

For brothers 'tis the only way,
    This co-operative plan,
By which labor may rule labor,
    And a man may be a man.

Then come and follow up our lead,
    It is one you all will praise,
For it denotes the dawn of a nobler manhood,
    'Tis the harbinger of brighter days.

But the tyrants watch us keenly,
Us the men they so oft stung,
They hope to see our prospects blasted,
And to hear our death-knell rung.

But we have nailed our colors to the mast,
So we are bound to do our best,
And thus, the co-operators of the East,
Send a greeting to the West.

Ajax. *Iron Molders' Journal*, May 1877

Contents

Acknowledgments

This book began too many years ago as a dissertation and has followed me through so many changes that it is just as much witness to, as product of, my life. As witness it has traveled the peripatetic and insecure world of the temporary academic worker. I hope it reflects empathy for the far harsher insecurity that Gilded Age workers experienced. It also accompanied me while I taught in a variety of institutions and met people who gave me their friendship, support, and insight. I owe them much and want to make special note of the following: Laurel Kelly and Walt Brode have been the best of friends through the final stages of writing this book. Jim McClure and Leigh Johnsen were my companions in exile, who commented on my work while also chasing thousands of unreadable documents. Larry Glickman and Ron Rothbart were there at the very beginning when we all began our research into the worlds of nineteenth-century working-class Americans. Sherri Katz read part of this manuscript and has been a wonderful commiserater on the state of our lives. Beverly Burch has helped me in ways I probably can't ever enumerate. My dissertation chair, Paula Fass, and advisors Kim Voss and David Brody, guided me expertly through this project's earliest incarnation. Finally, I want to thank my aunt and uncle, Bertha and Zeke, who sent me a subscription to the *Guardian* when I was an impressionable teenager.

I also want to note the various people, whose names I never knew or have unfortunately forgotten, who helped me in archives large and small, from the unheated Stoneham Historical Society, the Stoneham Public Library, the North Adams Public Library, the Wisconsin State Historical Society, and the Philadelphia Social History Project. Debbie Miller and Ann Kaplan of the Minnesota

Historical Society, two people I can name, were extremely helpful in the most recent phase of this project. Thanks also to the people at Wayne State University Press; Annie Martin and Adela Garcia were both extremely helpful and a pleasure to deal with.

Finally, to Chiye Azuma, my closest friend in the world, our lives are inextricably one.

Introduction

In 1871, a civic booster for the city of North Adams, Massachusetts, published a travel brochure to lure tourists and potential business investors to his small industrial city. Located in the remote and mountainous northwest corner of the state, North Adams, he boasted, had beautiful natural surroundings. The city he described, however, was also a growing industrial center that had nearly doubled its population during the previous decade to over twelve thousand people. Its various industries in 1870 produced cotton and wool cloth, shoes, carriages, sashes and blinds, and paper. As the author moved from factory to factory and shop to shop, describing the local merchants and their wares, he also mentioned, if only in passing, the presence of a shoe factory of some renown. The factory was a cooperative, owned and operated by the shoe workers of North Adams. It seems that the cooperative shoe factory, or more accurately the events surrounding its creation, had recently put North Adams on the map and had given the city a most unwelcome notoriety.[1]

About one year earlier, on June 13, 1870, a crowd of five hundred to a thousand townspeople met at the city's train station to witness a rather remarkable event. The first Chinese contract laborers to arrive east of the Mississippi River were about to enter this unlikely township to live and labor. A local shoe factory owner, Calvin Samson, had imported the seventy-five Chinese laborers, nearly all of whom were under eighteen years of age, from San Francisco in order to replace his workforce of Irish Catholics, native-born New Englanders and French Canadians. Anticipating an uncharitable welcome from his fellow townspeople, Sampson outfitted his factory with a dormitory, kitchen, and fence to protect his new workforce.[2]

The crowd fulfilled Sampson's expectations. The thousand or so townspeople jeered and shouted epithets as Sampson, seven of his own workmen, and three state policemen guarded the new arrivals. According to one account, Sampson emerged from a railroad car, his pockets bulging with six pistols, while his men armed themselves with revolvers and clubs. They then marched the Chinese laborers, phalanx-like, along the quarter-mile stretch to his factory, amid taunts of "rats" and rock throwing. Two townsmen would be arrested by the end of the day for assaulting the young men derisively known as "celestials."

Sampson's decision to import Chinese laborers was the last installment in his strategy to retake control of his factory from the well-organized initiatives of the Knights of St. Crispin, the shoe workers' union. In a larger sense, however, these events reflected the conflicting visions of factory owners and their various workforces all over post–Civil War America. Calvin T. Sampson, the self-made man, and the shoe workers of North Adams, organized into a formidable union, were locked in an ongoing conflict over shop floor control.[3] Sampson, angry and frustrated with the Crispins, described to a state investigator how he "could not stand it, and would not. . . . I found I could not govern my own business." Early in 1870 he reportedly said, "I will show the Crispins that they can't control my business. I will have the Chinese here the first thing you know."[4]

Calvin Sampson had established a reputation for hot-tempered, impetuous behavior, and his actions were anticipated by the shoe workers of North Adams for some time. He had already attempted, unsuccessfully, to lay off his own workers and hire other Crispins from a neighboring town. When this attempt failed to break the local union, Sampson sent his father-in-law to San Francisco to bring back the Chinese contract laborers. Angered by the Crispins' behavior, and apparently piqued by the town's opposition to the Chinese, Sampson continued to act with little restraint. On the evening of the Chinese workers' arrival Sampson accosted a local Crispin with a pistol.[5]

The appearance of the Chinese agitated more than just the laboring elements of North Adams. The *Hoosac Valley News*, a local newspaper, had earlier condemned the use of Chinese workers altogether, and later Lucius Ellis, a provisions retailer, complained to the State Bureau of Labor Statistics of a serious decline in his business: "My customers have largely been among the laboring class, perhaps one-fifth of them shoemakers. . . . The tendency of the coming of the chinamen has been to make trade dull." He was sure a third to a half of the displaced workers had left town with their families.[6] Besides the unhappiness of a retailer such as Ellis, according to one source, "continual pressure was exerted upon the owner [Sampson] by friends, associates, and local tradesmen" to rid the town of his new employees.[7] The arrival of the Chinese presented to the Crispins and to at least some other residents of the city an unwanted affront to the integrity of their community. Sampson's unrestrained self-interest menaced the interests of workers and merchants alike.

The Crispins reacted to the arrival of the Chinese in 1870 in a number of ways. While one account suggests that they attempted to organize the new workers into their union but failed, their overall reaction was quite hostile. Indeed, the new workers dared not venture outside of the factory for their first few weeks in North Adams. While they eventually could mingle in town, and middle-class townspeople attempted to educate them and convert them to Christianity, hostility toward them lingered for years to come. In 1873, a labor dispute between the Chinese and Sampson led to a brutal assault by white townsmen on a group of protesting Chinese laborers. In fact, the very presence of the Chinese in North Adams fueled anti-Chinese sentiment among the Crispins and others and contributed to the success of Chinese exclusion nationwide in 1882.[8]

The Crispins of North Adams developed a defensive and exclusionary labor strategy rooted in class resentments and racial hostility. However, they also challenged Sampson in a way that would resonate with American workers throughout the Gilded Age; that is, they opened their own factory, organized it cooperatively, and operated it democratically. They defied Sampson's power to mold their community in his image.[9] So if the North Adams Cooperative Shoe Factory emerged from a racial defensiveness, it also expressed a manly bravado that typified male working-class republican sentiment in the late nineteenth century.[10] Isaac Tyler, a former employee of Sampson's and soon to be director of the cooperative factory, showed some of this sentiment when he met Sampson on a North Adams sidewalk. Sampson, he recalled, said to him, "'I understand you are going to manufacture goods?' I says: 'We talk of it some.' He answers: 'I am glad of it; I have got my men all hired.' 'Well,' I says, 'we are going to put ourselves as close to you as possible, if we can get the land.'"[11]

In fact, Tyler and thirty other Crispins formed their cooperative in an established factory "only a few rods beyond Mr. Sampson's" a short time later.[12]

A few of the members of the cooperative, all officers at one time or another, Tyler, Oliver Wood, Timothy Riordan, Napoleon Poquette, and Sherman Bateman, reflected the ethnic makeup of the membership at large, a mixture of Irish, French Canadian, and American Protestants. Of the thirty-one initial members, all owned at least one $100 share of stock, which guaranteed them an equal say in the factory's operation. A correspondent for the *New York Tribune* described the cooperative factory as a "little democracy," where, "the men do as they like, and enjoy the privilege." There is, he added, "no one to command and none to obey." Indeed, the cooperative brought a variety of different ethnicities together in a remarkably democratic fashion. Without a hint of irony, however, the reporter also noticed that no woman employed in the shop held stock in her own name. "Several of the shares," he wrote, "set down to the husbands and fathers are understood to belong to the female members of their families."[13]

The exact fate of the North Adams Cooperative Shoe Factory is not known. It functioned well during its first few years of operation; the business grew, orders increased, and its future seemed assured. With the onset of the 1870s depression, though, the factory could not survive more than a couple of years. By 1876 no trace of the business remained. In all likelihood it suffered the consequences of undercapitalization typical of many small businesses. It simply could not ride out an economic downturn of any great magnitude.[14]

This factory was similar to thousands of other factories, workshops, and cooperative stores established by working-class Americans in the years following the Civil War. Through it, shoe workers in North Adams attempted to exert control over their work life and community under new conditions of increasing industrial inequality and instability. They set out with a bravado fueled by republican and democratic sentiments and they intended to build a model for what one well-known Crispin would call an "industrial republic."[15] They understood democracy and republican independence, however, in racial and gendered terms. Whiteness and maleness in North Adams, as in the nation at large, defined citizenship. Their self-made community would not include the Chinese, nor would women workers be visible in the democratic polity of the cooperative.[16]

Yet matters racial and sexual were not so simple in the world of working-class activism in late-nineteenth-century America. Over the next twenty-five years cooperators in the labor movement would tend to be the most liberal among their peers in expanding the pool of "acceptable" citizens. In addition, groups often excluded by the labor movement and cooperators, women and the unskilled, would use the stunted promises of cooperative democracy to demand inclusion in the cooperative polity for themselves. Women, in particular, would use their positions as stockholders to push and pull on the limitations of cooperative democracy, with some success.

Cooperation, as an ideal and as an integral strategy of Gilded Age labor movements, has never received proper scrutiny from historians of working-class America. The extraordinary extent to which untold thousands of American working men and women promoted and established cooperatives in these years alone merits investigation.[17] But rather than explore cooperation on its own terms, historians have generally approached the subject within the well-worn patterns of U.S. labor historiography. Pre-1970s labor historians saw cooperation as an expression of the ideological, middle-class, and backward-looking nature of the labor movement. It represented a utopian impulse appropriately rejected by the practical trade unionism of the American Federation of Labor.[18] Historians who hold to the more recent "republican synthesis" that attributes class consciousness to a working-class interpretation of republicanism identify the advocacy of cooperation sometimes as an expression of republicanism's most radical tendencies, but also, and more accurately, as the product of an ambiguous political legacy.[19] In a recent essay historian Gary Gerstle argues convincingly that republicanism, rather than supporting an unambiguously mature class consciousness, could both "sustain collective visions of escape from wage labor . . . [and support] with equal vigor individualist formulas for escape. . . . [T]he republican thirst for economic independence could lead the same individuals in profoundly different directions."[20] Rather than provide a clear vision for labor, working-class republicanism offered at best an ambiguous set of possibilities.

With all of the foregoing in mind, cooperation is best understood as an effort and vision inspired, in part, by working-class republican ideals. These ideals were, at best, vague and contested and therefore offered no explicit blueprint for cooperative activity. In theory and practice cooperation was contested terrain in which workers struggled over the meanings of independence, citizenship, and democracy, as well as their own ethnocentric, patriarchal, and racist tendencies.

However, the cooperative also functioned as an actual business enterprise designed to solve immediate problems. The workers who established cooperatives sought practical solutions to low wages, job insecurity, threatened craft skills, and community instability. They also created work environments as they would have them, seeking to rid their workplaces, in the words of one cooperative officer, of "unscrupulous bosses."[21] In the process they constructed functioning democratic institutions and they hoped to transform industrializing America into a more democratic society.

Most importantly, then, cooperative self-help was part of a larger struggle among wage earners to assess their democratic experience, ascertain how they would exercise their rights in the economic world, and determine who among them would function as the legitimate laborers and citizens in American society. Indeed, the cooperative expressed working-class America's many possibilities.

Finally, to understand Gilded Age labor's interest in cooperation, we must see it within the context of an increasingly national economy. American cooperators acted locally to establish their factories, workshops, and stores. This was, after all, the very locus of working-class life in late-nineteenth-century America, and where the actual building of cooperatives took place. Cooperators worked, however, within an expanding market economy, and over time, the nature and scope of the problems they faced suggested to them the necessity for some kind of centralized cooperative effort. Though they opposed direct help from the state, some activists in the labor movement of the period argued for a national financial commitment of their own organizations to cooperation. In order to survive the vicissitudes of a market economy, they required the capital or control that local sources alone usually could not provide. They would attempt to do this most notably under the aegis of the most powerful labor organization of the Gilded Age, the Knights of Labor.

The Knights of Labor, in Kim Voss's words, embodied "the second moment of working-class formation" in the United States. Unlike the labor organizations of the pre–Civil War era, the Noble and Holy Order of the Knights of Labor aimed its organizing efforts at a broad cross-section of American workers, skilled and unskilled, white and black, male and female, Catholic and Protestant. It also promoted a vision, rooted in nineteenth-century republicanism, that promised emancipation for wage earners from the "tyranny of wage slavery." Combining the attributes of labor reform and trade unionism, the Knights established a far-flung network of local, district, state, trade, and national assemblies. It reached its peak at seventeen years of age in 1886, the year of the "Great Upheaval," claiming a membership of 750,000.[22]

Many Knights believed they could achieve emancipation through cooperation, and the rapid growth of their organization in the 1880s convinced significant numbers that cooperation would ultimately succeed. However, the order's rapid decline in the latter half of the decade was both a cause and, in part, a consequence of the failure of many cooperatives. As these cooperatives failed, a major thrust of labor republicanism—the viability of collective emancipation from wage labor within a market economy—lost credibility among working-class Americans. When the labor movement regained its momentum in the 1890s, it did so through the American Federation of Labor and its pure and simple trade union philosophy. The AFL never officially repudiated the usefulness of cooperatives, but its leadership did reject the emancipatory vision that so inspired the Knights and other nineteenth-century labor reformers.[23]

Two recent books examining radical movements and labor in the mid- to late-nineteenth-century United States provide a suitable point of departure for this study of American cooperators. Timothy Messer-Kruse's *The Yankee International: Marxism and the American Reform Tradition, 1848–1876* examines the birth of the International Workingman's Association (IWA) in America and its split between American-born radicals influenced by abolitionism, woman's rights, artisanal republicanism, and spiritualism and German immigrant workers under the sway of Marx and his assessment of the American working class. Craig Phelan's *Grand Master Workman: Terence Powderly and the Knights of Labor* rehabilitates the leader of the Knights of Labor, not only from the condemnations of the old labor history but from the criticisms of recent historians who have judged him prickly, incompetent, and a cause of the Knights' ultimate failure. Powderly, in Phelan's view, was a model trade unionist and effective working-class leader. Both of these works are important and innovative contributions to American labor history and explore essential influences on cooperative ideas and activists in this period. However they both mold their studies around a peculiar trope, that is, they find the central struggle for these movements and people to be the conflict between open-minded, accommodating activists and closed-minded, "rule or ruin" radicals, if you will, good guys versus bad guys. Messer-Kruse counterpoises Yankees of the First International, like Victor Drury, radicals willing to fight for the rights of women, African Americans, and labor in a broad-based movement for reform, with Marxist radicals scheming to impose their narrow and ultimately incorrect ideology on the IWA in America. The conflict generated by the Marxists would lead to the demise of the International and the end of an effective native radical tradition. Phelan, on the other hand, sets up the same Victor Drury as the exact opposite, an uncompromisingly narrow-minded radical willing to impose his rule or ruin schemes on the Knights of Labor. He and his ilk did battle with the broad-minded and progressive leadership of Terence Powderly, leading ultimately to the collapse of the Knights.[24]

Clearly, Victor Drury could not be both a broad-minded radical and a sectarian schemer, but besides this contradiction, the two studies, by focusing on sectarian polarities, miss the complexity of "radicalism" in the late nineteenth century. This study will look closely at radicals of this period, including national leaders and local activists as they agitated for and actually built institutions to change the way business was carried out in America. To do this it is essential to examine the interplay between the often vague republican principles motivating reformers and the worlds they helped create. In building cooperatives within their communities reformers had to make choices and refine their ideas. They had to rethink the possible as well as the desirable.

The first chapter of this study presents an overview of cooperative movements and their influences as they emerged in the years before and just after the Civil War. It will argue that cooperators were practical utopians working to meet the immediate needs of their working-class communities while also building models of a new and more moral economic order. Their leaders' experiences, primarily with failed cooperative experiments, will suggest the need for larger national organizations to support new cooperative efforts. Chapter two examines the ideology of cooperation as it evolved from one immersed in a male artisanal ethos to one subject to the realities of community life, the market, and business needs, as well as to the demands of women for inclusion. Chapter three explores both the national and local cooperative activities of the Knights of Labor as the Knights embraced but ultimately cooled to this vision of reform. Chapters four and five study two local and quite successful cooperative movements in Stoneham, Massachusetts, and Minneapolis, Minnesota. Both examples show how central community life was to defining the parameters and definitions of successful cooperation.

CHAPTER I

THE PRACTICAL UTOPIANS

In 1865, a group of labor reformers in Philadelphia, the founders of Union Cooperative Association No. 1, appealed to their fellow workers to unite and "realize better times for themselves and families." They did not call on Philadelphians to join a trade union, though that would have certainly pleased them. Rather, they appealed to wage earners to embrace "cooperation" as the sure path to self-improvement. In the rhetoric of nineteenth-century labor reform, they implored their "brother workmen" to:

> Remember the "bundle of sticks," . . . and band yourselves together. Be of one mind in support of the truth; have faith in the lovely principle of Co-operation, and you may cast your mountain of woe into the sea of oblivion. Co-operation aims at elevating men morally, socially, physically and politically. This it does by freeing them from cankering cares of poverty and wretchedness which chain millions to a merely animal existence, and blessing with the plenty and happiness which come of sympathy and united action for a good end. Enough has been accomplished in a few years to make the hopeful happy and encourage the most desponding. Men of America! Co-operate. Women of America! BUY YOUR GROCERIES AT THE CO-OPERATIVE STORES.[1]

The Union Store activists imagined that this simple reform, the founding of a cooperative store, would materially and spiritually change the lives of American workers. As a practical device the store would supply unadulterated, fairly weighed, and reasonably priced groceries to wage laborers and their families. "Cooperation" would then bring plenty and happiness to working men and women and free them from poverty. The store's goals, however, went far beyond the cheapening of life's necessities. If men acted together for this common end and women purchased groceries at the cooperative stores, they believed, men could elevate themselves as citizens and women fulfill their moral obligations to the family as housewives and mothers. By acting on the "lovely principle of cooperation," the moral, social, physical, and political well-being of American workers could be transformed. Through operating a successful store workers could dramatically alter their world and build a more just republic. Cooperators were practical utopians.

The cooperative store, the very concept of cooperation itself, spoke to a moral vision of the marketplace holding that collective voluntary action could harness, temper, and ultimately transform the market economy. This faith in cooperation appealed to American workers as early as the 1830s, and gained increasing popularity among skilled trade union leaders in the years before the Civil War. After the war, cooperative ideals spread and inspired workers from a variety of trades and skill levels. Labor activists and organizations lent their support, both moral and financial, to the formation of worker-owned enterprises. Between 1865 and 1890, they established a minimum of five hundred producer cooperatives and possibly thousands of consumer cooperatives.[2] The practical experience and utopian goals of the cooperators would act as a dynamic force on the nineteenth-century labor movement.

During the 1830s cooperation first appeared, according to historian Bruce Laurie, as "a major tactical departure" for the fledgling labor movement in the United States. Anticipating an endless battle with employers over wages and working conditions, the National Trades' Union of 1836 recommended cooperation as a permanent solution to strikes and the dilution of craft skills. In 1845, another group of reform-minded mechanics established the Working Men's Protective Union in Boston, a network of cooperatively owned stores and buying clubs. Two years later wage earners in this association had organized forty Protective Union stores in the industrial areas of Vermont, Maine, New Hampshire, and eastern Massachusetts. By the late 1850s thousands of members from communities in New England, New York, and Canada sold basic provisions and groceries in over eight hundred union "divisions."[3]

In addition to these efforts, a small number of skilled workers established cooperative factories and workshops during the 1840s and 1850s. Cordwainers in Lynn, Massachusetts, Pittsburgh, and New York City; molders in Ohio, Pennsylvania, and West Virginia; tailors in Boston; and bakers, shirt sewers, and hat finishers in New York City set up workshops. Wilhelm Weitling and the cooperative movement in Germany inspired German tailors and cabinetmakers in New York City to do the same.[4]

The movement of the 1830s, the Protective Unions and the scattered efforts of craftsmen, did not survive the economic and political turmoil of the antebellum years. The Panic of 1837 drained the resources and the will of the first American labor movement and destroyed its cooperative experiments. Later the Protective Unions fell victim to internal discord, competition from other retail establishments, and the disruption of the Civil War. The fledgling efforts of craftsmen to produce cooperatively also collapsed due to economic decline and wartime disorder.[5]

The ideals of cooperation, however, continued to resonate with American workers as the labor movement reemerged in the 1860s. Cooperation, in fact, captured the imagination of postwar labor leaders. When a group of English immigrants established an insignificant storefront enterprise in Philadelphia, the Union Cooperative Association No. 1, they attracted as members such leading notables in the labor movement as William Sylvis, president of the Iron Molders' Union; Jonathan Fincher, the labor reform newspaper editor of *Fincher's Trades' Review;* and John Samuel, union activist, cooperator, and future Knights of Labor executive. The Union Cooperative Association, one of the first Rochdale cooperatives in America, was just the kind of working-class institution these men hoped would become commonplace among their constituencies.[6]

During the 1850s, American cooperators had learned through British immigrants and the labor press of the stunning achievement of England's Rochdale pioneers. A small group of weavers in the North of England had perfected a system that enabled cooperatives to survive and flourish. As Americans discovered, the key to Rochdale's prosperity was its adaptation to the market system. A Rochdale cooperative store did not rely on the meager resources supplied through small membership fees, the method employed by the Protective Union divisions. In the Rochdale method, members of a society accumulated capital, as in a joint stock enterprise, by selling shares to individual members. Though more securely capitalized than the Protective Union stores, Rochdale enterprises also differed dramatically from joint stock concerns. An individual shareholder held only a limited number of shares that allotted the owner one vote and earned a fixed dividend of no more than 5 percent on the investment. Rochdale stores sold all goods for cash at market prices, with the profits returned to members in proportion to their purchases.[7]

American workers attracted to the ideals of cooperation found such stores to be democratic and better capitalized then their predecessors. The stores also proved more practical, in that they could exist alongside, without directly antagonizing, neighborhood shopkeepers. Having reckoned with the marketplace, cooperators had learned the rules of the game. By 1863, cooperation in this new and more practical form emerged as a force in the labor movement. John Samuel, the cooperative enthusiast from Philadelphia, estimated that one hundred cooperative stores opened for business during the Civil War era, many of them built on the Rochdale system.[8]

More than in the antebellum period, many of the wage earners who promoted Rochdale stores also championed cooperative production, and they derived their principles, in part, from the propagandizing efforts of George Jacob Holyoake, one of England's preeminent Rochdale-inspired cooperators. His influential pamphlet, *Self-help by the People: History of Co-operation in Rochdale*, was first reproduced, in summary form, in the United States by Horace Greeley's *New York Tribune* before the Civil War. Union journals and labor newspapers copied additional Holyoake pamphlets as well as other sources of information on Rochdale with far-reaching effect. In 1864, one Philadelphian recalled how he often thought "of the first 'shilling' pamphlet we had from Mr. Holyoake," as he watched the proceedings at his own cooperative store.[9]

Holyoake described in *Self-help* how the Rochdalers implemented their system in stores and factories, and he established the model by which many American cooperators judged their own efforts. In Rochdale's factories, Holyoake explained, each worker was required to purchase five shares of stock. They received as shareholders 5 percent interest on their investment, and the association divided the surplus profits equally between members by share and workers in proportion to their wages.[10] In practice, Holyoake's pamphlet notwithstanding, the Rochdale movement in England had actually moved away from this form of cooperative production. By 1862 the English Rochdale societies had officially rejected any dividend to labor. Indeed, they grew increasingly preoccupied with retail stores alone. Though Holyoake and his allies continued to promote productive cooperation, the initiative fell to the advocates of consumer cooperation who came to dominate the English movement.[11]

Cooperators in the United States after the Civil War often cited Rochdale as their inspiration, yet they, too, deviated from Holyoake's model, as well as from the Rochdalers themselves. Unlike the English cooperators, who now focused primarily on stores, the Americans pursued both productive and distributive cooperation, and often advanced retail stores as a means to accumulate capital for production. In addition, only a small number of American cooperators ever paid a dividend on labor. Some associations required equal stock ownership among workers and paid dividends on that investment, while others simply paid a dividend on shares owned. Under American conditions, these deviations from the labor dividend did not necessarily violate cooperative principles. They did, however, indicate the variability and vagueness of the cooperative visions held by American reformers.

In the 1860s and early 1870s the Americans who experimented with Rochdale and its variations came largely from the ranks of shoe workers, molders, carpenters, machinists, clothing workers, cigar makers, and printers. Between 1866 and 1876, shoe workers operated at least forty cooperative factories, and molders ran at least thirty-six foundries. Both trades established cooperative stores. In addition, bakers, coach makers, collar makers, coal miners, shipwrights, nailers, ship carpenters and caulkers, glassblowers, hatters, boilermakers, plumbers, and iron rollers organized cooperative enterprises.[12]

These cooperators were most often, but not exclusively, skilled craftsmen or factory artisans, and they labored in a myriad of trades that varied significantly in skill level and degree of mechanization. Their decision to cooperate could, but did not necessarily, emerge from a direct threat to their skills. Shoe workers, for example, had long before left the artisanal milieu of the ten-footer and now worked as factory artisans in an increasingly machine-dominated environment. Though small shoe factories that employed all-around craftsmen still existed, by the 1870s they occupied an ever smaller segment of the industry. In the larger factories, production still required skilled labor (lasting remained an unmechanized craft for most of the century), but the heelers, trimmers, burnishers, and finishers often worked with machinery and had few of the skills of the old shoemaker.[13]

Iron molders also worked in a factory setting, but they were highly skilled craftsmen, unthreatened by machinery until the end of the century. They were menaced principally in this period by the reorganization and specialization of their labor and the breakdown of the apprentice system. In stove molding, for example, founders hired individual molders to produce separate pieces of a stove rather than the entire product and then had the pieces assembled by less-skilled workers. Employers attempting to further undercut the molder's power over his own labor trained apprentices in limited aspects of the molding process.[14]

Worker-owned factories reflected these differences in the uneven development of various industries. Shoe workers often used the most advanced machinery in their own factories. Molders established foundries to set union standards for apprenticeship and shop rules. Clearly, some cooperators attempted to preserve their craft traditions while others adapted factory production to their own ends.[15]

If the immediate threat of deskilling was not their universal experience or the recovery of lost skills their collective goal, the cooperators did face a common threat from wage reductions, vulnerability to market forces, and the constant threat of disruption to their community lives. After the war the conditions of a growing national market and prolonged deflation intensified competition among employers and made the wages and power of the workforce an obstacle to profitability. The increased, though uneven, mechanization and reorganization of production, as well as the conflict over wages that resulted are now well understood.[16] The workers who formed cooperatives perceived these developments through the artisanal ideology of the labor movement, yet they did not act simply to preserve or resurrect craft skills. They cooperated to protect their independence and build community while they approached production pragmatically with an eye to success in a competitive market.

This should not suggest that the cooperatives that preserved skills were quixotic gestures of status-threatened artisans. They could be, in many cases, viable economic alternatives to individually operated business concerns. Since traditional methods of production persisted well into the 1870s and the introduction of machinery did not necessarily foster economies of scale, small factories could be as, or more, efficient than larger ones.[17] If the capital requirements remained low enough, cooperators could enter a market and compete successfully. In addition, when skilled workers cooperated to protect their authority and power, they usually did so as long as it made for a viable business strategy. They reluctantly employed the newest machinery when competition required them to do so or face defeat in the marketplace. Cooperators could act pragmatically, and their objectives had as much to do with stability and efforts to create community than with a will to preserve craft skills.

The cooperators, in fact, acted as members of geographic communities, and they attempted to stabilize community life through their experiments with factories and stores. In cities like Charlestown, Massachusetts, and Philadelphia, Pennsylvania, city-wide trade assemblies or less formal coalitions of trade unionists established the first cooperative stores in the 1860s. Unionists created them as practical measures to lower the cost of necessities but also they celebrated them as centerpieces of the local labor movements.

Charlestown's cooperative, the Workingmen's Charitable Association, was one of over fifty cooperative associations formed in Massachusetts during and immediately following the Civil War.[18] Established by the city's leading trade unionists in 1864, its board of directors consisted of members of the Machinists' and Blacksmiths', Molders', Shipwrights', and Carpenters' and Joiners' Unions. The two top officers, president George H. Spaulding and secretary J. W. Simpson, were union activists in the Molders' and Carpenters' Unions, respectively, and they ran the store exclusively for trade unionists.[19]

Organized initially under the old Protective Union plan, the association managed to survive the first few months of operation. Meanwhile, an example of the Rochdale system thrived in neighboring Lawrence, Massachusetts, and the success of several stores in Philadelphia was discussed at length in *Fincher's Trades' Review*, the popular labor newspaper. Within a few months Charlestown's cooperators adopted the system and became Rochdale enthusiasts.[20]

The members of the association developed a broad agenda for labor reform. Promoting eight-hour legislation and cooperation, they gained control of the local Republican Party and, in 1865, Spaulding and other members of the cooperative store won election to the town's board of aldermen. At about the same time, the citizens of Charlestown sent a local shipwright, Jeremiah Remick, to represent them in the General Court. Along with other labor reformers in Massachusetts, they combined forces in a short-lived alliance with sympathetic members of the Republican party to pass reform legislation.[21]

In the early months of 1866, a committee of Charlestown's cooperators, flush with their recent political success, drafted a bill to present to the state's General Court. The bill established a legal corporate existence for cooperative businesses and codified changes they had instituted in their own store a few months before. Foremost among these changes was the main provision of the Rochdale plan, which allowed for the distribution of profits in proportion to members' purchases or the earnings of employees. Charlestown's local representative, labor reformer Remick, introduced the bill in February 1866 and it became law, with minor amendments, within four months. Massachusetts became the only state in New England to legalize cooperative associations during the nineteenth century.[22]

Simpson and Spaulding, the officers of the Workingmen's Charitable Association, had high hopes for cooperation and its capacity to alter working-class life. Practical in their efforts to answer the immediate needs of their working-class constituency, they developed a larger agenda for cooperation that pushed them beyond the limited efficacy of one cooperative store. In 1865, Simpson convened with other reformers to establish a central buying agency for all of New England's cooperative associations.[23] Spaulding, after organizing a cooperative foundry in Boston, called on the Molders' Union to encourage its members in similar efforts. He submitted, as a member of the union's Committee on Cooper-ation, a report recommending rules for worker-owned foundries similar to those recently enacted in Massachusetts. Under his plan the national union would have facilitated the growth of cooperation among iron molders by providing both the start-up capital and the guidance needed for success.[24]

The movement for worker-owned enterprises began in Philadelphia in the 1860s, as it did in Charlestown, as the work of trade unionists from a variety of occupations. In Philadelphia, however, the experiences of these men with the running of cooperative enterprises and organizations affected the national labor movement and its future development. The city's trade union movement produced an array of nationally significant leaders. Union men, such as William Sylvis, Jonathan Fincher, John Samuel, Thomas Phillips, James Wright, Frederick Turner, John Shedden, and Uriah Stephens, experimented with cooperation and directed the fortunes of nearly every major labor organization in the city. Their local efforts to ameliorate conditions for their working-class constituencies served as a starting point for a more grandiose cooperative vision. These men became key spokesmen for cooperation in the labor movement from the 1860s through the decline of the Knights of Labor.[25]

Philadelphia's labor movement had endorsed cooperation in the 1830s, and throughout the antebellum years workers in the city attempted to set up cooperatives. The first cooperative established after 1860 marked a qualitative change from the prewar period. Organized by a small group of English immigrants, the Union Cooperative Association No. 1 (UCA) was one of the first Rochdale stores in the United States. The principal organizer, Thomas Phillips, spent his early years as an apprentice shoemaker in England, and he rooted his political convictions firmly in Chartism. After he arrived in the United States in 1852, he immersed himself in the labor movement and a variety of reform causes. "[M]ovements," Phillips wrote, "such as the question of slavery, eight hours, and general labor matters engaged my attention; and among others was the co-operative, which was just beginning to be stirred up by the publication of [George] Holyoke's [*sic*] 'History of Co-operation in Rochdale.'"[26] The cooperative store was a product of this propagandizing effort and a magnet drawing other English immigrants of like mind to it.

Phillips and eleven other workingmen organized their cooperative association in December 1862. Gathering weekly for over a year in Phillips's South Philadelphia home, they studied the Rochdale system and slowly accumulated capital to commence

CO-OPERATIVE TRACT,

No. 1.

WHAT IS CO-OPERATION?

Co-operation is a united movement by working men to realize better times for themselves and families.

How?

Through Co-operation, or union, in getting and saving. Oh! the vast strength of unity! Remember the "bundle of sticks," brother workmen, and band yourselves together. Be of one mind in support of the truth: have faith in the lovely principle of Co-operation, and you may cast your mountain of woe into the sea of oblivion. Co-operation aims at elevating men morally, socially, physically and politically. This it does by freeing them from the cankering cares of poverty and wretchedness which chain millions to a merely animal existence, and blessing with the plenty and happiness which come of sympathy and united action for a good end. Enough has been accomplished in a few years to make the hopeful happy and encourage the most desponding. Men of America! Co-operate. Women of America! BUY YOUR GROCERIES AT THE

CO-OPERATIVE STORES,

where you can depend on the GENUINE ARTICLE and FULL WEIGHT. Hundreds of families have already felt the advantage of doing so. Nothing is tampered with to please the eye. There is no trust, therefore no risk. All who buy at those stores share the profits. Shares may be paid up at once, or by installments of ten or more cents a week. Working men and working women join the Co-operative corps, and together help to fight this great

A flyer promoting Union Cooperative Association, No. 1 of Philadelphia, 1860s. Wisconsin State Historical Society.

shopkeeping. Finally, after fifteen months of preparation, twenty-two members opened "one of the brightest spots in the earth . . . the little dingy one-story Co-operative shop."[27] At this inconspicuous storefront a handful of workers tried to eke out a better existence for themselves and play out their utopian aspirations.

Thomas Phillips, life-long advocate of cooperation and union leader from Philadelphia. Wisconsin Historical Society.

Like the shareholders of the cooperative stores that would open in Charlestown, the Union Cooperative Association's original members were predominantly skilled workers and factory artisans. In April 1865, they included eleven shoe workers, six tailors, four machinists, two molders, one carpenter, one car builder, one block maker, a glassblower, two clerks, two housekeepers (both women), two dealers, a corn merchant, and one editor. These activists also organized a broad cross-section of workers in their citywide trades' assembly.[28]

The cooperators built an organization to service their immediate neighborhoods. The majority of the earliest members resided within a few blocks of the store, where they could choose from an array of meats, fruits, and vegetables. The store, though faced with competition from retailers with greater resources and larger inventories, earned enough after the first quarter to pay a 5 percent dividend on stock and a 12 percent dividend on purchases to members.[29]

The Union Cooperative Association's significance for the labor movement loomed much larger than its meager resources justified. Prominent Philadelphia labor leaders William Sylvis, Jonathan Fincher, John Samuel, and John Shedden joined the association and fostered its growth through their publications and speaking engagements. These men gathered around the offices of *Fincher's Trades' Review*, agitated for unionism, and influenced the progress of cooperation well into the 1870s.[30]

Jonathan Fincher, one-time secretary of the Machinists and Blacksmith's Union and the owner and editor of the *Review*, orchestrated an effective campaign to promote cooperation far beyond the borders of Philadelphia. Correspondents from Charlestown, Massachusetts, for example, gave credit to the *Review* for encouraging cooperation in their city, and the newspaper's reports of the cooperative in neighboring Lawrence brought, in the words of the secretary, "deputations from various parts of New England and letters from Maine, Massachusetts, Connecticut, New York, Pennsylvania, Ohio, Indiana, Illinois, Michigan, Kentucky, and Missouri asking for information with regard to our system."[31]

William Sylvis, president for a time of both the Iron Molders' Union and the National Labor Union, was a principal figure in the cooperative movement of the 1860s. In 1866 he predicted that molders would one day control their own industry through cooperative production, and as editor of the *Iron Molders' Journal* and a frequent contributor to Fincher's newspaper he promoted that end in numerous articles. Well aware of European cooperative movements, Sylvis was particularly impressed by the Rochdale pioneers and reported efforts to establish cooperative banks on the Continent. Under his influence the Molders' Union established an "International" foundry in Pittsburgh in 1868 in what was to be a first step toward the end of wage labor among iron molders.[32]

John Samuel, born in South Wales in 1817, organized the Philadelphia glassworkers in the years before the Civil War. His first known role as public advocate of cooperation began in 1866 when the UCA authorized him to lecture to the trade unions of the city. Samuel moved to St. Louis in the early 1870s and championed cooperation as the associate editor of *Coleman's Rural World*, a Grange publication. He engaged in a succession of cooperative initiatives during the next two decades as an organizer for the Sovereigns of Industry (a cooperative reform association), a founder of a

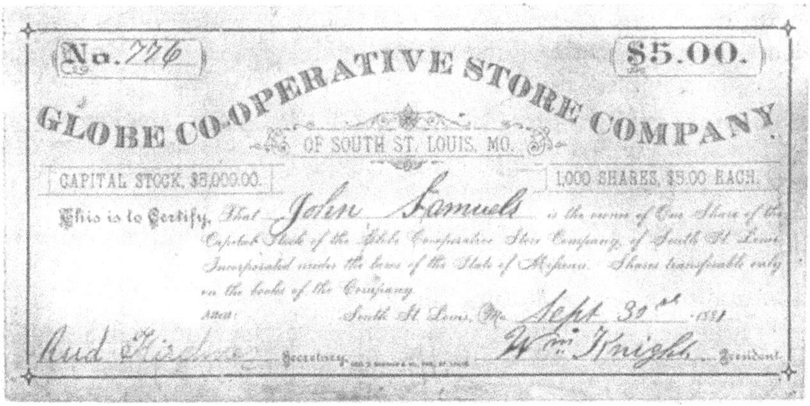

1881 cooperative stock certificate in the name of John Samuels. Wisconsin Historical Society.

cooperative labor newspaper in St. Louis in 1881, the force behind a cooperative coal outlet in 1883, the founder of a cooperative grocery store in 1885, and a member of the Knights of Labor Cooperative Board from 1884 to 1886. In addition, he authored the most influential how-to pamphlet on cooperation distributed by the Knights of Labor in the 1880s.[33]

John Sheddon, a Yorkshire-born tailor and labor activist before the Civil War, was well known in labor reform circles in Philadelphia. The local section of the International Workingmen's Association selected him as an officer, and he became state leader and ultimately president of the Sovereigns of Industry in the 1870s.[34]

To these men the Union Cooperative Association was the symbol of a new order, and they joined with the hope that their first cooperative endeavor would inspire the laboring population of Philadelphia and the nation. Thomas Phillips assumed the most prominent role as salaried chief manager of the store. He propagandized tirelessly in the *Review* under the pseudonym "Worker" and carried on an extensive correspondence with wage earners interested in cooperation. Phillips also organized a wholesale distributorship from which individual workers and cooperatives outside of Philadelphia could purchase goods. Each week, Fincher published the central store's wholesale list of approximately 150 items, and orders and inquiries arrived from all over the region. Miners from St. Clair, Pennsylvania, Mineral Ridge, Ohio, and Westernport, Maryland; railroad machinists and blacksmiths from Fort Wayne, Indiana; and other workers from cities like Beaver Falls, Reading, New Brighton, and Pittston, Pennsylvania, corresponded with Phillips to order goods or request information on cooperation. Though many faced obstacles, such as the closing of mines and unemployment in St. Clair or the opposition of shopkeepers in Reading, the movement appeared to have a promising future.[35]

Philadelphia's Union Cooperative Association, in fact, had grown and performed admirably. Its membership rolls, though never very large, expanded as the store grew from one main shop on Federal Street to include two stalls in a local farmers' market and a branch store on Market Street. The cooperators' success drew the attention of other workers, and in the early months of 1866 the association absorbed two pre-existing cooperatives from the northern part of the city. Having established a third branch store of the UCA, some members anticipated opening eight or ten more affiliated cooperatives.[36]

To Phillips and his associates the meaning of cooperation lay in its ability to meet the practical needs of a working-class neighborhood. "Cooperation," they stated simply, "is the united movement by working men to realize better times for themselves and families."[37] Providing its members with the necessities of life at fair prices, a cooperative store would rid them of retailers, the so-called middlemen, who produced nothing of their own yet added "five or six profits" to the price of goods.[38]

The Union Cooperative Association had, though, a more visionary goal. In their statement of purpose and in their own propaganda the founders spoke of a new way of conducting business. Cooperation would eliminate the dealers who "notoriously adulterate every article capable of adulteration and practice every spesies [*sic*] of fraud to such an extent as to render it almost impossible for a man or a woman to purchase good or wholesome articles for family use."[39] In a handbill promoting the store, a woman and shareholder described the benefits of the cooperative way of doing business to her neighbor:

> the simple honesty with which our business is conducted disarms suspicion, for we have no interest in deceiving or cheating our customers. . . . On the contrary our interest lies in the

> direction of removing all cause of suspicion, for we can assure you from experience obtained under the old system that it is a terrible thing to stand day after day in a place of business, subject to the suspicion and distrust of the customers as they come in, one after the other, doubting your every word, and suspecting your every act . . . and our present system of doing business is a wonderful and pleasant relief from it. It is worth something in this life to mingle in honest society, and realize that those around you trust and respect you, and require nothing of you but that which is consistent with honor. Under our system of doing business we can act in all things in the spirit of sincerity and truth, and consequently we consider the personal experience—the development of qualities simply honest—the strengthening of the whole moral character which results from our system, pays us well, independent of any moneyed gain.[40]

The cooperative, and the sense of community it hoped to foster, harkened back to the intimacy of the small town. To the participants this was no mere idyll. One member remarked on the patience of the customers, who, "knowing the attendants for old and tried friends, converse with them as such; so that the place has more the aspect of a social gathering than of an ordinary store." They encouraged this "social" atmosphere by setting aside a room "for the members to cultivate each other's acquaintance in," and they dedicated a percentage of their profits to a library and reading room fund.[41] Phillips even suggested that security requirements be lax for members occupying positions of trust. "Security," he wrote, "elevates the honor of property not what cooperators should have faith in which is human nature."[42] In the better world Phillips envisioned, "every member of the community would have an interest in every other member's welfare."[43]

The men of the association welcomed women's support for the ennobling moral power of the cooperative store. They welcomed women, however, not as participants in the labor movement but as wives and agents of virtue. Indeed, they conceived of the cooperative's moral universe as an extension of the virtuous home cultivated by mothers and wives. When we reflect, Phillips wrote, "on the destruction of morals which takes place under the old system of deception and fraud, we think we have a right to expect the support of the women in what we are doing; for what mother would not feel interested in supporting a system which would train her boy to be truthful in his dealings."[44] In the cooperative world, a moral space opened up for women to participate as virtuous mothers and wives in the public sphere of working-class life. This space, though, was riddled with ambiguities. Within the ideology and practice of cooperation lay contradictory notions capable at one moment of expanding the parameters of women's participation and at the next moment of reinforcing gender hierarchy and exclusivity.

The members of the Union Cooperative Association were enthusiastic and rapidly expanded their enterprise. According to Phillips, however, their missionary zeal overcame their good business sense and "the cry that the store must go to the people, instead of the people must come to the store, was the loudest. . . . Trade and membership did not increase in proportion to the outlay. Profits ceased. Business fell off and branch no. 1 was closed, being located among a class of people who cared not for cooperation. The summer soldiers and sunshine cooperators began to withdraw their stock and throw a wet blanket over the concern."[45]

As they spread their resources too far, members lost confidence and withdrew their shares. Yet not all shareholders removed themselves from the enterprise. One branch store defied the authority of the association and resisted its order to close.[46] In one last desperate attempt to preserve the cooperative, Phillips and six other members offered to subscribe $50 each if fifty more people would do the same. Knowing the significance of the store and the publicity it had received, they feared the consequences of its collapse: "If the Union Cooperative Association #1 of Philadelphia fails to carry out its objects it will entail a blow on the cooperative movement that will be felt not only in this city but throughout this country to the great and lasting injury of the movement, and to the disgrace of the working population of this city."[47]

The Union Cooperative Association was an important symbol to the participants as much as it was an enterprise designed to meet the immediate needs of its members. Yet Phillips was wrong. Its failure in November 1866 hardly dampened the enthusiasm of the cooperators and labor leaders. Sylvis, for one, continued to promote cooperation vigorously in the molders' union. His influence within the National Labor Union led that organization to champion currency reform and cooperation. Between 1866 and 1869, Philadelphia's molders, carpet weavers, machinists, and printers established productive enterprises. Cooperation, meanwhile, remained a priority for Thomas Phillips and John Shedden as well as the workers of Philadelphia, who nursed the fledgling Knights of Labor into the 1870s.[48]

Despite the passing of the UCA, the preeminent labor organization in Philadelphia, the Knights of St. Crispin, endorsed the principle of cooperation with much enthusiasm in 1869. The Crispins not only believed in the efficacy of cooperation but had organized factory workers into an effective national trade union of unparalleled strength. Though they considered supporting local cooperatives through a central union fund, the Crispins, like other national labor unions of this period, were decentralized. Their interest in cooperation remained enthusiastic but local. In Massachusetts, for example, the Crispins had already established between thirty and forty cooperative stores by October 1869. In addition, shoe workers started at least eight cooperative shoe factories in 1869, five in 1870, and eleven in 1871.[49]

The Crispins in Philadelphia grew rapidly and by 1870 had organized as many as three thousand members. Undeterred by the Union Cooperative Association's failure, they turned to cooperative production following two lockouts of their members in 1870. The state lodge, under Thomas Phillips's leadership, "decided to open a Manufactory that shall belong to the journeymen of Philadelphia." They did so "to enable the unemployed to earn the amount as wages which was heretofore given in like cases as a gratuity," but continued to operate the factory long after the lockout ended. The Crispins subsidized the factory with a $2 per capita assessment on the state's membership.[50]

Their enthusiasm, however, could not compensate for their lack of capital. Despite the fact that the state lodge required all members to purchase a five-dollar share in 1871, they had to solicit more donations within a year. At the same time bitter factional infighting developed over membership requirements for the cooperative. One group of shoe workers sought to restrict membership in some manner, while Phillips and his supporters "insisted upon the organization of a genuine cooperative association in which every member of the order could be members if they wished." Once Phillips's faction secured control over the factory, they procured a charter and required each member to purchase a $200 share in weekly installments of one dollar.[51]

As president of the factory, Phillips now had the opportunity to prove the efficacy of cooperative production. His ability to provide work for the Crispins, however, ebbed and flowed, as in other factories, with the seasonal nature of shoe production. In June 1872, for example, the factory employed between thirty-five and forty shoe workers and paid a total wage bill of $3,754.39. In November 1873 a much-reduced workforce received a mere $815.71 in wages. The following January the number of Crispins working increased and wages rebounded to $5,444.12. Though the members sacrificed 20 percent of their income to keep the cooperative afloat, they could not make it a paying or stable venture capable of surviving the rough years of the 1870s. Like many other businesses during this depression, the factory failed. The actual cause of the factory's failure is not known, though inadequate capitalization was one obvious problem. Clearly, the cooperative was as vulnerable as any other business to the vicissitudes of the market economy. Phillips, however, blamed the failure on inefficiency. The foremen, he claimed, operated with little supervision and failed to make good use of materials. He also blamed the defeated Crispin faction for thwarting his efforts to generate greater working-class support for the factory.[52]

Phillips was one of many reformers who attributed a cooperative's failure not to the system he championed but to inadequacies among the cooperators themselves. The cooperative plan was so straightforward in these reformers' minds that failure had to be the result of either working-class ignorance, apathy, or greed. As long as they believed this and their faith endured, they would continue to seek out ways to make cooperation work. As the Knights of St. Crispin and other unions in Philadelphia collapsed with the depression of the 1870s, the advocates of cooperation searched for more effective instruments to educate workers and generate broad community support. They joined organizations, such as the International Workingmen's Association, the Sovereigns of Industry, and the Knights of Labor, that promised to mobilize and educate masses of workers. The ubiquitous Thomas Phillips, for example, while president of the cooperative factory and former Grand Knight of the Crispins' State Lodge, was also president of the American section #26 of the International Workingmen's Association, an organizer for the Sovereigns of Industry, and the first shoemaker to join the Knights of Labor.[53] Phillips organized trade unions and a cross-section of skilled workers and sympathizers to supplant the wage system with cooperation. Ultimately, he would subsume both activities under the aegis of the Knights of Labor.

Phillips helped establish the American branch, Section #26, of the International Workingmen's Association in Philadelphia. The IWA, also known as the First International, absorbed a contentious collection of radicals in America influenced by Karl Marx and antebellum radical traditions. Its Philadelphia members included skilled workers from a wide array of trades as well as a number of small merchants, professionals, and manufacturers. The section's chief objective appeared to be the promotion of a cooperative economy through the education and mobilization of radically minded workers and reformers. They hoped to advance the interests of labor through regular meetings, public demonstrations, a cooperative newspaper, and a planned "Capital and Labor Cooperative Bank."[54]

The men who organized Section #26 had lived through a number of failed cooperative experiments. Phillips, of course, had experienced both the collapse of the UCA and hard times at the Crispin's shoe factory. Another activist, Isaac Rhen, had participated twenty-five years earlier in the short-lived North American Phalanx, a Fourierist community in New Jersey. He later joined the UCA and helped found Section #26 along with Phillips and John Sheddon. These reformers realized that the success of cooperation depended upon the organization of an entire community's resources rather than the restricted assets of a single trade union. Their efforts, however, proved futile. The International never attracted a large following, nor did it offer these reformers effective tools to educate and mobilize Philadelphia's workers.[55]

As the International in the United States disintegrated, the leaders of Section #26 joined a new national organization devoted single-mindedly to cooperation, the Sovereigns of Industry. The Sovereigns first appeared in Massachusetts in 1874, the brainchild of William H. Earle, a small fruit grower from Worcester. Earle had originally organized lodges of the Patrons of Husbandry but soon determined, so the story goes, that American producers needed a more inclusive organization, one that would embrace all varieties of workingmen. Having issued a call to interested reformers, Earle held a meeting in Springfield in early January 1874 with fifteen other men and founded the first council of the Sovereigns of Industry.[56]

The organization found a receptive and rapidly expanding audience. During 1875 and 1876 as many as 40,000 persons joined the order, in over eighteen states. While strongest in Massachusetts, the Sovereigns organized more than 11,500 members in seventy-eight local or subordinate councils in Pennsylvania, twenty-five of which were located in Philadelphia. Thomas Phillips, himself, organized five local councils in the city, two of which were composed exclusively of shoe workers and one of women. The original Pioneer Council #1 absorbed the city's most active cooperators and Internationalists. Eventually nineteen members of Section #26 enrolled, along with Thomas Phillips, John Shedden, and Isaac Rhen. The old Fourierist Albert Brisbane joined for a short time, as did William D. Young, a former UCA member, and two men of significance in the Knights of Labor, James L. Wright and Victor Drury. They organized the same base of skilled workers and middle-class reformers found in the International.[57]

In its official declaration of purposes, the Sovereigns proposed to render "impossible in the future the encroachments of oppressive monopolies upon the liberties or rights of individuals." By insuring "equal rights under the law, and equal privileges under the social systems of the land," producers would receive their "proportionate share" of the wealth and capital and a "suitable return" for the risk of investment. They believed, as well, that speculators and middlemen caused prices of necessary goods to increase and that these same middlemen compelled wages to fall by forcing "manufacturers to cheapen the cost of production in order to secure a fair profit to themselves." United under the banner of the Sovereigns of Industry, members "could purchase of such merchandise as we consume . . . [cheapen] production of such goods as we can produce with our labor, [and] . . . *best reconcile the interests of labor and capital*, which have been rendered antagonistic by the prevailing systems of trade."[58]

The Sovereigns instituted a fourfold approach to eliminate the inequities of the system of trade then "in vogue." First, the organization on the local, state, and national level contracted with wholesalers or manufacturers for goods in order to qualify for wholesale discounts. Second, through its local councils it formed cooperative grocery stores based upon the "Burton plan," their own version of the Rochdale system, though a competing plan took hold in some councils. Third, single- or multistate councils established warehouses and boards of trade to facilitate bulk purchasing direct from producers on a large scale. Finally, members of the order would eventually establish cooperative industries funded by the proceeds of the cooperative stores and administered by members trained in cooperative retail management.[59]

The Sovereigns of Industry came into existence during a period of economic and trade union decline and it absorbed a wide array of individuals and ideals. Considered the urban counterpart of the Grange, it served as a repository for labor reformers of all stripes. Only a few months after he founded the Sovereigns, Earle attempted to merge his organization with the Industrial Congress, the feeble descendant of the National Labor Union. Though the congress rebuffed his appeal, the order did absorb a number of trade unions. Its diverse membership agreed on the importance of cooperation but seemed to have less confidence in the leadership's analysis of the labor problem. In fact, considerable disagreement arose over the proper role of trade unions, the role of the state, and the very nature of the antagonism between labor and capital.[60]

In Philadelphia, the members of the Pioneer Council were not of one mind on these issues, either. They sympathized with the labor movement but disagreed over the utility of trade unions among themselves. Phillips believed that unions and cooperative reform could coexist. Cooperation, he wrote, was "the reform that contains all others in its germ," yet labor organizations could "attend to their own business[,] each trade meeting in its own private way[,] and at the same time reap all the advantages of the Sovereigns without interfering in any way with their own afairs [*sic*]." John Sheddon, on the other hand, shrank from endorsing trade union tactics even though he recognized the existence of an unyielding antagonism between labor and capital. When railroad workers rioted during the upheaval of 1877, he sympathized but looked to a greater reform that would transform the wage system permanently. "Our order," he said in July 1877, "looks higher than strikes for wages, if for instance we recognize wages, we then recognize the Political [*sic*] economy which sanctions the wages system. [W]hat then is the use of us recognizing conditions against which our principles war."[61]

Despite these dissenting opinions, the organization's members agreed on the importance of saving money through some form of economic cooperation. This is what the Sovereigns, for a time, did well. Philadelphia's twenty-five councils supported six cooperative stores in 1876, and the state council, headed by John Shedden, negotiated special prices with certain manufacturers for items such as coal and flour. In Philadelphia, two cooperative shoe factories, one carpet-weaving cooperative, and a saw and tool manufacturing association made special arrangements with the organization. The latter company discounted its prices 30 percent for council members.[62]

The Sovereigns of Industry as a national organization offered reformers what previous cooperative societies could not: the ability to both meet the immediate needs of working-class neighborhoods and exercise extra-local power. Since the 1860s, Phillips had believed in the emancipatory potential of cooperation, and in the Sovereigns of Industry he found the best vehicle to realize that vision. Practical and utopian, it was an organization, Phillips wrote, "that while entirely local in the benefits would be national in its schope [*sic*] and character. So that while we would feel its benefits immdiatly [*sic*] in our homes we could act as an united people in the direction of national efforts." He was confident that the time would come "when this Republic will in the fullest sense be a Cooperative body; and that the good work now being done in small local societies on cooperative principles, will one day be done in this Republic on a national scale."[63] The repeated failure of local efforts pointed to the real need for unified extra-local reform organization.

The Sovereigns' hope of transcending the wage system depended upon their ability to resist market forces. These forces could not be so easily overcome. As soon as the organization failed to deliver on its promise of inexpensive goods, national membership rapidly declined. By 1878, few of Philadelphia's twenty-five councils still functioned. With the economy depressed, workers needed credit for their groceries, a situation abhorred by the Sovereigns and rejected by the Rochdale system. To insure the security of their cooperatives and save their members from the trap of debt, the Sovereigns forced their own members to seek help elsewhere. Perhaps more significantly, a decline in prices during the late 1870s made discounting a difficult goal to negotiate with manufacturers. John Shedden explained, "the present conditions of the commercial world was such, that with the falling prices in the market, we could not make arrangements of a very profitable character hence the advantages at the present time were not so great as many might desire." By the end of 1878, the organization no longer functioned in Philadelphia.[64]

The failure of the Sovereigns, however, did not convince the labor movement or its leaders to reject cooperation as an alternative to private entrepreneurship. The Sovereigns, who had supplanted the decaying trade unions during the depression years, were now replaced, in turn, by a new organization that assumed the mantel of labor reform, the Knights of Labor. For a time, the two organizations had a simultaneous existence in Philadelphia. Important individuals, such as Phillips and James L. Wright, belonged to both, and the associations acted together, on occasion, for common ends.[65] Yet, by 1878, the Knights had subsumed the functions of the Sovereigns of Industry. Where the latter association offered the means to organize communities for consumer cooperation and to provide a national base for further reform, the Knights promised much more. The Knights of Labor organized as a labor union at the workplace and in the community as it promoted a vision of the cooperative republic through an ever growing presence beyond the immediate vicinity of the shop or neighborhood.

The Knights of labor originated in Philadelphia in 1869 with the attempt by former members of a garment cutters' cooperative association to form a comprehensive organization of workers. The order grew slowly during its first two years, expanded rapidly in 1873 to as many as sixty local assemblies, and then declined with similar dispatch as the economy plummeted. Only during the middle years of the decade did the Knights expand beyond the borders of Philadelphia into Pittsburgh and the coalfields of western Pennsylvania.[66]

The founders of the Knights designed the organization to act as both a trade union and a reform society, one that could organize at the level of the workplace, the neighborhood, and the nation. Thus even in their first years of existence they organized a variety of workers into trade assemblies, participated in the eight-hour movement, and endorsed cooperation. Uriah Stephens, Grand Master Workman of the Knights, and Henry Sinexon, a founder of the union, served as treasurer and auditor, respectively, of a carpet weavers' cooperative in 1874. District Assembly No. 1 of Philadelphia organized a Rochdale-style grocery in 1876, with Phillips,

James L. Wright, and Frederick Turner, the future General Assembly secretary, as president, treasurer and secretary of the association.[67]

Some of the key men who led the labor reform and trade union movements in Philadelphia during the 1860s and 1870s emerged as leaders of the Knights of Labor. John Samuel, then living in St. Louis, became the secretary of the Knights' Committee on Cooperation in 1884. James Wright, a cooperator and founding member of the Knights, continued to play a prominent role in the organization well into the 1880s. Thomas Phillips again organized the shoe workers of Philadelphia, this time into one of the strongest local assemblies in the entire order. Victor Drury, of the International and Sovereigns of Industry, left Philadelphia in 1878 to become an instrumental player in the Home Club of New York's District Assembly No. 49. Finally, Frederick Turner became secretary of the Knights' General Assembly in the 1880s.[68]

During the 1860s and 1870s the labor movement conveyed a cooperative vision, deeply rooted in the ethos of craft work, to skilled and less-skilled workers and, at times, to both men and women. These practical and utopian reformers had been drawn into the market economy as wage laborers, and they formed cooperative businesses to control that market, meet the practical needs of working-class communities, and create a more democratic community and polity. Their experiences pushed them toward politics but most importantly toward organizational innovation and ultimately to the Knights of Labor. In Philadelphia the practical utopians found that isolated cooperatives, trade union efforts at cooperative production and consumption, and reform organizations designed to create a cooperative economy regularly proved inadequate to the task. To combine trade unionism and labor reform in one organization and mobilize entire communities was their next logical step.

CHAPTER 2

TO SUBSTITUTE PEACE FOR WAR AND LOVE FOR HATE

The Cooperative Ideology of American Workers

In 1887, Master Workman T. W. Brosnan, of Minnesota's Knights of Labor District Assembly 79, declared that the competitive system under which Americans labored was nothing more than industrial slavery. "We must endeavor," he said to his fellow Minnesota Knights, "to abolish this system and substitute for it the cooperative system—substitute peace for war and love for hate."[1] According to Brosnan, cooperation was no simple reform of working conditions but a viable alternative to the prevailing system of "competition." Brosnan, and other cooperators, drew upon a working-class discourse of republican citizenship, democracy, and producerism to construct this cooperative alternative. The ideas constituting their belief system, however, were often vague and contradictory. At one moment hierarchical and exclusive, at another egalitarian and inclusive, the republican producerist discourse offered little specific guidance in the actual construction of cooperative enterprises. Originating in the trade union and craft experiences of the skilled white male worker, cooperation embodied the tension between hierarchy and equality that inhered in postwar labor reform. As the labor movement expanded and organized the less skilled, women, nonwhites, and whole communities, some cooperators challenged the essential categories and gendered nature of labor reform. By rethinking and remaking their workplaces and communities, cooperators like Brosnan gave new substance to the very ideas that constituted their republican worldview.

THE COOPERATION OF SKILLED WORKERS

Nearly twenty years before Master Workman Brosnan spoke of the reign of peace and love, a less expansive definition of cooperation held currency in the labor movement. Trade union leaders like William Sylvis, president of the Iron Molders' Union, articulated a cooperative vision rooted in the goals, hopes, and contradictions of the skilled male worker.[2]

William Sylvis discussed his vision of cooperative reform in a revealing exchange in 1868 at a meeting of the Workingwoman's Association of New York. The meeting, which was held in the office of Susan B. Anthony's *The Revolution*, hosted women from a variety of trades and professions, along with several prominent men from the National Labor Union Congress currently in session in the city. The topic under discussion, the differential treatment meted out to male and female typographers by union men and employers, engaged the group in spirited debate. When Susan B. Anthony suggested that female typographers establish a cooperative printing office, the audience responded warmly to the idea.[3] William Sylvis reacted with less enthusiasm. His response so clearly demonstrated the origins and ambiguities of cooperative ideals among trade union craftsmen that it is worth quoting at length. "I represent the iron molders," he said:

> The very first thing for labor to do is to organize trade unions. Had we started the co-operative movement ten years ago, we would have failed miserably. We spent $1,500,000 in sustaining strikes, lock-outs, and similar movements of the kind during the ten years. We had good schooling, and we cannot say that we have not paid for our education. We have since learned the value of work and co-operation. I am an iron-moulder, and I am perfectly willing that ladies should come into our business. (Laughter.) It is a very hard business. . . . All our present success in co-operation is because of the primary trade unions. The system of wages is the curse of labor all over the world. Labor, however, has been making steady progress everywhere. We have now come to the time when we can take hold of co-operation, and we shall yet utterly abolish the accursed system of wages for labor. I am in favor of universal liberty and universal suffrage, regardless of sex or color. They go hand in hand with universal labor and co-operation. I am not in favor

> of women working at all. I believe that every man should be able to derive enough profit from his toil to enable him to support his wife, daughter, or mother. I do not believe that woman was intended to live by the sweat of her brow.[4]

Sylvis, the labor leader, spoke to an audience of women aspiring to succeed in a work world dominated by male labor. He advised them that cooperation could not prosper without trade union strength, and he implied that women must form trade unions first before they could consider cooperation. His own experience in the Iron Molders' Union, he said, had taught him the value of such organization for the success of worker-owned enterprises. He also ringingly endorsed woman's, as well as African American, suffrage, linking it to "universal labor and co-operation." Yet, at the same time and not unlike many other men and women in the labor movement, he defined women as dependents who, under better circumstances, should not have to enter the workplace at all.[5]

Sylvis's sense of self, as a trade unionist and cooperator, was enmeshed in a worldview that defined universal values in gender-specific terms. Productive labor and cooperation, in his best of all worlds, would be male domains. His view of labor's emancipation, however, contained a more democratic dimension that insinuated its way into the separation of gendered spheres. This democratic ethos embraced a much broader notion of participatory citizenship than his cooperative vision allowed, and it would prove to be an irritant, pushing and pulling on those "universal" notions that excluded women, non-whites, and the unskilled. Cooperators like Sylvis found themselves caught between their own notions of exclusion and their inclusive ideals of democratic participation. This tension is what many active unionists were forced to reconcile as they articulated notions of citizenship in an industrial world of wage labor that included more and more women and unskilled workers. Sylvis's attempt to define cooperation was part of this larger struggle among wage earners to assess their democratic rights in the economic world and determine the nature of citizenship in American society.[6]

William Sylvis's ideas resonated with the craftsmen and wage earners who flocked to the postwar labor movement. They found in his vision of cooperation a means to address the immediate problems of wages and working conditions through a realizable form of self-help. The apparent practicality of cooperative reform also fired their imaginations and ignited a vaguely defined hope for change that could reverberate with extraordinary power in their daily lives. In 1868, for example, an iron molder from Troy, New York, described how profoundly the idea of cooperation had affected him:

> I do not think I ever thought so much upon any one subject before in my life. You know that workingmen do not have much time to think about anything else than how best to keep hunger, nakedness, and cold from becoming members of his family; but, somehow, this thing called cooperation got such a hold on me that I have been, in a manner, lost to everything else. I have dreamed about it, thought about it in the shop, on the street, at church, in fact, everywhere.[7]

Some workers aptly described this enthusiasm as cooperation "on the brain," a reflection, albeit pejorative, of the tremendous commitment cooperation could inspire. However, when the glass-blower and Knights of Labor cooperator John Samuel described cooperation as "simply an agreement between any number of persons to work together for the common good[,] [i]ts object, the physical, social & mental improvement of the condition [of the] working classes," he captured its essential indeterminacy.[8] The vagueness of this "agreement . . . to work together," allowed wage earners to imagine a future of their own design unhindered by rigid doctrine. Inspired and enthusiastic, they pieced together a future with their often contradictory values and half-understood notions of how the marketplace, workshop, and community should function.

The apparent practicality of cooperation inspired skilled male workers after the Civil War to dream of a utopian future, and they constructed that dream out of the ethos of craft work and their trade union experience. In letters and newspaper articles, and in an occasional poem, craftsmen depicted cooperation as the direct expression of craft virtues and trade union power. In "A Molder's Dream," a poem published by *The Iron Molders' International Journal* in 1876, a trade unionist illustrated these ideas and their inspirational power. The poem's protagonist, a Detroit iron molder and union member, found himself threatened with dismissal for his trade union associations by his anti-union employer. In response he packed his tools and quit his job. As he traveled by train to his new destination, the molder dreamt of waking twenty years hence in Detroit, "like Rip of old." Riding a horse car, he asked his imaginary driver to stop at his former employer's foundry. The driver replied:

> Let you off at the Michigan Stove Works, why there's no such place in town;
> There used to be, but then you know they had to close it down.
> What caused it? Why the Union men, they built a monstrous shop,
> And made the nicest kind of work, the others had to flop,
> Because their class of workmen, so all the molders say,
> Was composed of boys and scabs, you see the men were called away.
> They couldn't make the work to suit the purchasers' demands;
> So they took a little tumble, in fact the trade changed hands.
> Adair Street; here's the place, sir; and our hero left the seat,
> How often had he left the cars at this self-same old street?
> He saw a mammoth foundry on the cooperative plan,
> Right there on Miller's garden, close by the Michigan,
> A banner on the building, fully fifty feet in length,
> Had this motto worked upon it, "In Union there is Strength;"
> And just before you entered you would read above the doors,
> That none but Union Molders need apply in here for floors.
> Our hero's heart grew warmer as he gazed upon the scene,
> Was he not a Union Molder? aye, and he had always been;
> A stranger now no longer, there were men and brothers too,
> A score of hands to welcome him inside the wall he knew.
> For brothers, if you're in distress, there's none in this broad land,
> Who'll give it with a freer heart than an honest Union Man.[9]

This slumbering molder quit his job, like any self-respecting craftsman and trade unionist, to assert his independence and right of association. The spirit of independence to which he subscribed was rooted in his autonomy as a highly skilled and self-directed worker. Molders, like most skilled tradesmen of this era, jealously guarded their own independence and skills and joined in the trade union movement to enforce, as David Montgomery has argued, a mutualistic code of behavior that regulated the standards of the trade.[10] If our slumbering molder expressed this craft pride as an individual, he imagined its ultimate expression in the collective ownership of a cooperative.

In this molder's fantasy the cooperative's greatest virtue rested in the moral superiority of its unionized craft workers. Only properly apprenticed union molders could find employment in his shop, and they would produce what inferior boys and scabs could not, a quality product. They justified this far-reaching control by their knowledge and value as skilled men. "The whole business," union molder and poet Dugald Campbell wrote, "rightfully belongs to us, and not to those who, in nearly all cases, know not the first thing about it, and tell us that moulders have not the brains enough to conduct it if they had it. Well I hope, by and by, to show them whether we have the capacity to keep a 'hotel' or not."[11] If cooperation proved a success, one optimistic molder wrote, "in ten years we will control the foundry business in this country."[12]

Under their own regime, cooperators believed they could establish the conditions fought for by their trade unions and provide a haven for union members. In fact, a molder from Cincinnati wrote in 1866, "It is the only rock upon which a Trades' Union can stand and carry its members safe through the battle of life." Another molder maintained that cooperatives could, among other things, inaugurate the eight-hour system, raise wages, and employ all unemployed molders. "One Co-operative foundry," he wrote, "established by, and working under the laws of the International Union, will serve as a complete regulator for a certain number of shops in the vicinity." Similarly, William Sylvis believed that union foundries brought within their reach control over "prices, the hours of labor, and the rules of the shops."[13]

Ultimately, cooperation could achieve what trade unionism and the wage system could only approximate, that is, it could guarantee a worker the full value of his labor. If the laborer produced all wealth, and was, in fact, the essential producer, then trade unions could only compromise when negotiating a share of that wealth with nonproducers. The president of the Iron Molders' Union in 1876, William Saffin, recognized this dilemma when he explained that the trouble "has always been, and will continue to be, to determine, under the wages system, what is an equitable share that labor should be contented with. Is labor only entitled to a share? If labor is only entitled to a share, who is entitled to the balance?"[14] Labor's just reward, he continued, was "not a share," the mere byproduct of the wage system, "but all of what it produces."[15] Like Saffin, P. C. Forrester, an officer in the Machinists' and Blacksmiths' Union No. 1 of Illinois, promoted cooperation to "leave to a future generation not only a trade, but the means of conserving its best interests . . . and guaranteeing to every member the full enjoyment of the produce of his labor."[16]

When trade unionists opened a cooperative store in Troy, New York, in 1864, they similarly filtered their understanding of consumers' cooperation through the ethos that animated these craftsmen. In fact, they organized their store in a manner clearly compatible with a craftsman's understanding of production. The founders adopted the Rochdale method—that is, they distributed dividends in proportion to purchases, and they believed this would

> invariably work beneficially and profitably because the most profit goes to the best customer. And the best customers will be found among the one-share members—men with large families, spending about all they earn in their support; while those who are able to pay out the money for ten shares are men who do not spend all they earn in the support of their families, and do not bring so much profit into the Association as the one-share member; yet, were dividends declared upon shares, he would receive ten times as much profit as the one-share member, notwithstanding the latter may bring ten times as much profit into the Association as the former; thus virtually taking from the poor and paying over to the rich, defeating the object of the Association, and perpetuating one of the greatest evils it is designed to counteract.[17]

As the labor movement based its main demand that the producer receive the full value of his product on the labor theory of value, the city's artisan cooperators believed that the consumer deserved the full return on his expenditures because he contributed most in purchases to the store.[18] The consumer added value to the store through his purchases in the same way a producer added value to material by his labor. If an individual received more than he contributed to the store, the system had allowed the rich to rob the poor. The Rochdale method clearly appealed to the producerism of skilled male workers, which was an essential component, as will be shown in the following, of their cooperative ethos, whether manifest in stores to distribute goods or in factories to produce them.

REPUBLICANS, PRODUCERS, COOPERATORS

The cooperators' contest for control over their working conditions went beyond the workplace and store and was part of a larger struggle over the distribution of economic and political power in a republic. Democratic rights, they insisted, superseded the power of money, and they made the principle of one member-one vote the defining characteristic of a cooperative institution.[19] Indeed, labor reformers understood cooperation in highly charged political terms. In the late 1860s, John Samuel contended that

> the principles of Co-operation are more in harmony with the principles of our form of government than our present social system. Our social system in many things is at variance with our political institutions. The relation of Employer & Employed is not the normal condition of Freemen. Superiority & Inferiority is implied in the relation. . . . Co-operation supersedes this relation and places men just where the Declaration of Independence was designed to place them—equal—& with equal rights to liberty & the pursuit of happiness.[20]

Writing soon after the end of the Civil War, Samuel was particularly sensitive to labor's subordination to capital, a condition labor reformers branded wage slavery.[21] He believed that factories and stores operated upon cooperative principles would remove the inequalities of wage labor, eliminate dependency, and guarantee equal rights. The principles of cooperation would fulfill the egalitarian promise of a democratic republic.[22]

Cooperators believed in their reform as the consummate expression of republican rights and, like labor reformers before them, appropriated the symbols and rhetoric of the American Revolution. They regularly invoked the paternity of the Founding Fathers and their republican legacy, whether it was to "revive the Republic" or to perfect that "social order which guarantees equality of rights, privileges and opportunities to all."[23] This invocation was by no means a dull repetition of eighteenth- or early-nineteenth-century republicanism. As other historians have now long argued, various sectors of American society contested the meaning of the republican legacy throughout the 1800s, and by midcentury a distinct working-class version had emerged within the labor movement. In fact, the "practical workingmen," who while on strike established Boston's *Daily Evening Voice* in 1864, realized that it was their responsibility to reinterpret republican principles. The Founding Fathers, so the printers believed, had laid down a foundation for a new order and left to "their successors the duty of rearing the superstructure." Their newspaper, "a little commonwealth" and advocate for the rights of labor, would do this and ensure that "the rights of one are the rights of all."[24]

Cooperators believed that under the rubric of legitimate republican rights fell the privilege to set the price of their own labor and to receive the full value of its product.[25] As William Forbath has argued, these rights would establish the conditions for the successful participation of a fully functioning republican citizenry. In fact, when workers referred to cooperation as "republicanized labor," they meant to possess a power, albeit an ill-defined one, that would reclaim their sovereignty lost, according to cooperator Hugh Cameron, when "the spirit of competition grew and the corrupting reign of the almighty dollar was inaugurated."[26] They sought vindication as competent citizens capable of managing their own affairs and controlling their own fate in an industrialized republic. Through cooperation they could exercise the power over their lives that would give democracy meaning.[27]

The rhetoric of labor reform notwithstanding, in the 1860s "republicanized labor" included a very narrow spectrum of skilled white male workers. Since the early nineteenth century the labor movement had bestowed republican legitimacy on these men by distinguishing them as producers. The labor of skilled producers, it was argued, created the wealth and independence a republican citizenry required, while nonproducers lived off the wealth created by others. The concept of "slavery" captured the dependence to which wage labor reduced producers. It also, however, revealed the racialized nature of the producer as American workers understood him. As a number of historians have recently argued, the racial definition of slavery demeaned black labor, slave or free, and led white workers to exclude African Americans from the very definition of the independent producer. Irish workers, in particular, excluded black laborers from certain jobs in order to legitimize themselves racially through defining those jobs as white.[28] This notion of white labor clearly resonated with many cooperators. When they spoke sympathetically of the "white niggers" or the "emancipation of the white slaves," as they on occasion would, cooperators equated the degradation of white labor with slavery.[29] They also excluded the many black workers among them from the category of the oppressed producer.

At the same time, and in contrast, a few of the leading exponents of cooperation put themselves at the forefront of the advocacy of racial inclusiveness. Their democratic sensibilities, at least in part, pushed them toward a broader conception of the legitimate producer. It is also true that practical concern with the threat of unorganized black workers to the well-being of whites aroused some cooperators. William Sylvis was an important example of both tendencies in the 1860s. Another advocate of cooperation, Terence Powderly, as the leader of the Knights of Labor, strongly favored the organization of African American workers and their admission into the order on an equal basis with whites. Furthermore, at a time when anti-Chinese sentiment was a given in the labor movement and advocated by Powderly, Victor Drury of New York led the city's Knights of Labor in organizing cooperatives as well as Chinese workers.[30]

Despite the more typical attitudes of white workers, black laborers saw themselves as legitimate producers, and they formed cooperatives to advance their interests as black producers in a racist environment. The most notable example of such activity took place in Baltimore, Maryland. In 1866, Isaac Myers, later a leader of the Colored National Labor Union, along with black ship caulkers and members of the black business community, helped organize the Chesapeake Marine Railway and Dry Dock Company. They designed this cooperative to employ black workers shunned by white-owned businesses. The Colored National Labor Union, of which Myers was president, also endorsed cooperation for black workers in 1869.[31]

As the century progressed and the ranks of wage labor grew and diversified, labor reformers attempted to redefine the concept

General Master Workman Terence V. Powderly of the Knights of Labor. Ohio Historical Society.

of the producer in other ways as well. They narrowed what was in reality a vague moral category that could include businessmen as well as wage workers. Cooperators had a particular interest in understanding the difference between themselves as worker-owners and entrepreneurs. In the process they challenged certain ambiguities of producerism and explored the boundaries of legitimate participation within the labor movement.[32]

Ostensibly, nineteenth-century laborers easily understood who fit the profile of a producer. In the early years of the century, journeyman and small business owners considered themselves the quintessential republican producers. By the Civil War years this had changed. Cooperators, above all others, recognized the moral deficiencies of shopkeepers and employers. In 1864, the founders of the Troy Workingmen's Co-operative Association condemned in no uncertain terms the "idle horde of speculators" that fed off the retail system, and Trenton workers formed their cooperative store a year later to protect "the laboring classes from the monopoly of speculators in all the necessaries of life."[33] In regard to their employers, a Massachusetts machinist wrote in the 1860s, "Those really desiring work to be done invariably prefer to go direct to the men who do it, and leave unnoticed the employer, who stand[s] only as a middleman between those who want the work done and those who do it."[34] A Kentucky molder similarly asked, "Why should we maintain a set of middlemen, when we have capital enough among ourselves to carry on our own business and trade directly with the consumer?"[35]

For many skilled craftsmen these statements rang true. Among skilled men though, even those who began to speak disdainfully of nonproducers as "capitalists," the producer was not so easily defined. The activist cooperator from Philadelphia, Isaac Rhen, for example, wrote in 1872 that by capitalists

> [we mean] those who are mere traders and speculators, and such as put their money into industries in the way of stocks, on the profits of which they may sit in their easy chairs, pull the wires perchance, and open their bags to receive the revenues. By producers, all those who by their manual labor fill the earth with the necessaries of existence, and those who by their more special devotion to the artistic, scientific, aesthetic, embellish our homes with the beautiful, unlock the mysteries of nature, and reveal her powers and perhaps her purposes, give us poetry, history, ethics, whose combined industry makes the world better for their having lived in it.[36]

Rhen began his analysis with a simple structural distinction: Producers performed manual labor and capitalist nonproducers invested capital. These categories, however, could not clarify the roles of capital and labor with much precision, and in a diversified economy failed to account for all the varieties of productive work. The producer, Rhen realized, had to be much more than a manual laborer. He was, in fact, a moral agent who made the world better by his creativity and industry. What defined him as a producer was his behavior rather than his structural location within the economy. Who, then, ultimately fit into these groupings? Rhen's account certainly left this unclear. Moreover, he believed that his categories were both "sufficiently defined to be dealt with as classes," and "to some extent mixed."[37] A manufacturer or businessman who invested his capital as well as his ingenuity and labor, it seems, could fall on either side of the producer/nonproducer dichotomy.

In the postwar years what increasingly marked a businessman as an acceptable producer to labor reformers was not his industry and creativity but his attitude toward labor and the role he played in the community in which he lived. In the 1880s, when labor organizations still admitted businessmen into their ranks, they admitted only those individuals uniquely sympathetic to labor's interests. The one manufacturer-delegate who attended the Knights of Labor General Assembly in 1886 hardly fit the profile of a typical nineteenth-century entrepreneur. The delegate, John Best, was a former factory worker, cooperator, trade union leader, and labor reform representative in the Massachusetts General Court and, though now a small shoe manufacturer, had recently helped organize his city's striking shoe workers along with other labor activists and cooperators. The very nature of community life for working people throughout this period, its mixture of neighborhood shopkeepers and wage earners, made it possible for someone like Best to embody the interests of labor. As the labor movement, particularly the Knights of Labor, organized whole communities, it looked for support from such neighbors and sympathetic businessmen.[38] However, if someone like John Best worked against the demands of the labor movement, he might easily slip from legitimacy into illegitimacy.

John Samuel, a member of the Knights of Labor Cooperative Board, confronted this issue of the producer businessman's relationship to labor when in 1886 a member Knight wrote to him concerned for the stability of his local assembly. S. L. Gault belonged to LA 3396, located in the small city of Cheboygen, Michigan. Members of his local, Gault wrote, had proposed the establishment of a cooperative store, a move he vigorously opposed. It was sure, he informed Samuel,

> to cause a divided feeling in our Local and probably break it up. Last winter I kept groceries and would certainly have been opposed to this move if made then. I would be opposed to a co-operative Dry-Goods store now, because I am in that business myself. There are 5 grocers here who are knights, (out of about 25 grocery stores altogether). The grocery business is overdone here. These 5 grocers know nothing of this move yet, for

> they do not attend the meetings very often. If they knew it, they would surely enter a protest. My advice at the meeting last night, was to start in some kind of co-operative manufacturing. This would not create any dissensions. The store keeping plan, I think would.[39]

The Knights' local in Cheboygen, a mixed assembly with as many as 212 members in 1885, included shopkeepers sympathetic to the interests of labor.[40] Yet the economic self-interest of this latter group could, Gault made clear, threaten the stability of the assembly. It was the principle of cooperation made potent by the threat a cooperative grocery posed to his own livelihood and that of his fellow shopkeepers that disturbed him. That threat could tear asunder the forces of solidarity in his community.

Samuel answered Gault eleven days later and counseled caution in any move toward opening a cooperative store. "It would be neither safe nor wise," he wrote, "to make any attempt in that line." His response, however, was uncharacteristically harsh in tone. The explanation, he wrote, for the divided feeling in the local assembly was clear:

> What motive dear brother prompted those 5 grocers & yourself in seeking admission into the order? Don't you admit for yourself & them that it was personal gain & selfish interest? It was to bring all business down to a legitimate basis that the order was instituted & to prevent such results as the 'grocery' or any other business being 'overdone,' it is intended that the members when properly educated shall carry on all business productive and distributive, in the interest & for the welfare of all & not for the benefit of a few.[41]

Samuel questioned the fitness of these shopkeepers for membership in the Knights of Labor. Not only did their selfishness contradict the Knights' ultimate goal of cooperation, but private ownership of business itself benefitted only the few, while the Knights hoped to conduct business in the interest and for the welfare of all. The labor movement, it appeared, would be better off without them. Yet the plan of action Samuel suggested to Gault was as astounding as it was contradictory.

> My advice to your members is, take no step that will jeopard-

> ize the existence of your A[ssembly], its progress & prosperity— Cultivate patience harmony, & good feeling & all will come out right. Those of your members in business are engaged in a legitimate calling as the world understands it today, any change must come slowly & with as little disturbance to existing interests as possible. This is the true foundation & law of sound social progress.[42]

Samuel seemed to fear most the breakup of community solidarities that gave the Knights their strength. Even though as a cooperator he renounced privately operated businesses, he recognized the significant interdependence of shopkeepers and laborers within a working-class community, as well as the high regard in which labor still held the fair-minded independent producer.[43] If the Knights would organize such communities, they would have to, in Samuel's view, mute their members' conflicting notions of producerism, one of which hallowed the welfare of all, while the other operated for the "benefit of the few." As workers organized cooperatives, the constituencies formerly joined under the rubric of producerism no longer coexisted without conflict.

The concept of the producer had additional complications for the skilled workers who formed the core of the labor movement. They understood their world as a contradictory dialogue between inclusive democratic principles and the hierarchical exclusivity of both skill and gender. So while cooperators insisted on democratic rules as they sought to include their fellow skilled workers in efforts at self-help, their craft pride could leave helpers and the less skilled beyond the protection of cooperative membership. They would, at times, cooperate in order to preserve their privileges as skilled workers. On occasion, cooperators spoke of their factories as levers which would elevate them to their proper position in society.[44] Looking directly into the eyes of the manufacturers, as well as down at the unskilled, increased their status and respectability in an increasingly mechanized economy.

Moreover, cooperators understood their world of skilled work and republican rights in gendered terms. The labor press consistently declared any denial of a worker's rights an affront to his manliness and any assertion of power an expression of his manhood. When Thomas Phillips, a well-known trade unionist and cooperator, described the defeat of his fellow Crispins in a strike in 1869, he described their humiliation in terms repeated endlessly for the next twenty years. Their defeat was a "surrendering of their manhood, their rights and privileges as men and citizens."[45] "By all that is sacred in manhood," another worker wrote, toilers should receive the just equivalent of their labor.[46] A cooperative could guarantee a citizen's rights because each member would, according to "Earnest" from Charlestown, Massachusetts, "stand upon his manhood, as a voter in the government of the association."[47]

Cooperators appealed to wage workers as journeymen but also as men who were heads of families and had the responsibility to support dependents. The Journeymen Shoemakers' Co-operative of Philadelphia addressed each shoe worker "as a workman, as a man, as the head of a family," and offered him the means to provide more for his family.[48] To the dissolute, a cooperative store might offer the discipline necessary to alter habits uncongenial to family life. *Fincher's Trades' Review* wrote:

> With a praiseworthy economy in family expenses [from membership in a cooperative store] is blended a restriction of such indulgences as tobacco, segars, ale, or frivolous amusements; and in proportion as these are curtailed, he [the member] finds he is not only providing for a 'rainy day,' but his morals have improved. He no longer deserts his home for the dram-shop, his wife has ceased to frown, and his children look happy. He begins to feel the pride of manhood, and is now better prepared to resist the tyranny of an avaricious task-master.[49]

Cooperation could then maintain the integrity of the male breadwinner and provide the necessary resources to keep women out of the workforce. It could, in addition, instruct its own followers to act responsibly and sustain those values most supportive of family stability and trade union discipline.

Moreover, cooperation itself, according to the Crispins' newspaper, the *American Workman*, was the metaphorical "marriage of capital and labor."[50] In the language of manhood used by working men this rang true. In a cooperative, the producer asserted his manliness and rightful authority over nonproductive capital. In the family, a man's rightful place was as producer and provider, and as the authority over his dependent, nonproducing wife. Capital, when dominant, denied labor its manhood, but when properly dependent upon labor it created a harmonious unit. Similarly, when the uncertainty of a husband's employment and his inadequate wages made the labor of women and children vital to a family's survival, a father's manhood was placed in doubt. The capacity of a man to keep his wife out of the workplace was the same expression of manliness through which the cooperator subordinated capital. The refrain often uttered by labor reformers that cooperation was the harmonious union of labor and capital can be understood in this light, as a balance of power equivalent to the "natural" balance of the family.[51]

Cooperators constructed their alternative businesses to include men and women in what they believed were their appropriate and natural roles. During the postwar years the entrance of women into the labor market posed a threat and a challenge to this model of the family. Subsequently, laboring men often chose to carry the family's exclusionary and hierarchical tendencies into the workplaces they themselves defined. Cooperators often excluded women from membership, pegged them to limited roles, and kept them from positions of authority in their stores or factories.[52]

The categories they created, however, were not entirely exclusive and could suggest an expanded role for women. Here the ambiguities of democratic cooperation opened space for subordinate groups to act. When a handbill for Philadelphia's Union Cooperative Association No. 1 read: "Men of America! Co-operate. Women of America! BUY YOUR GROCERIES AT THE CO-OPERATIVE STORE,"[53] it implied that men and women both had important, if different, roles to play in the life of the cooperative. The ill-fated *Labor Champion*, a short-lived cooperative newspaper, stated this more explicitly but also more ambiguously. Women were to consume and invest their dividends from the cooperative store, "as capital for workshops, etc., in the interest of their husbands, sons and others."[54] Men and women would function as a family unit, the men as producers and the women as consumers.[55] This was, however, a dynamic role for a consumer to play. Here cooperators exhorted women to make an investment decision, to exercise control over the financial resources they mustered from their frugal cooperative purchases.

At the same time that these skilled workers restricted, with some ambiguity, women's participation in cooperation, they consistently advanced woman's suffrage. The "equal rights" tradition within the labor movement carried many of its most important leaders to the conclusion that "universal suffrage" was necessary and just.[56] The evidence suggests that when, out of either need for capital or conviction, male cooperators welcomed women as shareholders, women participated and exercised their votes. This development notwithstanding, unless women established their own cooperatives, they did not occupy positions of authority in their associations.[57]

Even when women were admitted into cooperatives as workers or as members, male workers often qualified their involvement with the conventional logic of separate spheres. The Knights of Labor of Eastport, Maine, who resolved in 1887 to open a cooperative sardine-canning factory, were quite willing to hire women. Yet they insisted: "We will employ no married woman unless she can give positive proof that her husband is physically unable to support her. The husband is the natural and legal breadwinner, and we consider that we should be doing injustice to the large army of single women who are bravely fighting the battle of life, should we give employment to their married sisters, who could be as well employed at home, their natural sphere."[58]

Within the skilled workers' understanding of cooperation, space existed for the limited expansion of gendered roles. Yet these wage workers would overcome notions of exclusivity based on skill or gender only when they understood cooperation in different terms. There is some evidence that by the 1880s, the increased deskilling of labor and mechanization of production had convinced some cooperators that the less skilled were legitimate laborers. Most importantly, however, the rise of the Knights of Labor, whose aim was to organize all workers, transformed cooperative thought. This new thinking, which occurred among some women, and with the approval of some men, can be characterized as the feminization of cooperation.[59] C. Fannie Allyn's cooperative vision was one example of this tendency.

C. Fannie Allyn, a well-known labor feminist among Massachusetts shoe workers, and the daughter of a shoe cutter, believed the Knights of Labor and co-operation could achieve equality for women and the end of wage slavery.[60] She based her analysis on the family and the experience of self-supporting women. Allyn was enraged that a woman who "molds the future of the world" as a mother was denied the vote, paid lower wages than a man for the same work, and forced by poverty to turn to vice for survival. If a woman's moral significance was degraded by the conditions of employment, the experience of work convinced Allyn of her capacity for independence. "Sister workers," Allyn wrote, "The pleasant fiction about our being 'angels,' and 'clinging ivy,' is over. Angels don't wash, iron, bake, mend and darn hose. It would wear out their wings and temper. Ivy, that fails to find an oak to cling to, gets along by supporting itself, and often grows beautifully."[61]

Understanding women as independent, Allyn did not reject family life but wished to transform it from an institution based on economic necessity to one based on freedom and choice. If men and women received their just wages the family could become a very different institution.

> Sisters, we need in this beautiful land, happy homes, made by marriages based on love. Yes! I repeat it, real reasoning, ennobling love; not respect and esteem merely, but love that appeals to the physical, mental and spiritual needs of both parties. When women receive a just proportion of what they earn few will marry merely for a home. When men receive their share of the wealth they produce, they will have more time to make home happy.[62]

Cooperation and the ballot box would ensure equal pay for equal work and provide working men and women with the tools to harmonize familial relations. This would form the basis of a new world. "When laborers become capitalists by co-operation," Allyn argued, "when back into the pockets of the producer comes a just share of the product—then will the 4,000,000 white slaves be free."[63]

Fannie Allyn understood cooperation in "producerist" terms, as did her male colleagues, and those terms were white. Allyn suggested, however, that self-assertion and the demand for full value of one's labor were not only expressions of white manliness but of woman's nature as well. Furthermore, once she defined women as producers her concept of cooperation changed from that of her male counterparts. The cooperation of male and female producers that she hoped for would transform rather than reinforce the very basic institution of society, the family.

In the 1880s, another line of cooperative thought developed among the Knights of Labor that also challenged the "manliness" of cooperation. It appeared as members debated the appropriateness of a plan for centralized cooperation and a compulsory tax to support it. Promoted by Henry Sharpe, the president of the Knights Cooperative Board, the plan called for the creation of a central Cooperative Guild to establish and control factories and stores among the Knights. The guild, in order to eliminate competition among cooperative factories, would bring its cooperative producers into direct contact with its cooperative consumers. In effect, the decisions of the guild concerning prices and production would replace the competitive market. This was the most ambitious of a number of plans to control the market economy that labor reformers considered during the postwar years. The significant opposition that arose among the Knights to the guild's compulsory tax and its centralized authority, to what was in reality its own alternative version of bureaucratic modernization, culminated in the General Assembly's rejection of the plan in 1884.[64]

A revealing aspect of the guild debate centered on the opposing virtues of compulsion and voluntarism. One supporter of Sharpe's guild wrote, "your plan of [the] co-operative guild will make many a heart glad and stimulate the most timid to take hold—if put in force by the word 'shall.' The word 'shall' gives strength. . . . The word 'may' gives weakness."[65] Compulsion in this cooperator's eyes meant strength. The opposition opposed the compulsory 'shall' with their own voluntary 'may,' and defined it, as a "sister knight" did in verse, in gendered terms. Her allegorical poem, which appeared in the Knights' *Journal of United Labor*, described four children sent by their mothers to gather plums but who bickered among themselves instead, shouting, "you shant, I will, you must, I say," while birds devoured the fruit they came to collect. This continued until "the Dame Maternal" of mutual aid appeared. Under her chiding gaze one boy volunteered to pick the plums. His grandfather neared, however, and disapprovingly noted, "How weak, to me, seems woman's way; Where we say must she still says may." Such self-centeredness, the poem explained, had lost man his heavenly place and forced him to enter a world of labor and necessity. Yet:

> To freedom, love still paved a way,
> And framed, for every must, a may.
> Labor we must, in field and State,
> Blest truth, we may co-operate.

Must suffer, oft the lived long day,
With heav'nly comfort comes M.A. [mutual aid].[66]

Mutual aid and voluntary cooperation were the products of female virtue, compulsion the result of men's selfishness. Freedom, the poet asserted, was to be achieved through the feminine virtues of love and cooperation.

Hugh Cameron, a member of the cooperative board and a leading critic of Sharpe, agreed. He had already written that "Cooperation voluntary and practical [was] Democracy enlightened, purified and rightfully applied," while compulsory cooperation was despotism.[67] In his response to this woman's poem he called for women to join the labor movement, where they, with their special virtues, could help men cooperate.

Between her lines, so full of thought, there is an argument,
Stronger than words could well express for her enfranchisement.
While honest toilers count her out and count drunk loafers in,
They still "must suffer," "go to dust," be punished for such sin.
Think of it, Brothers, when you speak, and boil your speeches down;
Burn up the rubbish, lift the scum, with M. A. woman crown.
That she may in all proper fields of handicraft and state
With her blessed influences for the right help us CO-OPERATE.[68]

While women, in Cameron's view, still had "proper" roles to play based on their uniquely feminine moral authority, cooperation was no longer to be the fulfillment of manly selfishness, but of the voluntary, peaceful, and democratic virtues women carried. These same virtues justified women's political enfranchisement as well as their participation in the labor movement.

The triumph of "voluntary" cooperation and its democratic inclusiveness over the centralized guild did not signal the general triumph of womanly virtue among all cooperators. It did, however, signify the relative plasticity of cooperative ideology. Cooperation was a vital, if ill-defined, tool with which workers explored their possible identities in an industrializing republic. Skilled workers often envisioned a cooperative future that would fulfill a male trade unionist's dream of craft control and equal rights. They did not understand in any consistent way how to settle the conflict that flared between their democratic ideals and their desire to exclude the unskilled and women. Yet cooperation provided the free space where their vision based on manliness and the craft ethos could be recast both by themselves and by the self-activity of subordinate groups. Some workers accomplished this under the influence of the Knights of Labor, which welcomed both women and the unskilled as well as black workers into its fold. When these workers cooperated they struggled along with many wage-earning Americans to assess the democratic experience and determine who were to function as legitimate laborers, producers, and citizens in nineteenth-century America.

A Practical Utopia?

If cooperatives provided a free space for working men and women to test their understanding of gendered rights, producerism, and citizenship, no single plan unified them in their pursuit of reform, nor did they have a generally accepted theory of organization to guide them. While most labor reformers did adopt the Rochdale method of consumer cooperation by the late 1870s, the workers who established producer cooperatives had no such uniform plan. They would have to resolve the dilemmas of self-help in a market economy on their own as they actually cooperated. Subsequently, in their determination to resist the discipline of the market, distribute profits justly, and live harmoniously within the labor movement, they were never conflict-free.[69]

Central to much of their conflict was the labor theory of value, or the commonly held assumption that labor produced all wealth. It served as the ethical basis for cooperation's claim upon the profits of a business enterprise. This theory, however, had to be applied in practical terms in a cooperative, and disputes surrounding the distribution of profits arose frequently among cooperators. The labor theory of value, it seems, offered no unambiguous solution for cooperators to follow.

A Kentucky iron molder, for example, helped organize a cooperative foundry in 1867 and found the nature of profit an issue of immediate concern. While his colleagues disagreed among themselves, he decided that shareholding as the basis for profit distribution was "altogether wrong." Part of the profits of any manufacturing enterprise "belonged" to labor. Yet he believed that profits should go to capital as well. Money, he contended, "is worth just what the laws of the different States say it is worth, and no more; the rest of the profit belongs to labor, and whoever takes more, (after paying for their services) takes that which does not belong to them. The saying, that the 'bosses' have the right to all they can get, is wrong; they simply have the power, and they use it."[70] This Louisville molder had found an arbitrary solution to his problem. If manufacturers could take more than their share of profits by force, fairness dictated that capital should only receive a percentage decided upon by the state.

The members of the Cooperative Shoe Company of Philadelphia addressed a similar issue of concern to the shoe workers of their city a few years later. The cooperators had decided to distribute all of their profits to shareholders. It appeared from a handbill issued by the cooperative that the city's other shoe workers objected. They preferred to see profits distributed only to workers employed in the factory. In the handbill the cooperators responded to their concern:

> But [the typical shoe worker says, the cooperative proposes] the very thing I have all my lifetime been trying to shake off, "The Power of Concentrated Capital."
>
> Why, my dear sir, can not you see our proposition is, to make you, as an individual, one of those very capitalists. By every journeyman subscribing for One share of Stock, are not thereby the whole 4,000 of us the capitalists who receive this return of profits,—how else, pray, could it be done?[71]

The cooperators had made a virtue out of necessity. In order to accumulate the needed resources, all four thousand journeymen shoemakers in Philadelphia had to become capitalists. Yet in the minds of ordinary shoe workers the need for capital alone could not justify the distribution of profits to nonproducers.

Cooperative shoe workers from Nyack, New York, wrote to John Samuel in 1885 for advice after they had predictably disagreed among themselves over the distribution of profits. "Is it right," they asked, "that after a Cooperator [*sic*] receives his wages at the end of the year say he earnes [*sic*] $800.00 in the year and he has $200.00 Capital invested in the Company at the end of the year a five cent dividend is declared now is it fair or not for the Cooperator [*sic*] to receive a dividend on $200.00 or $1000.00."[72] They could not decide whether it was "fair" to give priority to capital or consider labor its equivalent. Their decision would have a significant impact on who among their members would benefit most from the success of the factory.

The Illinois coal miners who formed the Peoria Co-operative Coal Association in 1882 faced the same questions and resolved them on the side of labor. Duncan McPhail, the master workman of the miners' local assembly, explained how they formed their cooperative to employ members blacklisted after a recent strike. "At our first preliminary meeting," he wrote, "an effort was made to have the association based on a money foundation, but fortunately for all concerned, the scheme was killed." Instead they required only a small initiation fee for membership and distributed dividends according to the labor performed by each worker. "By this law," McPhail boasted, "it will be seen that an interest or share in our association is of no benefit to those who do not intend to work for the association; beside, we pay no interest on money paid by members. . . . We have no applications from capitalists for membership because that class will never invest unless they can get something without working for it."[73]

The cooperative solidarity McPhail advocated, however, was problematic. The cooperators had undersold local competitors in order to break into the market, and they soon developed problems with workers in those mines who saw this as a threat. McPhail had little sympathy for them and condemned their objections as the work of wage slaves. He welcomed them to join the Knights of Labor and make their way into the cooperative.[74]

A carpenter and member of a Knights of Labor cooperative from Austin City, Texas, wrote to John Samuel in 1885 for advice on a number of similar issues. Like his counterparts in New York, the carpenter had trouble deciding whether profits should be distributed according to the contributions of labor or of capital. A more significant issue that went to the heart of cooperation as an alternative to competition, however, troubled this member. He wondered how they would operate their business successfully on a day-to-day basis and maintain a broad commitment to labor. It appeared that certain foremen preferred to exclude "slow or common" carpenters for the sake of greater income. It would hardly be fair, the member insisted, to leave the slow man out, but "we are at a loss," he wrote

> how to start the 'Austin Carpenters Cooperative Association' on right & just cooperative principles. So that all will feel as if he was at home & with Brothers. . . . This business is new to us. We have been used to every Carpenter working for himself under the Old cut-throat plan but we are Knights of Labor & we wish betters [*sic*] things. We hear of the success of all other Co-operatives elsewhere. We are Fraternal to each other & would like to form a Co-operative of Carpenters if we had a good plan of constitution.[75]

A commitment to labor, in this cooperator's mind, went beyond the just distribution of profits to the inclusion of as many carpenters as possible in the firm's fraternal fold. How, he asked, could they design their cooperative to succeed and at the same time supplant cut-throat competition? Would their cooperative ultimately meet the needs of a few or the many?

These difficulties notwithstanding, cooperation inspired labor reformers with an exhilarating sense of its practical possibilities. Cooperators, from William Sylvis to most leaders of the Knights of Labor, believed in the very real practicality of worker-owned enterprises. Given the uneven development of industry and the continued viability of many small factories, this was not an altogether unreasonable assessment.[76] However, many labor reformers of the postwar years were also remarkably naive. They envisioned a comprehensive cooperative system of workers' control functioning within a market economy in which wage earners collected their small resources, formed businesses, and then challenged hostile manufacturers. They could successfully challenge their competitors because of their willingness to sacrifice wages and their ability to marshal resources.[77] The severity of competition and the vicissitudes of booms and busts offered scant discouragement to the cooperators. William Sylvis, in fact, believed in the salutary benefits of competition between union foundries and private manufacturers and was convinced that a cooperative could handle any problem posed by the marketplace.[78] All labor had to do, contended the machinists of the Equitable Co-operative Machine Manufacturing Association in 1866, was

> devise some plan by which we may command the necessary capital to yield us the full fruits of our labor. . . . As our united labor forms for him [the capitalist] a large establishment, why not unite our many small capitals, thereby in the aggregate, forming a large one, and already possessing the mechanical skill, forming for ourselves a great establishment, in which the profits would be diffused among those from whose labor they had been accumulated."[79]

The certainty many labor reformers felt in their ultimate triumph was based on their confidence in the practicality of cooperation as well as in their own knowledge and moral place as producers and trade unionists. Yet this cannot explain adequately their enthusiasm and expectation of success. Their expectation of success was buoyed by a combination of Christian triumphalism with an abiding faith in reason, natural law, and self-help. Inspired by an evangelical fervor, labor leaders, like Philadelphia's Thomas Phillips, exhorted their followers to transform their world. Phillips, in his many newspaper columns and published letters, told his readers again and again to contribute their savings to cooperative stores or factories and make of them a practical success. They would, in short order, earn profits, reinvest the proceeds into new stores and factories, and become a power in the land.[80]

The utopian future Phillips and other cooperators nurtured was to be built, moreover, with the mortar and stone of Christian brotherhood and science.[81] In an address to the Knights of St. Crispin, Phillips demonstrated how these ideas could commingle in one man's mind as he spoke in the biblical voice of the cooperative ideal:

> Remember Capital that from the date of my advent . . . thy share of earths treasures must be determined by the rules of arithmatic [*sic*] in accordance with the laws of justice.
>
> I know that thou will resist this . . . —thou will point to the customs and usages of men: but when we compare notes

> as most certainly we shall thou will find that these will not bear the test of reason and science and morality—thou will no doubt call to thy aid man made laws backed by human authority but that will avail the [*sic*] nothing—for I will stand on the higher laws—laws which eminate [*sic*] from; and bear the seal of the highest authority; and from which there is no appeal.[82]

Phillips juxtaposed the "advent" of cooperation, or the coming of the millennium, with the rules of arithmetic or natural law. These rules expressed moral truth, and Phillips and other cooperators appealed to fellow workers with the simple logic of numbers. Invest so many dollars in the cooperative system, they asserted, add to that sum the profits certain to accrue, and you will soon control your economic life. They repeatedly presented such figures as if their very recitation would conjure the necessary belief in cooperation and its essential reasonableness.[83] If only the Crispins, or the iron molders, or the Knights of Labor would contribute a particular sum of money every month or every year, their respective organizations could establish a vast network of cooperatives. The system would work if wage earners recognized their self-interest, made evident by reasoned argumentation, and acted accordingly. All workers, in fact, were obligated to cooperate both by religion and science. "Every man is duty bound," Phillips wrote, "to use his powers for the good of all. We believe in the doctrine that no man made himself and has no right to claim exclusive ownership of his powers." Man, he implied, was the product of divine forces as well as human society, and both obligated the individual to work for a good greater than his own personal welfare. Cooperation, Phillips maintained, would bring about "as fast as the ignorance and selfishness of men will let it—the good times that is [*sic*] coming. . . . [It] would make the prophysey [*sic*] that we are to have heaven upon earth, no longer a promise . . . but a thing realized—a fact accomplished."[84]

Thomas Phillips, as well as the iron molder who in 1868 had cooperation "on the brain," held an abiding faith in the power of cooperation to change the lives of American workers. He believed that a cooperative future could and would be achieved as soon as working people overcame their deficiencies. To most cooperators this idyllic future remained compellingly vague and contradictory. How would cooperation define and reflect the values of manhood and womanhood, producerism, and citizenship? Only as working men and women actively promoted and constructed cooperatives within their organizations, like the Knights of Labor, and their communities, would a cooperative future assume definite shape.

CHAPTER 3

COOPERATION AND THE KNIGHTS OF LABOR

In late May 1886, Leonard Wheeler of Gilbertville, Massachusetts, wrote a heartfelt letter to J. P. McGaughey, then secretary of the Cooperative Board of the Knights of Labor. Wheeler, a factory worker, Master Workman of his local assembly, and father of six children, described to the secretary his experience of joining the Knights in the mid-1880s:

> I suppose I am like hundred's [*sic*] of others who a few years ago could look ahead and see nothing but missery [*sic*], hard work, and starvation, but what a change, when I first heard of the K's of L [Knights of Labor], I immediately subscribed for a daily paper so as to learn all I could of the K's [Knights.] [I]t seemed as if the Cloudy Heavens had opened and I could faintly see a little bright clear sky. Finally I became interested and with about forty others we were organized into an Assembly. We now number over three hundred and a good field before us. I have taken more interest in Cooperation than in Strikes and if this whole country could be managed on that plan how much better it would be for all[.] Bro Powderly says that the next five years will see the emancipation of the white slaves. I do not believe that strikes will do it, but think they will assist. Legislation will also be a great help but cooperation must after all do the whole business.[1]

Leonard Wheeler had discovered a source of great hope in the Knights of Labor, and, as this letter indicates, the rapid growth of the order encouraged him to believe in the likelihood of social change. His letter provides an example of how, in the aftermath of the Civil War, many American workers characterized desirable social change as some form of "emancipation" from wage labor. Though the concept was ill-defined and complicated by the racial strictures of post-Reconstruction America, Wheeler believed emancipation to be eminently achievable through a judicious mixture of strikes, political action, and cooperation. He believed in the efficacy of various types of actions and, like many Knights, assumed these three strategies to be mutually supportive. Yet cooperation was unlike other union strategies involving politics or strike action. It promised a final answer to the labor problem. After all, cooperation, alone among the three, would "do the whole business."[2]

Cooperation, however, proved attractive to many Knights precisely because it aimed to ameliorate specific labor problems, such as low wages, insecure employment, and declining craft control. The final and utopian nature of the Knights' cooperative project only complicated their formulation of effective policies. If the Knights were to form a consensus on this issue they had to both define and then sustain a social vision as well as offer a practicable method to meet the challenges of the marketplace. This proved unusually difficult to do. Under the ironic rubric of cooperation, the Knights fought among themselves. Debate over the means and ends of cooperation became a regular feature of the yearly General Assembly meetings.

As the Knights of Labor grew from a small regional organization to became a formidable national force, its leadership failed to advance cooperation in any substantive way. By the mid-1880s, the initiative fell to local and district assemblies, and they established hundreds of cooperative stores and factories. They, not the national leadership, developed "centralized" approaches to cooperation from the bottom up. Though influenced by the policies of the national organization, their actions would determine the success of cooperation for the Knights of Labor as a whole.

The Knights, like most American workers in the post–Civil War years, could agree only on the most general definition of cooperation as a democratic form of self-help. As late as 1887, the secretary of the Knights' Cooperative Board could still believe cooperation "has so broad a meaning that it designates nothing more than working together," and then implore the General Assembly to "decide what kind of co-operation it desires to establish."[3] This characteristic uncertainty hardly tarnished cooperation's luster. The General Assembly had long embraced worker self-employment as an official and desirable end of labor reform. In fact, the Knights' earliest recruits had participated in cooperative enterprises in Philadelphia, and their first constitution, adopted in 1878, endorsed "the establishment of co-operative institutions, productive and distributive."[4] Uriah S. Stephens, a founder and first Grand Master Workman of the Noble and Holy Order, conceived of the Knights as an emancipator of wage labor through cooperation. While he envisioned local assemblies fighting for the amelioration of working conditions, he defined the district assembly as "the 'strong right arm and the intelligent head of the institution through which in time financial and industrial emancipation of the world's workers from Corporate Tyranny and Wages Slavery is to be achieved." As the locus of cooperative activity, the district would "secure to the toiler all the advantages and possibilities now retained by the banker and manufacturer, the broker and middleman, the gambler and speculator, all the channels of a vicious civilization, through which the profits and rewards of productive labor are now so fatally diverted from him into the possession of idle, absorbent capital."[5] The Chicago General Assembly of 1879 altered this vision only slightly. The assembly approved a resolution that, among other things, called for "Locals . . . to become manufacturing, and Districts, commercial or distributing agencies."[6]

Terence Powderly endorsed cooperation, as well, after he assumed the duties of Grand Master Workman. The problems inherent to wage labor, he argued, could be overcome only if workers challenged the very essence of their relationship to capital. In his address to the General Assembly in 1880, Powderly lamented the seemingly endless antagonism between capital and labor. "So long," he declared, "as a pernicious system leaves one man at the mercy of another, so long will labor and capital be at war, and no strike can hit a blow sufficiently hard to break the hold with which unproductive capital today grasps labor by the throat."[7] If not the "suicidal strike," Powderly continued, than only "thorough, effective organization" could remedy labor's ills; organization, that once perfected, put itself

> to some practical use by embarking in a system of COOPERATION, which will eventually make every man his own master,—every man his own employer; a system which will give the laborer a fair proportion of the products of his toil. It is to cooperation, then, as the lever of labor's emancipation, that the

Terence Powderly and associates John Devlin and Alexander Wright stand before a chair Powderly received in 1887 from a Toledo, Ohio, cooperative chair company. The Powderly Papers. The Catholic University of America.

> eyes of the workingmen and women of the world are directed, upon cooperation their hopes are centred [*sic*], and to it do I now direct your attention. . . . The laboring man needs education in this great social question, and the best minds of the Order must give their precious thought to this system. There is no good reason why labor cannot, through cooperation, own and operate mines, factories, and railroads.[8]

With guidance and education, Powderly observed, laboring men and women could emancipate themselves.[9] Yet, after years of diligent education, the Knights failed to devise a consistent strategy for cooperative production or distribution. When they established a fund to support cooperatives in 1880, rather than plant the seeds of industrial self-management, they managed to argue for seven years over how to collect it. When, during those same years they created a central cooperative board, they gave it power enough only to understand its own limitations.

The Knights' effort to establish cooperative policy began in earnest in 1880, when they first allocated funds for cooperation. The delegates to the 1880 General Assembly earmarked 60 percent of the order's regular per capita assessment for cooperatives, 30 percent for strikes, and 10 percent for education. The following year, the Assembly established a compulsory Cooperative Fund based on a $.10 per capita monthly tax on men and $.05 tax on women which was collected and safeguarded by the various local assemblies. The order issued certificates for every thirty cents a member paid in, and in exchange for ten certificates issued a $3.00 share in the Cooperative Association of the Knights of Labor of America. When needed, the Executive Board would call on each local to send their accumulated funds to a designated authority.[10]

Significant opposition to the compulsory nature of the fund developed over the year, and the next General Assembly in 1882 converted the tax to a voluntary contribution. Indeed, during the previous year few members of the order had paid in their assessment, and few local assemblies later willingly transferred their funds when called upon by the authorities to do so. The General Assembly continued, though, to maintain the fund as a depository for voluntary contributions, and established a Co-operative Board in 1882 to examine opportunities for its investment. In 1884, the Cooperative Fund amounted to no more than $974.52.[11]

It soon became apparent to the men sitting on the new Cooperative Board that they had little authority or money to advance their cause. They grew increasingly frustrated with the duties they described as "honorary" and "administrative." George Holcombe, the board's president in 1883, criticized the "discretionary" nature of the cooperative fund and lamented the board's inactivity. In his view, the order should have mandated an assessment for cooperation and then employed the individual cooperative as a tool to win strikes. Money spent on strike support, he argued, was money lost.

Yet a cooperative factory opened during a strike could provide the necessary edge to defeat an employer. Even if the order itself met defeat, the cooperative would serve "as a landmark to show others the right direction." John Sanderson, the Cooper-ative Board's secretary, called similarly for a compulsory fund. An equal assessment on all members, he argued, would "harmonize with one idea of brotherhood," unlike local cooperative efforts. The nature of the assessment was an essential element of, and necessary step toward, an egalitarian system. "'Call no man master, all ye are brethren,' can only be realized," he wrote, "when the wage system is substituted by that of mutual co-operation."[12]

The delegates to the 1883 convention were swayed halfheartedly by these appeals. They, like their predecessors in 1882, rejected the compulsory tax. Yet, they also refused a motion to dismantle the cooperative fund and turn over the accumulated assets to the District Assemblies.[13] Moreover, they elected Henry Sharpe to head the Cooperative Board, a man who championed the compulsory tax and an integrated system of cooperation. These mercurial positions indicated both how much the delegates wanted a plan of action and how unsure they were of their goals. Sharpe's actions as Cooperative Board president would help to resolve their uncertainty, by defining not what they wanted but what the order as a whole found unacceptable.

Henry Sharpe was the guiding light and founding member of the Grand Cooperative Brotherhood headquartered in New York City in the early 1880s. He and other society members established an agricultural colony in Eglinton, Missouri, in 1880 and three years later constituted themselves Local Assembly 2776 of the Knights of Labor. As a self-described "integral cooperator," Sharpe carried forward a long tradition of communitarian labor reform dating back to the antebellum Owenites and Fourierists. What made his plan of "Integral Cooperation" more a product of the 1880s than of the 1830s was the absence of the well-defined social blueprint of the "utopian socialist" or the doctrinal commitment of the religious communitarian.[14] Integral cooperation, Sharpe explained,

> may be summed up in these words: If a body of men sufficiently numerous, with sufficient variety of skill, establish themselves in a favorable locality, they can produce by their

> own labor all those things necessary to the comfort of their lives; they can arrange their labors and distribute their products according to their own ideas of equity; producing all that is necessary to their comfort, they are not compelled to buy or sell; they become self-supporting, they become independent of capital, they become, in fact, the arbiters of their own fate. Panics cannot frighten them. They have solved the wage question.[15]

The Knights of Eglinton, Missouri, hoped to establish such a self-sufficient community, replete with agricultural and industrial facilities. Unencumbered by a preconceived plan, they would construct a system of their own design, produce the goods they needed, supersede the wage system, and serve as an example to the world of a non-market-driven cooperative order. They strove to free themselves from the forces of dependency through separation from the marketplace and complete self-sufficiency.[16]

Over the course of its existence, Eglinton's isolated utopia grew less and less utopian. The colony collapsed after three hard years in a tumult of internal bickering, and the few members who remained in Eglinton charged Sharpe with a variety of bizarre crimes. They expelled him from the order soon after. A full-scale investigation by the Knights' Executive Board exonerated the erstwhile communalist, but by that time he had completely severed ties with the integral colony.[17] Meanwhile, Sharpe's perspective on isolated cooperation began to change. Self-sufficiency, in the form of an independent colony, had obviously failed. Sharpe, undaunted, found inspiration in the expanding membership of the Knights of Labor. "The power to cooperate," he asserted, "had to be obtained by organization and numbers. The growth of the Order has been so rapid, its numerical strength has increased so fast, that the power to cooperate has now been attained."[18]

Sharpe, like so many other members, witnessed the power and prestige of the order grow and the remarkable potential of the Knights as an organized force increase. To say he was intoxicated with its potential power is no exaggeration. The actual liberation of wage earners from dependency, the slavery of the "money market," "wage market," and panics seemed possible; and to this end Sharpe and his sympathizers attempted to harness the Knights' energy.[19] However, the order had to have proper direction; without it, Sharpe argued, its potential would come to naught: "As individual atoms, the members of our Order are helpless; as the cohering atoms of a mighty association, they become a power, but a power that needs direction to become efficient. The atoms cannot cohere and move in association without direction."[20]

In what direction the Knights should wield their power was not yet clear in Sharpe's mind. While still associated with the Eglinton experiment, he suggested the order invest its cooperative fund in cattle, to be cared for by the settlers. He also called on all Knights wishing to participate in cooperative colonies to raise a special fund through cooperative stores. In this plan, every local assembly interested in colonization would open a store under the aegis of the Cooperative Board. A colonization fund would absorb all profits to the credit of individuals in proportion to their purchases, as the Rochdale plan required. The order would then establish colonies and sell their products in the various assembly stores.[21]

Sharpe assumed the presidency of the Cooperative Board in September 1883 and, over the course of his tenure, slowly articulated a new and farsighted cooperative plan. He recognized what most cooperators failed to acknowledge or refused to believe: the marketplace was an insuperable enemy. Isolated cooperatives that continued to function within the marketplace, Sharpe argued, could not liberate workers from wage dependency:

> That co-operation which does not seek to become self-contained, but which rather seeks to live on its environment, does not help to abolish the wage-system; Nay, it thrives by the necessities of the wage slaves, and is in fact only a corporation of competism [*sic*]. The Knights of Labor were organized to abolish by supplanting the wage-system, it therefore as an Order should not lend its power, authority or prestige to any institution, even though it creeps under the shield, which does not mean ultimately death to the wage-system. Integral co-operation does mean that, therefore it is the only kind of co-operation which should be protected by the aegis of the Order. The individual co-operative institutions are good as far as they go, for they give experience, encourage fraternity and kindle hope, but they are part and parcel of competism and must go with it. We must have the Exodus.[22]

To eliminate "competism," Sharpe devised a plan in mid-1884 that would supplant the market for wages and goods with a system owned and controlled by the Knights of Labor. He described this plan as "cooperation of the Order, by the Order and for the Order," and he tirelessly promoted it through correspondence and in his column for the *Journal of United Labor.*[23]

Sharpe submitted his program to the General Assembly in September 1884. He proposed the establishment of a separate division within the Knights of Labor, a virtual parallel organization, known as the Cooperative Guild. Complete with its own assemblies and executive board, the guild would assume all of the order's cooperative functions and create a system of production and exchange open only to members in good standing. Membership in the guild was voluntary, yet Sharpe tentatively proposed a compulsory tax on all Knights to fund its cooperative enterprises.[24]

The guild, in a fashion similar to Sharpe's cooperative colony, would focus its productive efforts on one geographic area. However, unlike the Integral Colony, it would not be limited to a single locale and could establish businesses elsewhere, if necessary. Ultimately, the Knights of Labor would become "a great industrial union, self-employing, self-sustaining, self-governing." The group would absorb all other labor unions and include every worker wanting "equity" in its plan of cooperation.[25]

Unlike the vast majority of his compatriots in the labor movement, Sharpe envisioned a highly centralized bureaucracy administering this new industrial system. He likened the guild to "a State," and believed

> the Order has arrived at the time when its organization should be at least as complex as that of a State; when, in fact, its members should be taught to look upon themselves as a 'people,' or, so to speak as a nation, and the legislative, the executive, the judiciary, the industrial, the police, the insurance, the educational and the charities departments should all be well defined, properly officered and actively employed. It is high time that members be found whose special aptitudes incline them to one or the other of the departments, and who, finding therein a field for their activities, develop their aptitudes still further and become specialists.[26]

All successful organizations, whether states or armies, and "modern fortunes" accumulated through commerce or industry, cooperated in order to succeed, and "the law of social progress" demanded that the Knights either "co-operate and prosper" or "disintegrate and perish."[27]

Sharpe was disappointed in the cooperative movement as it existed in England and the United States. The English movement, having started with "aspiration and zeal," had "settled down to mere shopkeeping." The Rochdalers failed, according to Sharpe, despite their great "wealth and ability," to articulate a program of any long-term significance. In the United States, the Knights could learn from this experience. Rather than form local market-oriented cooperative institutions, they could develop an entirely new program, one that would call upon the Knights to "organize the consumers and produce for them."[28] "In the labor propaganda," Sharpe contended, "men have been taught to look upon themselves as producers. Far better were it to teach them that they are consumers, and that the interest of the consumer is to get all he needs, and to get it at the lowest cost."

> Now if we start out with this idea that we are consumers, and that the best thing we can do is to produce for ourselves the things we need, we shall advance rapidly to that condition in which we become self-employed and independent of masters. In that case, when the Order, as part of its programme, establishes, say a shoe factory, every intelligent member of the Order would understand that it is his factory, and he had better patronize his own factory, so at once the market for shoes is made. . . . "Organization of the producers" has been the watchword long enough. Organization of the consumers is the real work that should engage us. When this great system has . . . its thousands of members busily working, with no idlers to maintain, then its members, being self-employing, self-sustaining, not beholden to any master for work or wages, can reap the full fruits of their labors.[29]

The Cooperative Guild attracted considerable attention and praise from the standard bearers of cooperation, even if their own visions differed from Sharpe's. Quite possibly these men would have found any alternative to the aimless drift of the previous cooperative policies acceptable. Longtime cooperator John Samuel, for one, accepted the underlying principles of the guild if it was to be carried out simply and unambitiously, even though he could not "accept in every particular" the theory of integral cooperation. Richard J. Hinton, a noted socialist and former member of the International Workingmen's Association who had toured European cooperatives in the late 1860s, supported the guild and saw in such cooperative enterprises "the economic emancipation of the wage slaves, and . . . their permanent enfranchisement through the evolution of the New Republic." At the General Assembly of 1884, the Committee on Co-operation, which included such notables as Ralph Beaumont, Gilbert Rockwood, and John Samuel, proposed the guild plan for consideration by the order. Indeed, Henry Sharpe recommended that these men, as well as other prominent Knights and cooperators, including Henry Fecker of Indiana, Amos Fayram of Detroit, J. S. Rankin of Minneapolis, Frank R. Foster of Massachusetts, and T. B. Barry of Michigan, become charter members of the guild.[30]

Despite the support of some leading Knights, the guild plan failed to gain the approval of the General Assembly or of the rank-and-file members of the order. The Assembly considered the plan in 1884, supported both by a voluntary fund and by a compulsory tax. During the course of a rather long debate the majority arrayed itself squarely against the compulsory tax plan. This, however, was no indication of the assembled representatives' sentiment toward cooperation. In what must have been a moment of frustration, if not high drama, Powderly requested the delegates to rise if they were "in favor of co-operation" at all. The delegates rose in a unanimous response. When the General Master Workman asked those in favor of compulsory cooperation to rise, only fourteen responded. Seventy-three delegates later stood opposing any form of compulsory cooperation. On the guild plan without a per capita tax, the delegates could not agree, and they postponed the debate until the next General Assembly meeting in 1885.[31] The guild, for all practical purposes, had been defeated.

Before the convention began, Sharpe had sent questionnaires to each local assembly to assess rank and file interest in the guild. He was disappointed in the response. Only 212 out of as many as 3,000 locals returned the survey, and only 132 of those approved of the guild. Ninety-eight respondents favored the compulsory plan and 34 approved of the voluntary scheme.[32] Sharpe realized that the order had thoroughly rejected his plan. "This, to my mind," he wrote before the General Assembly adjourned, "puts an end to co-operation of the Order, by the Order, and for the Order."[33]

Sharpe had received letters objecting to the guild and its compulsory tax months before the Assembly convened in September. Fearing the defeat of the guild altogether, he decided not to insist on the tax at the General Assembly. The members, he wrote, "are not yet educated up to it."[34] The tax, however, was not all that disturbed the Knights. Members of the order expressed a profound uneasiness with the guild's centralized authority. One local assembly denounced the guild as "no more nor less than a joint stock concern," where the funds would be managed by a few unaccountable officers.[35] Another district assembly looked askance at the plan, "savoring as it does strongly of State Socialism."[36]

Such objections, alternatively accusing Sharpe of capitalist and socialist inclinations, betrayed the members' discomfort with an issue far more elemental than either taxes or centralization. The Knights perceived the guild as a threat. It appeared, in fact, to challenge not only their accepted notions of cooperation but the fundamental ideals of the labor movement.

When Sharpe spoke of the guild, he did so in the familiar idiom of working-class republicanism. Like most nineteenth-century labor reformers, he sought independence for the wage-laborer from the whim of the employer and the caprice of the market, and he fought to return to producers the full fruits of their labor. The means he promoted to achieve this end was, unsurprisingly, cooperation or worker self-employment. All this was evidence of his unimpeachable nineteenth-century reform credentials. When he belittled the efforts of individual cooperators, however, he must have baffled his listeners, who expected to gain power from the cooperative control of their respective shop floors. Yet even more bewildering was his insistence that successful cooperation must mirror the bureaucratic enterprises of the age: namely, the army, the state, and the corporation. The evolution of society, he argued, demanded this, and the creation of the guild, a highly departmentalized and specialized organization, was a necessity if the Knights would ever achieve independence.

The incompatibility of republican independence with the complex organization of bureaucratic forms, though, never troubled Sharpe. In part, this can be ascribed to his definition of independence as a general freedom from market forces and not, in the first instance, the autonomy found in the direct collective ownership of a cooperative shop. Yet most significantly, a bureaucratized order, in his view, could not violate the sanctity of personal independence because its membership was a "people," and, like the state, it embodied the people's interests and will. The phrase, "cooperation of the Order, by the Order and for the Order," having exchanged the word "order" for "people," clearly expressed the equivalence of the two terms in Sharpe's mind. When the guild controlled a cooperative, it took no authority away from the participating members because it was by definition the members. They could achieve independence only through the actions of this organization, not the petty activities of individual men.

Sharpe placed one foot clearly beyond the republicanism of labor reform and, as a result, stepped closer to a variant of socialism and the organizational realities of the new industrial economy. Though he did not see control of the state as a means of liberation, he believed that a cooperative society could be achieved only through the power of a highly specialized organization. Such an organization could act with impunity because it embodied the will of its membership. Sharpe, in addition, asked the Knights to identify, not with their local community or shop floor experience, but with all members of the order in the form of such an organization. He suggested that they understand brotherhood in more distant and abstract terms than was their wont. In a similar way, he asked them to organize as consumers and not as producers. Acting in concert, consumers could guarantee the market for goods and only then control production. By making a priority of consumption, however, Sharpe slighted the most important issues for the Knights as wage-earners, those emanating from the workplace itself.

The Knights' rank and file would not accept the creation of a parallel organization within the order, especially one that so completely redirected members' loyalties from the local assembly and shop floor to a more abstract peoplehood and consumerism. Sharpe called on the Knights to abandon the local experiences that defined them. He encouraged them to place their trust in a bureaucracy that would free them from market forces and grant them independence. Simply put, the Knights would not do so.

This opposition was exacerbated by Sharpe himself, who had an obstreperous personality and an uncompromisingly zealous position on cooperation. His behavior alienated key members of the order, who organized against him and eventually expelled him from the organization.[37]

With the abandonment of the guild plan, the Knights of Labor did not then devise a simple or straightforward policy. At the same time that they rejected an organized system fostered from the top down, they sanctioned an attenuated version of cooperation "by the Order." In fact, before Henry Sharpe formulated his guild plan and set the terms for the debate in 1884, the Executive Board had assumed control over a coal mine in Cannelburg, Indiana. This cooperative mine was one of two enterprises owned in whole or in part by the order during the mid-1880s.[38]

The order assumed control over the Cannelburg mine in April 1884. About a year and a half earlier, the Buckeye Coal Company had locked out eight Cannelburg miners for refusing to withdraw from the Knights. Rather than leave the order, these men acquired a lease for forty acres of coal and opened their own mine. They worked the mine for about a year, with little success, and when their lease payment fell due they called on the Knights for assistance. The Executive Board implored the order at large to contribute funds, and the glass workers' Local Assembly 300 came forward with a loan of two thousand dollars. The board then constituted itself the company's directors and issued $5.00 debenture bonds to raise money for the operation of the mine and to repay the loan.[39]

Despite the *Journal of United Labor*'s praise for the Cannelburg mine as an assured success and "a new departure for the Knights of Labor," the rank and file responded lethargically. In a period of economic decline, very few members purchased the bonds. Delegates to the 1884 General Assembly, however, expressed more interest. These representatives, who rejected the guild in its compulsory form, authorized the executive board to assess each member $.20 to support the mining enterprise.[40] Their effort, backed wholeheartedly by Terence Powderly, was an acceptable form of "centralized" cooperation, while the guild plan was not.

When the order attempted to collect the tax, the rank and file responded, as they had previously, with little enthusiasm and some resistance. Frederick Turner, the Knights' general secretary treasurer, complained of their vocal "impatience" and "dissatisfaction" with the assessment. Yet, by the end of the year the order had collected over $10,000 for the Cannelburg mine. More than fifty thousand Knights had, at that time, paid their $.20.[41] During the life of the cooperative, the Knights of Labor would spend more than $20,000 to support the enterprise.

Why, after rejecting the Cooperative Guild, did the order dedicate such enormous resources to the Cannelburg mine? Certainly, it presented a less than ideal investment opportunity. The mine required machinery, pumps, and engines to make it operational, as well as a switch for rail service, all of which required a large subsidy. The leaders of the order accepted this, despite some resistance to assessments from the rank and file, for one primary reason: the mine represented their organization's potential as a force for change. Having conceived of this project during a small but typically bitter labor conflict, various Knights vested the mine with a symbolic power they wished the order could exercise. For a General Master Workman wary of strikes, it was a "sensible" and "practical" measure, "the biggest card for the Order we have ever played."[42] General Secretary McClelland described it as the first favorable opportunity for the order to control resources and begin in a small way "the transition from the wage system to the cooperative system."[43] John Samuel, as secretary of the Cooperative Board, believed its success would "exert a powerful influence throughout the Order & advance the cause of Cooperation by inspiring confidence in those who now hold back from making any effort to carry it out."[44] The fact that the mine presented obstacles to profitability did not, at first, deter their enthusiasm.[45] The mine was a small but potent symbol of the order's potential strength.

As the Cannelburg mine progressed, the newly elected Cooperative Board replaced Henry Sharpe and announced its policy of "voluntary" cooperation. Under this rather vague rubric, a number of ideological tendencies coexisted. The board itself attempted to continue a policy of centralized aid to cooperative enterprises, though when local and district assemblies deluged its members with requests for financial aid, they were unable to offer assistance. The board was constitutionally limited to investigating requests for aid and presenting findings to the Executive Board. This latter council reserved the final say on money matters for itself. In addition, if the Executive Board agreed to provide support, the Cooperative Board had to assume control over the business.[46]

Given these strictures, the Cooperative Board members emphasized self-reliance to the Knights in local and district assemblies. J. P. McGaughey of Minneapolis, Minnesota, secretary of the board in 1886, actually pleaded with the membership to stop requesting aid. He had received hundreds of applications for assistance during his tenure as secretary and had been forced to deny them all. Influenced by the ideas of Henry Sharpe and an advocate of agricultural colonies, he despaired of ever implementing cooperation "by the Order."[47]

John Samuel experienced similar frustrations. Samuel had been an active cooperator and trade unionist since the 1860s in Philadelphia. When he arrived in St. Louis in the early 1870s, he was already an ardent Rochdale enthusiast and, within a decade, he became the preeminent voice for cooperation in the Knights of Labor. In 1884, he and several other men replaced Sharpe's contingent on the Cooperative Board. Although he had previously supported the guild plan, he also implored American workers to proceed like the English Rochdale Pioneers. Start first, he suggested, with cooperative stores, accumulate capital, and then venture into production:[48] "While under peculiarly favorable conditions productive co-operation may be made a success, it has been the settled conviction of the most experienced co-operators that the store is the first step to be taken. Where the Rochdale plan has been the most closely adhered to the greatest success has followed."[49] He counseled patience and conservatism, fearing the results of haste and bad planning. "Many an attempt at co-operation . . . has broken down & confidence consequently destroyed," he argued, when cooperators acted too hastily.[50]

Samuel, despite his admonitions to others, often made exceptions to his own rule. For example, he supported funding cooperative enterprises, and early in his tenure as secretary of the board sought aid for a proposed saw mill in Wisconsin. When the Executive Board rejected his request because of its preoccupation with the Cannelburg mine, he came to view the order as an unreliable source of revenue. He did not, however, reject control of cooperation by the order on principle, like board member Hugh Cameron, who feared the "corruption" of centralized authority; neither did he long for an "integral" colony, like McGaughey. Samuel was pragmatic. He understood the limits of what the order could provide at any given time and pursued the avenues of opportunity open to him. When the general secretary treasurer denied his request for aid, he first counseled Knights to rely on their own resources, waited seven months, and asked again.[51]

Samuel's requests notwithstanding, the Knights of Labor did not extend aid to any other cooperative until early 1886. During that time the order spread rapidly and faced a growing number of labor conflicts. One such conflict involved the wagon makers of Homer, New York. The wagon factory proprietors in this small upstate New York town had locked out their employees in an attempt to break the Knights' organization. Terence Powderly took a personal interest in the plight of the affected workers, and he visited their small town to mediate the conflict. The employers, however, slighted him, and Powderly advised the wagon makers to build a cooperative factory in response. Soon after, the order contributed $2000 to the town's fledgling cooperative factory. Nearly a year later, the Knights had invested $8,000 in the Homer Manufacturing Company.[52]

Investments of this kind tended to develop their own peculiar and revealing problems. In Cannelburg, Indiana, for example, the Executive Board of the Knights, headquartered in Philadelphia, directed the mine's operation and made decisions for workers hundreds of miles away. The miners, as indirect owners, had no authority over the mine. When they had cause to complain of their superintendent's incompetence, they could confront their directors only as workers would an absentee owner. Indeed, they had to appeal to an emissary from the board to have their grievances heard. Unlike most "capitalist" mine owners, the board heeded their request and replaced the offending superintendent. This had, however, little impact on the viability of the business. For a variety of complicated and still unclear reasons, the mine failed by the end of 1885.[53]

In Homer, the Executive Board was the principal stockholder, rather than the actual director, of the wagon works. As in Cannelburg, though, it could control the factory and impose its own decisions on the workers involved. This was most apparent after mismanagement, a dearth of capital, and the absence of needed machinery nearly led to the company's collapse. The Executive Board instituted two unilateral changes they believed would save the cooperative. First, they replaced the original trustees who worked in the factory with men whom the company did not employ. According to one investigator's report, the trustees resisted the shop floor directions of the superintendent, and the cooperative, he implied, suffered from an excess of democracy and inefficiency. Second, the Executive Board planned to move the factory to larger quarters in Cortland, a neighboring town. This particularly irritated the Homer wagon workers. They brought charges against the administration of the company, accusing it of mismanagement, incompetence, and contemplating "removing the works to Courtland [*sic*]." They raised $500 to induce the Knights to change their mind and keep the factory in Homer but ultimately failed to change their decision.[54] The factory was moved to Cortland, where it operated successfully for six more years.[55]

In these instances the Knights were unable to reconcile the demands they imposed on cooperation both to represent the power and interests of the order as a whole and to operate in the interest of its member-workers. Only the broadest needs could be met by cooperatives controlled from the rarefied atmosphere of the Executive Board. That is, the order could operate cooperatives in its own interest but the workers involved would have little say in the daily operation of the enterprise. The order's concern for all of its members, then, took precedence over the concerns of individual local or district assemblies directly involved in the cooperatives. These latter knights, so the Executive Board seemed to say, were too particularistic to act in the interest of the entire order.[56]

Despite these difficulties and disagreements over cooperation, the General Assembly of 1886 reversed its long-standing policy against establishing a compulsory fund. The delegates agreed, on former grand secretary Charles Litchman's suggestion, to set aside $10,000 quarterly from the general revenues for cooperative purposes. Whether they agreed to this out of enthusiasm for the order, out of discouragement with the defeats of 1886, or both is impossible to say. Regardless, the fund itself never materialized. Though the order did lend money to a few enterprises over the next two years, it never had the resources to dedicate $40,000 a year to cooperation. At the General Assembly of 1887, Litchman again introduced an amendment successfully, this time to reverse policy and make the contribution to cooperation voluntary.[57]

The Knights of Labor believed in their power to resist market forces on a grand scale, yet failed during their most influential years to establish a meaningful, consistent, or workable policy for cooperation. Cooperation by the order, in the abstract, was a powerful guarantor of liberty and challenge to capital. Conceptually and in practice, however, it distanced itself from the shop floor issues that resonated with the rank and file. It tended, as well, to generate, among hard-pressed members, resistance to taxation. Combined with divisive ideological tendencies, this prevented the Knights from reaching a consensus on an effective policy. The order then surrendered the initiative to the members of local and district assemblies, who, acting largely out of their own needs, became the innovators in cooperative organization.

By the mid-1880s, the order had grown to a size unprecedented in the history of the American labor movement. Between 1885 and 1886, the year of the Great Upheaval, membership in the Knights of Labor increased from 110,000 to 750,000 and the number of strikes more than doubled. At the same time, Knights in their local and district assemblies established hundreds of cooperatives in at least thirty-five of the thirty-eight states.[58] Buoyed by their organization's success but without a clear design to guide and assist them, the cooperators were influenced more by local conditions than by national policy. The circumstances of a particular city, town, or industry had a decisive impact on when and how cooperation would develop. At the same time, market conditions prodded some locals toward more centralized cooperative efforts, picking up by necessity where the general officers left off.

Local assemblies considered cooperation a formidable weapon for their purposes. "We have organized an assembly here," the recording secretary from a Meridian, Mississippi, local wrote to John Samuel, "and by a decree of vote I was instructed to correspond with you. We intend to bring ourselves to a higher standing and mean to use cooperation [as] a means by which we may make capital humble itselves [*sic*] to us and not us to it any longer."[59] Indeed, the local assembly was the most common venue for any form of cooperation, and a strike the most common precipitating event. District assemblies became actively involved in the planning or running of cooperatives as well. The district assembly in Williamsport, Pennsylvania, for example, operated a cooperative store while Newark, New Jersey's District Assembly 51 planned, as early as 1883, to open both a store and a building and loan association and to publish a cooperative newspaper. District Assembly 76 of Grand Rapids, Michigan, opened a cooperative coal yard in 1884 at the same time the shoe workers' District Assembly 70 in Philadelphia considered buying a shoe factory in Riverside, New Jersey.[60]

Among the workers who established cooperatives in the 1880s, coal miners were the most prolific. These men were particularly vulnerable to the authority of their employers and attuned to issues of dependency. Hounded by the blacklist, dependent upon company housing, and forced to shop at company stores, miners experienced a particularly intense variety of industrial inequality.[61] Cooperation represented their potential independence from, and collective power over, a closed and hostile environment.

For a number of miners in Illinois, Indiana, Kansas, Missouri, and Pennsylvania, the cooperative store provided some of the independence they desired.[62] For others, the store simply couldn't do enough. One organizer, writing to John Samuel in 1885 from Kentucky, found little hope in cooperative distribution and believed it would be quite impossible to achieve, "under our circumstances": "[I]n the first place there are but one craft employed, namely, miners, the moment any or all of them undertake to deal with an individual store keeper, he or they guilty of the offence, are discharged, and there being no other workmen or craft or enterprise and the opperators [*sic*] or company haveing [*sic*] a store compel men under their employ to patronise [*sic*] them, regardless of the prices charge [*sic*] for goods[.]"[63]

"What we want," he contended,

> is to free ourselves from the Iron hand of monopoly, through productive Cooperation. . . . [O]ur membership in the five L.As. at present is 250, and are working very Secretly, on account of the Tyranny imposed on the workers hear [*sic*] in the past. . . . [I]t would seem after a visit to places I have visited, that free speach [*sic*] is taken entirely from the wealth producers. . . . The plucmee system is very bad all along this line, and in order to compell [*sic*] men to deal in Company store I have Known different Corparations [*sic*] to with hold [*sic*] the hard earned money belonging to the workers from three to six months at a time, so you will see at once, nothing save Productive Cooperation can free, and elavate [*sic*] the poor but Honest workers of this locality.[64]

With such powerful employers, mine workers had, at best, a tenuous grip on their rights to organize, to speak freely, or to even shop at a store of their own choosing. James Beck, a master workman in Belleville, Illinois, also worried that his blacklisted union friends would be forced to leave their community and families in order to find work. They could conceive of only one solution that could "avoid or prevent such a calamity," he reported: "[and] they had come to the conclusion in the Ay.[assembly], after patient & mature consideration, that through co-operation only, productive & distributive, could they hope or expect to secure for themselves, 'just remuneration for their labor & the exercise of their art.'"[65]

The notion that cooperation should serve to stabilize community life was taken quite literally by the Belleville Knights, as well as by the Knights of Alabama. In December 1887, three members of the order from Birmingham formed the Mutual Land and Improvement Company to purchase property and settle a Knights of Labor town. Their efforts were so successful that within a year they had established two towns, Powderly and Trevellick, named after the two labor movement leaders. They laid the towns out in a series of 50-by-120-foot lots on which they intended to build houses for members of the order. About a third of the lots were reserved for sale to businesses, while only Knights in good standing could qualify to buy the rest. The owner of a lot then became a stockholder in the company and waited for his house to be built.[66]

The Knights who established Powderly set out to create a cooperative community and provide stability for working-class families. To that end they built their own affordable homes at half the price they would have had to pay outside of the town. Moreover, they envisioned operating all businesses on a cooperative basis. Members of the order established the Powderly Cooperative Cigar Works and sold four hundred $25 shares to members. Local miners purchased over half of the stock. The cooperative gave priority to the employment of married men, and all employees could become stockholders in the factory. Within a year the Powderly Knights had created a community out of nothing, a place where wage-earning families could build their own affordable homes and at least hope to operate their own businesses collectively. According to the historian of the Alabama Knights, by the end of its first year the town had "200 inhabitants, a school, a general merchandise store, a market house, a Knights of Labor Hall, a free reading room, a railroad station, and a cigar store."[67]

The autonomy provided by cooperation, both real and symbolic, resonated with the Alabama Knights, as it did with Kentucky and Illinois miners. Within the context of their neighborhoods,

Trademark from the letterhead of the Knights of Labor Cooperative Soap Factory of Chicago. Wisconsin Historical Society.

cooperators attempted to protect themselves, assert their rights, and provide for their immediate needs. Their desire for protection, though, took them beyond neighborhood and shop floor issues; they became more than simple "localists."[68] Virtually all cooperators, at one point or another, realized that the success of their own businesses depended on the power of the Knights' extralocal organization. Many expected the order to help with their cooperative efforts, and that very expectation of mutual assistance signaled a new sense of their own obligation toward other workers. Many Knight-cooperators, in fact, began to think in larger terms than their immediate environs as they looked to their organization in a variety of ways to make cooperation work.

The Knights of Belleville, for example, turned expectantly toward the District Assembly in nearby St. Louis for protection and aid. Anticipating far more than conventional strike assistance,

Trademark of the Cooperative Shirt Manufacturing Co. of Baltimore, from the *Journal of United Labor*, 1887. Wisconsin Historical Society.

James Beck proposed the formation of a cooperative coal outlet to District Assembly 17 to be operated under its auspices. He suggested this as a way of bringing into practical operation "one of the fundamental principles of the Order," the primary object of which "[was] to bring producer and consumer together, & do away with the middleman." When the Belleville Co-operative Coal & Mining Company opened for business, its fifty-two members expected the District Assembly to "furnish a market for their product."[69] Indeed, the District Assembly, under John Samuel's tutelage, established a cooperative outlet to sell their coal.

The Knights of Powderly, Alabama, having created their own community, seemed to recognize rather quickly their need for additional funds. The town's local assembly wrote to the General Executive Board and requested an investigation "of the chances and inducements this place can offer any cooperative enterprise and also to reccomend [*sic*] that the Order at large will demonstrate the success of co-operation by establishing some enterprise at Powderly."[70] The board refused their appeals. At the General Assembly of 1888, the Alabama delegate requested an appropriation of $30,000 to open a cooperative in Powderly.[71]

Many members of the order grew to expect a new level of mutual assistance from their fellow Knights. They looked upon the expanding network of local and district assemblies as a potential market for goods and a source of capital. Practically speaking, this was essential if cooperation would succeed at all. The typical cooperative, undercapitalized and marginal, could survive only if it found a ready market among the members of the Knights. This was most evidently true for the cooperative stores that served a local clientele. In one typical case, the coal yard established by District Assembly 76 would certainly have failed, its Master Workman admitted, without the "organized patronage" the Knights could guarantee. "A private enterprise," he assured John Samuel, "with such a small capital and the sharp competition would have been a dead failure."[72]

For producer cooperatives, the widespread organization of the Knights presented promising possibilities. A local or district assembly that planned to open a factory would typically appeal first to Knights within its own geographic area for stock subscriptions. If it failed to generate enough capital by this means, the members would appeal in a circular to the Knights at large. In this manner, the molders of Bloomington, Illinois, first raised $4000 from nearby local assemblies and then petitioned other members of the order for assistance. They sold the idea of stock ownership to the Knights as both a profitable venture and an act of mutual assistance. They stood ready at all times, they maintained, to help those who subscribed for stock in their enterprise. Other prospective cooperators promised, as did the tobacco workers of Raleigh, North Carolina, to pay a fixed portion of their profits into the general cooperative fund of the order. The Raleigh cooperators succeeded in selling stock to over one thousand assemblies scattered throughout the country.[73]

K. of L. Brand

COSSACK.

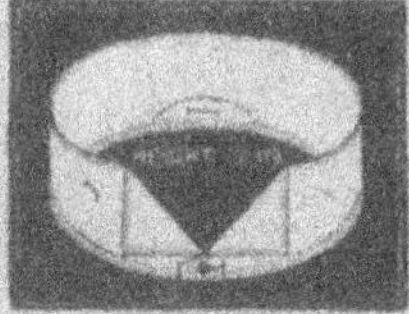

LEIPSIC.

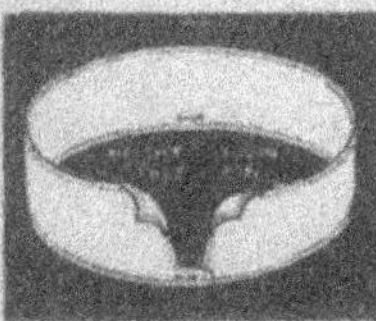

HECTOR.

CO-OPERATIVE COLLARS AND CUFFS

The Only Union Made Collars

The above Cuts are Selected from our Variety of Styles in Popular Demand.

These Celebrated Goods are made by the

Co-Operative Collar and Cuff Co.,

TROY, N. Y.

We use the Best Linens and Spare no Expense in Making our Collars Heavy and Durable. They are all 4 ply and the Workmanship is Unsurpassed.

Every Collar and Cuff Bears our Trade Mark.

TRADE MARK

Ask your Merchant for Them.

Endorsed by D. A. 68.

Advertising flyer for the Cooperative Collar and Cuff Co., of Troy, New York, circa 1887. Wisconsin Historical Society.

Taken from the letterhead of the National Knights of Labor Cooperative Tobacco Co., Raleigh, N.C. Wisconsin Historical Society.

To the Knights of Labor of America.

☞ To the Secretary.—Please read to your Local, and urge the importance of this matter among your membership and report the action taken. It is a co-operative and mutual association combined.

WATERFORD, N. Y., April 29, 1886.

To the Knights of Labor of America:

Brethren: For the past few weeks our local assembly, No. 4,865, of Waterford, N. Y., has been considering the propriety of organizing in Waterford a *National K. of L. Co-operative* Linen Collar and Cuff Manufactory.

Situated, as we are, on the Hudson river, almost directly opposite Troy, N. Y., the great head quarters of this industry, and our assembly being attached to D. A. 68, of Troy, N. Y., and being strongly urged to said action by D. A. 68; and also being assured, after a careful consideration, that such industry in this place would thrive and prove helpful to the cause of labor, and furnish employment to those in need, we have therefore organized the *National K. of L. Co-operative Linen Collar and Cuff Company*, of Waterford, N. Y., on a basis of $15,000 capital, to be taken in shares of $2.50 each. We propose that the profits arising from this enterprise shall first pay 6 per cent. on the paid up capital stock, and the remainder shall be divided between labor and the co-operative fund of the General Assembly. Thus, while helping ourselves, we hope to help others.

The hope of labor is in co-operation, and we promise to bring to this work all the energy and capacity that we possess, to the end that others may be encouraged by our success to do likewise.

We are nearly ready to begin operations, having secured ample room and nearly all the machinery necessary, including a good steam boiler and engine. We are anxious to commence manufacturing by June 1st, and invoke the influence and help of all true knights to bring success to this enterprise. We therefore earnestly request that your Assembly respond to our appeal by taking at least one share.

HOW WE PROPOSE RAISING THE MONEY!

First. The members of the assemblies here have taken every share they can pay for.

Second. We ask each assembly in the bounds of our order to subscribe for at least one share (Two Dollars and Fifty cents) of the capital stock. If the individual members of your assembly are willing to take stock, we shall be pleased to have them do so. But we especially desire that each assembly, as a body, shall take at least one share.

We hope that you will not delay the matter one week, but act *now*.

Send your subscriptions by check or postal order for the amount to Edward VanKleeck, Waterford, N. Y., who will immediately issue to you certificate of stock for the same.

N. B. Employees to work eight hours with full pay in this shop.

A stock solicitation for the National Knights of Labor Cooperative Linen Collar and Cuff Company of Waterford, N.Y., directed at all members of the Knights of Labor. Wisconsin Historical Society.

Cooperators also defined the purchase of cooperatively made goods as an act of solidarity with other Knights of Labor, an expression of their common "brotherhood." The small local assemblies in Gibson City, Illinois, and Canton, Kansas, both sought out cooperative mines, in preference to others, to purchase coal for their members. An assembly from New Britain, Connecticut, pledged itself, "in view of the noble work that our brothers in South Norwalk have accomplished," to buy hats only from that city's cooperative hat makers. G. A. Fleischer of Toledo, Ohio, set himself up as an agent for Knights of Labor Cooperative Manufacturers and promoted sales for the social good they would achieve. Buying cooperatively produced goods, he claimed, would help do away with strikes, as well as "decrease pauperism, landlordism, and millionarism and increase the welfare of the wage workers, and their families. . . . By promoting the betterment of their condition," he added, "you advance your own interests." District Assembly 148 in Olean, New York, established a cooperative oil refinery in 1887 to challenge the monopoly of the Standard Oil Company. These cooperators relied quite self-consciously upon the patronage and support of the Knights of Labor to succeed and appealed to them again in the name of "common brotherhood."[74]

C. Fannie Allyn, the Stoneham, Massachusetts, labor feminist, went beyond this notion of a common "brotherhood" when she attempted to form a market for cooperatively made goods. An outspoken advocate of equality for women, Allyn inspired a group of twelve women and six men from Cincinnati, all members of the same local assembly, to plan a unique event. These young men and women, all but six under twenty-two years of age, appealed to cooperatives from around the country to display their products in a grand "Cooperative Fair" to take place in Cincinnati. Calling themselves the Fannie Allyn Cooperative Association and Local Assembly, they held their weeklong fair in the Knights of Labor Hall, where Allyn opened the event and served as its "chairman."[75]

Inspired by Allyn, this group displayed the exhibits of ten different cooperatives from at least nine states. According to George Kuechler, secretary of the association, their goal was to form "a cooperative concern" of their own with the proceeds of the fair. Through the fair and the store they acted on their belief in cooperation as "one of the leading principles of our noble order." In their new cooperative they would sell only Knights of Labor products and by doing so "establish a market" not for any particular cooperative, but "for the cause."[76] If most Knights opposed any attempt to centralize cooperation from the top down, these knights found one way to give substance to their ill-defined cooperative future. Under Fannie Allyn's tutelage, both men and women constructed the rudiments of a distributive network without central-

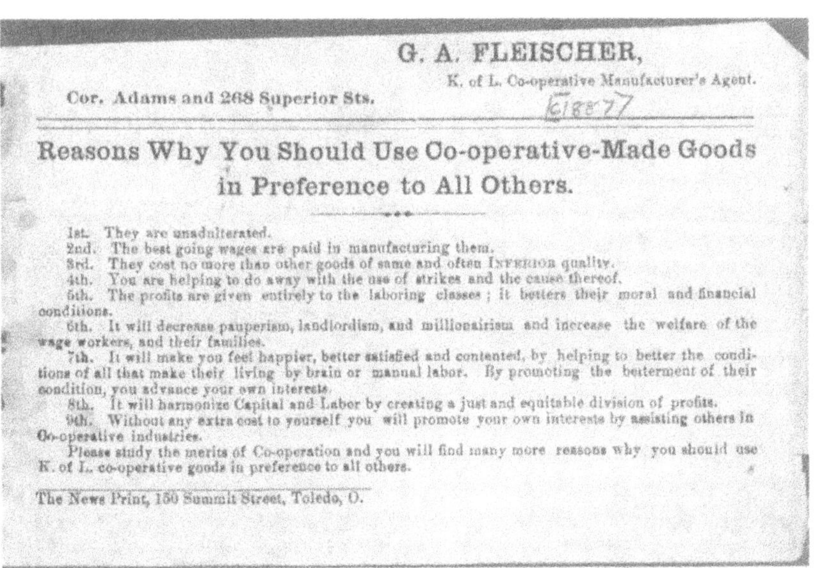

G. A. FLEISCHER,

K. of L. Co-operative Manufacturer's Agent.

Cor. Adams and 268 Superior Sts.

6188 77

Reasons Why You Should Use Co-operative-Made Goods in Preference to All Others.

1st. They are unadulterated.
2nd. The best going wages are paid in manufacturing them.
3rd. They cost no more than other goods of same and often INFERIOR quality.
4th. You are helping to do away with the use of strikes and the cause thereof.
5th. The profits are given entirely to the laboring classes; it betters their moral and financial conditions.
6th. It will decrease pauperism, landlordism, and millionairism and increase the welfare of the wage workers, and their families.
7th. It will make you feel happier, better satisfied and contented, by helping to better the conditions of all that make their living by brain or manual labor. By promoting the betterment of their condition, you advance your own interests.
8th. It will harmonize Capital and Labor by creating a just and equitable division of profits.
9th. Without any extra cost to yourself you will promote your own interests by assisting others in Co-operative industries.

Please study the merits of Co-operation and you will find many more reasons why you should use K. of L. co-operative goods in preference to all others.

The News Print, 150 Summit Street, Toledo, O.

Flyer issued by G. A. Fleischer from Toledo, Ohio, promoting cooperatively made goods, circa 1887. Wisconsin Historical Society.

ized coercion and without the intervention of the Executive Board.

Cooperation in the 1880s could also serve the immediate needs of a distinct constituency. Some women workers, for example, used cooperation to meet their own particular needs and aspirations. Indeed, cooperative production, they believed, could alleviate the most egregious conditions under which women worked, and Leonora Barry, the Knights' investigator of women's work, recommended that the order "turn [its] whole undivided attention to the forming of productive and distributive co-operative enterprises."[77] The cooperatives formed by women workers in the 1880s protected them from the blacklist and gave them the opportunity to prove themselves to their male colleagues. The Our Girls' Cooperative Clothing Company of Chicago and the Martha Washington K. of L. Co-operative Overall Association of Indianapolis made a special point of the fact that women workers would control the companies.[78]

In New York, the members of District Assembly 49 had their own vision of an industrial future and experimented with a form of

Feb. 1886

CO-OPERATIVE FAIR.

Fannie Allyn L. A., 4457.

CINCINNATI, O.

Believing that our only salvation lies in co-operation, and that being one of the leading principles of our noble order, we therefore, having full confidence in each other, make a bold attempt in forming a co-operative concern.

L. A. 4457 has announced that a Fair is to be held at K. of L. Hall, south-east corner of Abigail and Main streets, for said purpose, commencing March 21st, ending March 28th.

We would like all co-operative concerns to correspond with us and give statements of articles manufactured and prices therefor. We will be thankful for any information of the above description, as we are anxious to exhibit all K. of L. goods manufactured or made by members of the order.

We have enclosed tickets for various articles to be raffled for at said fair, and we hope the Assembly will use its influence in the disposal of the same.

All articles that are raffled off will be made public through the Journal and the labor papers of the country.

All remittances to be made by March 15th.

C. Fannie Allyn, Chairman,
Geo. Kuechler, Secretary,
Miss Mary Healy, Treasurer,
Fair Committee.

Address all communications to Geo. C. Kuechler, 495 Walnut st.

Flyer announcing the Fannie Allyn Cooperative Association and Local Assembly's Cooperative Fair held in Cincinnati in 1886. Wisconsin Historical Society.

cooperation unique to the Knights of Labor. The Knights of this powerful district sold shares in an organization of their own design called the Solidarity Co-operative Association. Controlled by the district assembly, the association raised and invested over $6,000 in various enterprises. No interest was paid to the shareholders, nor did they have any control over the management of the firms. The association planned, in time, to buy back the shares, reinvest 50 percent of its profits in cooperation, and deposit the rest in land and insurance funds.[79]

District Assembly 49 attempted to organize production and distribution as if it was an urban cooperative guild, and for a short time succeeded. In 1887, eight cooperative businesses thrived under the aegis of the Solidarity Association. The most successful company, the Solidarity Knights of Labor Watch-Case Company of Brooklyn, operated with a capital of $67,000 and employed over one hundred workers. At 136 Canal Street, the association opened a store and sold cooperatively produced goods from as far away as Raleigh, North Carolina, and Spencer, Massachusetts. In the same building they ran a Knights of Labor restaurant, and next door, the Solidarity Co-operative Clothing Company.[80]

If cooperators established institutions expecting to meet their specific needs and achieve independence, they soon had to face the reality of their failure in the marketplace. Most cooperatives lost their egalitarian features or went out of business with a swiftness both unpredicted and devastating. By the late 1880s, the Knights no longer maintained their faith in cooperation as a viable industrial alternative. They disbanded the Cooperative Board in 1890, and few local assemblies dared venture into production or distribution.[81] How could the enthusiasts for reform explain the failure of their one great hope?

To reformers in the Knights of Labor, cooperation was the quintessential expression of self-help, and they understood its failure in terms of their own deficiencies. They berated themselves or their fellow Knights for their apathy or for lacking the necessary knowledge of cooperative principles. Without this proper knowledge, cooperators allowed businesses to degenerate into corporations. Workers, they often suggested, were selfish, interested in quick profits and unable to choose the best men to lead them. Cooperative stores failed once they succumbed to the ruination of the workingman, credit. Others failed when members went to the

COLLARS AND CUFFS

Ask your merchant to send for samples of TRIANGLE and DOUBLE TRIANGLE BRANDS. The only K. of L. or Union-made collars in the United States.

MADE BY

Co-operative Collar and Cuff Co.,

TROY, N. Y.

See their trade mark in column of K. of L. labels. tf.

Ask your dealer for the **Watch Cases** made by the

SOLIDARITY WATCH CASE COMPANY,

CO-OPERATIVE.

Purchase none other. See that our stamp is in the case.

THIS STAMP IS PLACED IN EVERY CASE OF OUR MAKE AS A GUARANTEE THAT THE CASE IN ALL ITS PARTS IS THE QUALITY OF GOLD REPRESENTED.

ALL OF OUR SHAREHOLDERS ARE MEMBERS OF THE KNIGHTS OF LABOR AND WE EMPLOY NONE OTHER.

FACTORY, NOS. 11, 13, 15 AND 17 HOPE STREET, BROOKLYN, N. Y.

N. Y. OFFICE, 84 BROADWAY, ROOMS NOS. 5 & 6

PRACTICE WHAT YOU PREACH

This Label is endorsed by the General Ex. Board A fac simile appears in all garments made by us

SUITS TO ORDER............$14 AND UP.
PANTS TO ORDER.......... 5 AND UP.
OVERCOATS TO ORDER... 16 AND UP.

Send for self-measuring blanks and samples; good-fitting garments guaranteed.

Advertisement of cooperatives in the *Journal of United Labor*, 1888. Wisconsin Historical Society.

corner store for last-minute purchases rather than planning ahead to patronize their more distant cooperative groceries.[82] In the end, the moral deficiencies of the Knights sabotaged their own emancipation.

The Knights could also cite specific problems that typically afflicted cooperatives. They complained of inadequate capital, their members' meager resources, and the ill-effects of mismanagement. Hard times debilitated many cooperatives, while others often had to face opposition from grocers or manufacturers. In the instance of the Cannelburg mine, the Knights blamed the obstructionism of the local mine operator and railroad company for its failure. They also found fault with the state laws of incorporation that offered inadequate protection against predatory stockholders.[83]

To some degree, all of these factors rang true. Mismanagement, undercapitalization, and ignorance could present formidable obstacles to a cooperative's success. It is also true that individual worker-owned stores and factories had often failed in the past, but as long as the labor movement continued to grow, the Knights remained optimistic. By the late 1880s this optimism had dissipated. After a cooperative grocery in Chicago failed in 1887, one Knight wrote, "we have learned a good lesson, and it will be a long time before anything of the kind starts here again. . . . In Chicago nothing is good in the shape of organized labor, after all its every body for himself whether its in co-operation as a grocery or political."[84]

Conditions had changed drastically for organized labor. The Knights' growth of the first half of the decade reversed itself, and the membership roles decreased dramatically after 1886. If its progress had generated great hope, the Knights' collapse must have engendered a very real despair.[85]

Terence Powderly lost faith in the ability of cooperative enterprises to succeed under prevailing conditions. In his address to the 1888 General Assembly he said:

> So long as the entire control and management of the public highways of the country—the railways—remains in the hands of private individuals while doing the work of the nation, just so long will the operation of co-operative enterprises be attended with failure. We may manufacture the best quality of goods and be prepared to sell at the most reasonable rates, but

> we cannot depend on having these goods transported to market so long as the transportation facilities of the nation are controlled by monopoly.[86]

The Knights would first have to attack this problem politically before cooperation could succeed.

At the same time, the meaning of the term "cooperation," as advanced by the Knights, changed. Under the guidance of Henry Beckmeyer, a leader of the Knights in Newark, New Jersey, the Cooperative Board "extended" the word to denote "an organized demand for Knights of Labor goods." Beckmeyer introduced this new notion through a series of articles in the *Journal of United Labor* after the 1888 General Assembly. He argued that the practical work of cooperation had been retarded by the diversity of opinion in the order and the unwillingness of members to compromise their points of view. Their inflexibility notwithstanding, Beckmeyer found nearly all their plans for cooperation inadequate and defective. They approached the problem, he wrote, from "the wrong end." Rather than emphasize production and distribution, he implored the Knights to focus on consumption and expend all efforts at mutual assistance on developing the market for fairly produced goods. Knights, in his view, should buy only union-labeled goods produced by organized workers under acceptable conditions. Once practiced in fair consumption, Beckmeyer asserted, "the transfer of patronage from Knights of Labor goods in general to a particular variety, those that are co-operatively Knights of Labor made, can be brought about without any particular difficulty." Having developed an adequate demand, cooperative production would follow.[87]

The distance Beckmeyer had traveled from the cooperative schemes of Henry Sharpe, despite his emphasis on consumerism, or even John Samuel, was enormous. There was, in fact, in his roundabout path to cooperative production, an entirely new dimension. "Do not imagine," he wrote,

> as some do, that the sum and substance of co-operation is contained in running a little supply store in combination with a savings institution, where, after a good deal of trouble, you merely succeed in eliminating the retail dealer, the weakest element in our faulty system of distribution. As matters stand now the retail dealer should be made our friend, so that he may

> regard K. of L. goods with favor and assist us to extend our market. I would recommend the establishment of an independent K. of L. supply store just now only as a measure of last resort.[88]

Not only was the cooperative store no longer desirable, but the goal of a "complete chain of correlated cooperative industries under the immediate direction and control of the central authorities of the Order" seemed possible only "in the dim and distant future." Beckmeyer's vision of "universal co-operation" was nothing more than the organized consumption of union-made goods. He admitted that his ideas represented a break with the past. "Extremists," he said, generally understood universal cooperation to exclude the "capitalist employing class." He, however, welcomed the cooperation of fair employers. His system, he maintained, was practical and "the best possible use of existing conditions."[89]

What would Leonard Wheeler have thought in 1889, three years after his letter to the secretary of the soon-to-be nonexistent Cooperative Board?[90] Then his local assembly had grown from forty to three hundred members. The General Master Workman had predicted the "emancipation of the white slaves" in five years, and Wheeler sincerely believed this could be accomplished through the use of strikes, legislation, and, most importantly, cooperation. In the meantime, he had seen the order admit thousands of new members and watched as local assemblies opened hundreds of cooperative stores and factories. If he was like most other members of the order, he imagined the Knights to be a powerful force for change. The group's massive organization provided workers with both the confidence to act locally and a network of potentially sympathetic organized workers. He also witnessed the order do battle over cooperation and fail, not only to devise a workable policy, but to come to the aid of enterprises in need of support. In a few short years the order, which had once hailed cooperation as a pragmatic reform, would reject it as visionary and extremist. The order would also lose, rapidly and decisively, a large portion of its membership. Wheeler could only have been profoundly disappointed as his faith in a cooperative future waned.

The failure of the Knights to devise a successful cooperative policy precluded any systematic use of the order's resources for cooperation. It is doubtful, given workers' local orientation, that such a policy could ever have been implemented. Yet through their debate, the Knights attempted to clarify their prospects as workers in an industrial republic. What kind of future would, or could, they create? The diversity of opinion reflected both the period's ill-defined belief in a more benign industrial society and the Knights' de facto decentralized structure. Members experimented with cooperative production and distribution in their local and district assemblies, and the experiences that defined them occurred in their own cities and towns. Though buoyed and disappointed by their leaders' actions, rank-and-file Knights of Labor made cooperation a reality and, as the next two chapters will show, through their own actions gave substance to its promise as an alternative industrial system.

CHAPTER 4

COOPERATION AND COMMUNITY

The Shoe Workers of Stoneham

The men of Stoneham, Massachusetts, assembled before dawn on July 4, 1873, to celebrate their nation's birth and independence. Gathering at the Farm Hill railroad station in one of the poorer sections of the city, 127 masked and costumed shoe workers, tradesmen, manufacturers, and professionals formed an extraordinary procession of characters. They called themselves the Antiques, Horribles, and Jim Jam Convulsionists and, according to a description in the local newspaper, the Stoneham *Amateur*, they were "of an amusing, ludicrous and burlesque character, well made up of local hits and allusions." Indeed, the grotesquely clad townspeople formed a more than unusual array of floats and displays. Their parade was a mockery of Boston's annual march of the Ancients and Honorables and was similar to a parody that yearly graced the streets of the capital city.[1] Now the residents of Stoneham, both high and low, proudly displayed themselves in the regalia of the absurd.

The parade began with the march of the Stoneham police, followed by the august General Neverready and his retinue. The general carried a sword "of enormous size, being some eight or ten feet in length and of graceful proportions." His compatriots, including a General Crockett and B. R. Guzler, were followed by the Regimental Band of Stoneham. Conspicuous in the procession, the *Amateur* reported, was a carriage carrying the orator of the day, Hon. Peletire B. Snodgrass, Jr., 2nd of Squashboro, Me., and the "ancient lady and gentleman, associates said to be renowned graduates from old Harvard." The revelry continued with the appearance of a horse-drawn wagon known as the "female battery." This display carried men "grotesque in form, feature and dress; the dress a burlesque on female costume." "Upon the rear of [this] carriage (if such it might be termed) was placed a blacksmith's heavy anvil, from which occasionally on the route issued the deafening sounds of a cannon. Various mottoes were placed upon this vehicle, some of which were: 'Anvil Chorus,' 'Crispins wanted,' 'Give us more room,' 'Let virtue be rewarded,' etc."[2] The most novel feature, according to the *Amateur*, was a carriage carrying a man and a woman, "riding upon a single wheel lying horizontally and dragged upon the ground, which gave [the wheel] a revolving motion . . . presenting a most ludicrous spectacle." Another wagon displayed a man and woman "dressed in the most fantastic and uncouth manner, with countenances not to be envied . . . and [who] were observed to be remarkably gifted with good and evil, at one time being very tender and loving, and the next moment full of spite and fight." The "Drum Major," clothed in Indian costume "remarkably characteristic of a bloody Modoc warrior," and the "desperado" "Klu Klux Band" toting "mammoth" instruments followed.[3]

As the parade filed into an already crowded town center, the Independence Day ceremonies began. On the square's center stage six men assumed their places. Snodgrass, the orator, sat alongside General Neverready, Capt. Provisor, the reporter for the Amateur, the Drum Major, and "a noted Modoc." The part of Captain Provisor was played by William Marden, the local secretary of the Knights of St. Crispin. He started the proceedings by calling the role of "this antique company," and the *Amateur*'s reporter noted the presence of "shoe manufacturers, traders, lawyers, doctors, and many of the most prominent citizens of the town." General Neverready, a local tradesman, introduced the speaker of the day, Peletire Snodgrass, a machinist and former shoe worker named Myron Ferren. Surrounded by his fellow Civil War veterans on stage, Ferren launched into a hilarious lampoon of the self-serving politician. With feigned inebriation he ridiculed political fortune hunters, lambasted the pretensions of the wealthy, and poked some fun at women temperance workers.[4]

As the speech ended, the crowd nominated three men, John Best, Samuel Trull, and Francis L. Whittier, to award prizes to the participants. More than any other event of the day, the selection of these men captured the parade's significance. By bringing different classes together, the Independence Day celebration reflected the social solidarities that made the city a cohesive community. John Best and Samuel Trull were both shoe workers and Civil War veterans. Best, a popular local leader of the Knights of St. Crispin, had three months earlier assumed the leadership of the Stoneham Cooperative Boot and Shoe Company. Trull, also an officer in the local Crispin lodge, served as Labor Reform representative to the Massachusetts General Court for a term in 1870. The last of the three, Francis Whittier, was the third son of the local newspaper publisher and erstwhile Postmaster. Unlike Best and Trull, Whittier had not served in the army, though his family had sacrificed much for the Union. His two oldest brothers had both perished in the war. Under the banner of national unity these two labor leaders and the son of a middle-class family stood comfortably together. Nominated by acclamation, the three men awarded prizes to the Female Battery, General Neverready, and the Drum Major. The festivities ended soon after.[5]

Such frenzied celebration reflected, in part, the cohesiveness of community life. The parade was an act of definition, an attempt to designate the parameters of legitimate community membership. The tradesmen and professionals stood alongside the workers of Stoneham on this day of national unity and agreed on certain common enemies, the corrupt politician and elitism. The contemptuous portrayal of Indians and Southern "desperadoes" showed how they collectively defined specific groups as outside of their community. These definitions bound them together and reinforced their sense of commonality.

Community life, however, had changed since the pre-war period. In the early years of the nineteenth century, Stoneham's residents had practiced the shoemaker's craft in small "ten-footers." Prior to the outbreak of war, they, like other shoe producers in Massachusetts, had already abandoned this method and had begun to consolidate production in central shops. The war intensified the transition to factory methods, and by the 1870s mechanized shoe manufacturing was becoming the principle industry of Stoneham.[6]

These changes in the methods of production materially affected the life of the city. The new technologies of the era, such as the sewing machine and the McKay Stitcher, reorganized and deskilled the work process. This reduced outwork and prompted men and women to enter Stoneham's factories. Both sexes came in relatively large numbers, and between 1865 and 1870 the influx of factory workers increased the city's population of more than three thousand residents by 37 percent. With 17 percent of its workforce foreign-born, Stoneham now had a mobile and unstable working-class population.[7]

The men who led the labor movement in Stoneham, and who were among the most visible participants in the July Fourth exercises, had witnessed these changes firsthand. John Best, Samuel Trull, and William Marden made Stoneham their home in the years before the war. They enlisted in the Union Army along with other young men from their city and, when mustered out, settled back into Stoneham's working-class community. All three were shoe workers, and their prominence in the parade was symbolic of their personal importance and the self-confidence of the factory workforce at large.[8] In public procession their pride as citizens of Stoneham, as veterans of the war, and as leaders of the labor movement blended together. This identity with the Northern victory contributed to their assertiveness as it legitimized their integral role in the local polity.

The workers who labored in the new shoe factories and who clearly dominated the Independence Day street-level celebration were a force to be reckoned with. In the years following the Civil War they organized in both the political and economic arenas, with real impact. As early as 1867, male shoe workers established the Pioneer Lodge of the Knights of St. Crispin, and in 1869 their female counterparts founded their own Excelsior Lodge of the Daughters of St. Crispin. In 1872 these women mobilized three hundred of their associates in an unsuccessful strike for higher wages.[9]

During this postwar period, Stoneham's workers were active in politics and achieved notable successes in their reform-oriented campaigns. The gubernatorial candidate of the Labor Reform Party, a Crispin-dominated organization, received 48 percent of Stoneham's vote in 1869, 66 percent in 1870, and 44 percent in 1871. Statewide the candidate received no more than 15 percent of the vote in any one year. In 1870 the local party sent Crispin officer Samuel Trull to the state legislature, and two years later supported Stoneham's Amos Hill, who won his bid for a seat in the General Court.[10]

So when the workers of Stoneham paraded through the central square on the Fourth of July, 1873, they did so with self-confidence. They exuded an elan, a sense of power and the right to mock with laughter and derision the place of privilege in American life. The address of the inebriated Hon. Peletire B. Snodgrass, Jr.,

2nd of Squashboro, Me., the grotesque figure of General Neverready, and the derisive portrayal of the ancient Harvard graduates were irreverent assaults on what they considered corrupt American institutions.

Yet something more obscure infused this parade with meaning. The sheer madness of the events, the bizarre nature of the costumes and floats suggested an underlying confusion. In part, this may have been related to the national disarray of the Knights of St. Crispin and its major defeat in Lynn in 1872. Though Stoneham's locals were still functioning, the Crispins felt hard-pressed by their organizational decline and the severe competition in the industry.[11] They were confronted with the possible loss of power after years of successful organization. Yet when Best, Trull, and Whittier, buoyed by the crowd, awarded prizes to the Drum Major and General Neverready, their mockery and laughter seemed brazen as it subverted authority and subordinated the outsider, the Southerner, and the Indian.

When the committee of three awarded the second-place prize to the Female Battery, their choice pointed to a different threat. In nearby Lynn, manufacturers had violated the sexual division of labor that restricted women to the factory stitching room. Women were now potential competitors for portions of the work formerly delegated to cutters and lasters. In Stoneham, women had entered the factory workforce and had taken a prominent position in Stoneham's labor movement. The Battery, with its cross-dressed anvil drivers, who at a later date were described as representatives of women's rights, clearly mocked these women workers and reformers.[12] Moreover, the imagery of gender conflict was hardly isolated to one display. During this parade women and men moved circularly and uncontrollably, screaming at each other one moment and loving each other the next. In all of its ludicrousness, the parade suggested a fear of the unconstrained, of a society turned upside down, where men were women and women were men. Male shoe workers of Stoneham, it is clear, sensed the very real threat that industrial change brought to their homes, workplaces, and community.

In the city of Stoneham, shoe workers organized as a powerful economic and political force. Through their integration into the community they felt capable of asserting authority and they acted to stabilize their family and work lives. These acts of assertion included the establishment of four cooperative shoe factories, two cooperative stores, and a cooperative tannery. Activists discovered, however, that community life could cut two ways. When the inadequacies of cooperation became manifest and conditions suggested a need for new ideas, the cooperators were immobilized. Their very integration into the city limited their ability to produce alternatives. Moreover, their cooperative vision was riddled with contradictory impulses. Profoundly democratic, cooperators transformed their workplaces into miniature republics. Yet they attempted, as well, to reassert their power and dominance as male workers and to create a cooperative hierarchy. Ultimately, they were trapped within the confines of the community they helped create and the power they had achieved.

In January 1873, twenty-five wage earners, including John Best, organized the Stoneham Cooperative Boot and Shoe Company. Nearly all were formerly employed in two of Stoneham's shoe factories, and though the financial panic of 1873 had not yet set off the mid-decade depression, their former employers had experienced the pinch of hard times and competition. Consequently, one of the manufacturers had moved his factory to the cheaper labor market of rural Maine, while the other one had simply closed up shop. These workers, however, assumed they would succeed in Stoneham where their employers had not. This confidence was hardly based on a realistic assessment of their business skills. Nearly three-quarters of the cooperators worked as narrowly trained factory artisans. They were, like the rest of the city's workforce, from New England, Ireland, and Canada. With only about half of the members born in Massachusetts and another 17 percent of foreign birth, they made up a representative sample of Stoneham's mobile industrial population.[13]

These men, nevertheless, were unique in several ways and, in a manner of speaking, formed an advanced guard of the factory workforce. When compared with other shoe workers in Stoneham, the cooperators had a set of interests that marked them off as particularly concerned with community institutions. The story of John L. Cotton, one of the earliest cooperators in Stoneham, illustrates this well.

John Cotton was a native New Englander born in his parents' home state of New Hampshire in 1836. As a maturing young man in his early twenties, Cotton headed west for Ohio. Though his wife gave birth to their first child there in 1862, he and his small family soon moved again, resettling in the northeast. He enlisted in the Union Army from Stoneham and served for nearly two years. After the war he returned to Stoneham, where his second child was born, and in 1866 this thirty-year-old father of two invested his savings in a modest home valued at $400. Four years later he reported to the federal census taker that he worked for wages in a shoe factory. By 1873, the year he became a charter member of Stoneham's first cooperative factory, he had accumulated $3,710 worth of real property. Furthermore, though a comparatively recent arrival to Stoneham, Cotton was elected to a series of offices in both voluntary organizations and city government. He served on the cooperative factory's first board of directors and "had charge" of a unit in the factory known as the sole leather room. The Cooperative Union Store elected him treasurer in 1874, and six months later the citizens of Stoneham designated him constable at their town meeting. As a sign of his increasing stature in the city, he won his bid for the office of tax assessor the following year.[14]

Far from unusual, John Cotton's age, marital and family status, occupation, property holdings, and involvement in town affairs were typical for a cooperator. On the whole, in fact, cooperators from the Stoneham shoe factory tended to be older, more often married, and more likely to have children then other shoe workers in the city. Between the years 1870 and 1885, while 51 to 63 percent of Stoneham's male shoe workers had passed their thirtieth birthdays, 70 percent of the cooperators were thirty years of age or more when they joined the company. These older shoe workers, unsurprisingly, also tended to be married and have children more often than their wage-earning counterparts. In 1870, 57 percent of all male shoe workers were married and 67 percent of these men had children. In 1873 65 percent of the cooperative's founders were married and 80 percent had children. Throughout the lifetime of the cooperative, 70 percent of all of the male cooperators married, and 73 percent of these men had children before they purchased their first share of cooperative stock.[15]

Not unlike John Cotton, nearly 70 percent of the cooperators had accumulated some real property on or before 1873. This was in striking contrast to the 72 percent of all shoe workers (not including cutters) who were propertyless in 1870. Over the next fifteen years nearly all of the cooperators would acquire modest property holdings, usually a plot of land and a house. Only a minority of these men would fail to establish their own homes in Stoneham.[16]

Clearly, the men who founded the Stoneham Cooperative Boot and Shoe Company had entered the mature years of their lives. Some of them, born in Stoneham, had experienced the changes of the 1860s as young men and wanted to continue living in the town of their birth as economic conditions demanded otherwise. Others had settled in Stoneham after a period of uncertainty and geographic mobility. They, too, were at a stage in life when stability was most prized; when the demands of raising a family literally required a shoe worker to defy the business cycle. Yet almost above all, they, as property owners, had a stake in the community. They were now rooted in Stoneham, and there they would try to determine the world in which their families would live. As the treasurer of one cooperative said, successful cooperators were those who felt they belonged to a place and had a permanent interest in it.[17] These men, in fact, set out to secure a place for themselves in the city of Stoneham.

By the late 1860s, the men who would experiment in the years ahead with cooperation had already put down roots. Their names soon appeared on the roles of local churches, voluntary associations such as the Grand Army of the Republic, the International Organization of Odd Fellows, fire departments, temperance societies, labor reform organizations, the Democratic and Republican Parties, and, of course, the trade unions. In 1870, six of the eight officers of Stoneham's Post 75 of the Grand Army of the Republic were future cooperators. Their names appeared in the transcripts of town meetings, and they filled, or ran for, at one time or another, almost all of Stoneham's offices, including selectman, assessor, and policeman. Three were sent to the Massachusetts General Court to represent Middlesex County, and many others participated in their election. When conflict arose in the workplaces of Stoneham, they often took leading positions in the formation of strike committees or offered relief to strikers. In the 1880s they joined with the Knights of Labor in large numbers and avidly pursued third-party politics.[18]

Workers felt their influence and control grow over a town that, in these years, had a relatively small population and few large manufacturers.[19] Because of the town's size, workers had direct access to Stoneham's political process through town meetings, where they met, participated with, and defeated middle-class residents on issues of local importance and for political office. Their participation in city government gave them a sense of power. Yet their interaction with their middle-class neighbors had other, more ambiguous, consequences.

As evidenced on the Fourth of July, the middle and working classes of Stoneham had developed very real bonds. In fact, the town's professionals and shopkeepers rarely hesitated to support the wage earners of the city in labor disputes. Yet they offered support strictly on their own terms. When a shoe manufacturer cut wages in 1876, he was anathematized by the local press not for his violation of workers' rights but for his violation of community responsibility, as someone who took the counsel of "men with no aim in life but self advancement, and whose motto is 'That will be a dollar in my pocket and a feather in my cap.'"[20] In 1884 another manufacturer cut wages 20 percent, the second wage cut in a year, and the local newspaper condemned this as "an impolitic, selfish and indefensible attempt to crowd to the wall good, honest workmen and force their own brother manufacturers to make a similar reduction . . . to the injury of our whole people. . . . A general reduction, after the ratio of this firm, means a decrease in the wages of Stoneham shoe operatives in the course of a year of $30,000, which must affect every store in town."[21] They fashioned their commitment to Stoneham's workers out of provincial loyalty and self-interest. Such support could be lost when workers acted more like workers than like citizens of the city. In 1885, when a group of one hundred Knights of Labor traveled to Lynn for a coffee party, the editor of the *Independent* responded with palpable bitterness:

> Our interest in the laboring people prompts us to say that to us there was [a] very evident mistake in regards to the transportation of the party . . . that putting money into strangers' hands is very inconsistent with the principles that wage-working organizations generally advocate, such as 'patronizing home industry,' 'helping each other,' 'keeping their money among themselves.'. . . Now, if there is a likelihood of a similar misunderstanding, and it cannot be otherwise harmoniously arranged, we would suggest that the committee keep it a little more in their own hands. We expect no thanks for our ideas or suggestions,—they are gratuitous—and our only object in thus

> parading them is the firm belief that it is the lack of forethought in hundreds of such little matters that engender hard feelings and dissatisfaction, and eventuate is [*sic*] the dissolution of working organizations.[22]

Mutual assistance in the middle-class mind of Stoneham seemed more akin to chamber of commerce boosterism than sympathy for the working poor. If the tradesmen and professionals of Stoneham could support the abrogation of individual property rights during a labor dispute, it was because the community had been violated by a manufacturer's selfish actions, and the consequences were theirs to suffer as well.

Even this support, however, could evaporate if workers organized as business competitors. When the two original cooperatives, the shoe factory and the grocery, were founded in 1873, some of Stoneham's businessmen were appalled. They had been accused by the cooperators of reaping "a larger profit . . . than was consistent with justice," a charge that not only impugned their moral standing in the community but threatened their livelihood as well. In response the shopkeepers organized collectively to oppose the grocery. At the same time, the shoe cooperative faced opposition from "parties with whom business relations were necessary or desirable." According to a report of the Massachusetts Bureau of Statistics of Labor, hostile businessmen feared the enterprise would be controlled or managed in the interest of a trade union.[23]

The cooperators, though, were defiant of authority and believed themselves capable of governing their own work lives. They derived this belief, as we have seen, from power they exercised within their community. At the same time, their participation in societies like the Odd Fellows and the Grand Army of the Republic, and in town meetings, actually taught them the substance of democratic participation. It provided them with a model of social behavior and democratic practice: a model that invoked the notion of republican citizenship so elemental to the working-class mentality, so much a part of the rhetoric of the age, but one so little practiced in economic life. This process of integration gave Stoneham's workers confidence to recreate the city in their own image.

When shoe workers established their first cooperative in 1873, they organized themselves as they had in voluntary associations and town meetings, first by electing their officers through popular vote. Then, more significantly, the cooperators appeared to mimic the procedure of Stoneham's town meetings, where every action, no matter how minor, was made a motion, voted on, and recorded; where little was done without a committee being formed to form a committee to do something. A typical case in the town meeting was the "committee appointed to nominate a committee for making arrangements to attend the celebration."[24] The meetings of the stockholders of the Stoneham Cooperative Boot and Shoe Company could be, in similar ways, painfully meticulous and democratic. Such a meeting in 1876 read as follows:

> Called to order by the President.
> Records of last quarterly meeting read and approved.
> The treasurer made his report of the business transacted as follows:
> Voted that the report of the Treasurer be laid on the table.
> Voted that [we] proceed to election of officers.
> The president appointed John S. Gilmore, Dudley R. Barnes and John L. Cotton a committee to sort collect and count votes.
> Voted that there be a recess of five minutes to prepare ballots.
> Voted that we reconsider the vote by which we voted to proceed to election of officers.
> Voted that there be a committee of five nominated at large to prepare a list of officers.
> [Six were then nominated and five were elected and then the committee reported a list of officers.]
> Voted that the Report be accepted
> Voted that we proceed to election of officers
> Voted that we ballot for each one separately
> Voted that we proceed to collect votes for Pres.
> [They then voted for president, voted to vote for officers, and then voted for the other officers]
> Voted that we proceed to elect two auditors to audit the accounts and report of the Treas.
> Voted to adjourn[.][25]

The general meetings in the Stoneham Cooperative were characterized by a nearly obsessive concern with democratic process. By extending this process into the workplace, worker-owners demonstrated the pervasive role those ideals played in their lives. Community life had provided the cooperators with both an education in democracy and the determination to exercise power.

Like most shoe workers in the 1870s, the cooperators were neither unskilled factory operatives nor craftsmen, but factory artisans, workers with highly developed skills confined to very narrow areas of production. Their self-confidence came, in part, from this work experience, and they carried with them the cultural emphasis on independence characteristic of skilled workers. In the early years of the Stoneham Cooperative the shareholders acted out the familiar patterns of this independence. Member-owners, at times, rebelled against the restraints imposed by their duly elected board of directors and refused to work when dissatisfied with their pay. Indeed, they governed shop life with an ambivalently enforced discipline and unstructured supervision. In 1873 the directors took the first step to control their members when they voted to have "card playing . . . stopped in the shop while the shop [was] running." The supervisor, who in any other factory would normally dictate this kind of decision, had such diverse duties he couldn't monitor the shop floor and accomplish his required tasks. As agent of the company, he traveled, represented the cooperative to buyers, managed day-to-day operations, and, when able to, performed "his regular day's work in the factory" as well. When he disciplined workers on the shop floor, he acted with the board of directors' approval or instructions and then only with caution. In July 1873 the board instructed the agent to "notify the bottom finisher that unless he do better work he must give up the job," and three months later he was "instructed to discharge any workman who persistently refuses to do good work."[26] Yet, there is no record of a cooperator fired for insufficient output or bad workmanship. The cooperative was simply not in the business to discipline, punish, or deprive its members of work.

Though cooperation emerged from the community and work experiences of factory artisans in Stoneham, it had, as part of the labor movement, a loosely defined tradition and ideology of its own that promised emancipation from the daily indignities of dependence. If shoe workers, the "white niggers" of Stoneham, as one shoe worker opined, were compelled to accept the dictates of their more powerful employers, cooperation would redistribute power and redefine the republican citizen in the economic sphere.[27] Yet this process of redefinition occurred within a small and integrated city, among workers who were neither completely independent in their shops nor independent of their community. The nature of this dependence determined how profoundly they would critique and transform their economic world.

In all of Stoneham, no one person's life better illustrated the relationship between cooperation and community than that of John Best. In 1873, this shoe worker and Civil War hero was a respected citizen of Stoneham and a spokesman for its factory artisans. When he appeared in the Independence Day parade he had already served as the town's assessor and tax collector and as secretary to the Knights of St. Crispin and president of the Stoneham Cooperative Shoe Company. Twenty-two years earlier, Best had arrived in Stoneham as a fifteen-year-old factory employee. Now, at the age of thirty-seven, he provided a house of his own for his family and held positions of authority in an appreciative city.[28]

For over two decades Best made Stoneham his home, and he played an integral part in various aspects of its community life. As a citizen he occupied town offices; as a shoe worker he was a committed trade unionist; as a the head of a family he owned a home; and as a resident he joined a fire company and led the local post of the Grand Army of the Republic.[29] As a cooperator he combined the concerns of all of these roles in a grand vision, one that called for the simultaneous preservation and transformation of his city's communal life. Faced with economic uncertainty, John Best the cooperator acted to stabilize his community through the control of production and consumption. In the instance when a shoe manufacturer abandoned Stoneham for cheaper labor markets, Best and his associates chose to operate the business themselves in their own interest. When grocers charged "unjust" prices, the cooperators sold their own groceries "at the lowest cash price." Best, who was an officer in both the factory and the grocery and worked on the state level with the Sovereigns of Industry, labored with other cooperators to replace exploitative businesses with democratically controlled organizations.[30] They acted to contain and direct the forces that affected their everyday lives. They acted, in effect, as the guardians of the community of workers.

Politics was as central to their agenda as cooperation, and in 1874 Best campaigned for a seat in the General Court on the

John Best from William B. Stevens, *The History of Stoneham, Mass.*, 1891.

Republican ticket. The local enthusiasm for labor reform swept him into the legislature with the largest vote a citizen of Stoneham had ever received in a town or district election. This enthusiasm was for a man whose concerns as a legislator mirrored his activities at home. Best served on the Joint Special Committee on the Labor Question, voted against abolishing the labor bureau, and designed his first bill to protect working-class homeowners from excessive taxation. If this bill had become law no worker would have been taxed on the unpaid portion of his home mortgage.[31] This surely would have enabled more workers to own homes and live with less fear of dislocation. It is clear, however, that Best had no intention of using the state to direct or participate in cooperative enterprises. Cooperation, he apparently believed, should remain a voluntary activity.

John Best was now a well-respected townsman, politician, and reformer. For some unfathomable reason, though, he sacrificed all he had accomplished for the paltry rewards of a petty crime. In the words of the *Independent*, he simply "succumbed to temptation." On May 8, 1875, Best walked into a local grocery, one that he regularly patronized, reached into its safe, and removed $16. He was apprehended and sentenced to serve two years in the state penitentiary. Within weeks of his arrest he resigned from the cooperative and stepped down as commander of Post 75 of the Grand Army of the Republic. In February 1876 he relinquished his share in the cooperative factory and retreated to the anonymity of the city's factory workshops.[32] Yet after, and possibly because of, his ignominious fall, Best continued to personify the interests of community and the forces and ideals that held Stoneham together. As we will see, when he opened his own small shoe factory in 1880 he reemerged to spearhead the city's most important labor confrontation of the decade.

John Best epitomized the interests and growth of the labor movement in Stoneham, and his style of political and trade union activism endured, despite his embarrassment, well into the 1880s. Just months after Best's conviction, nearly a third of the city's population rallied in support of striking factory workers. They watched as three hundred Crispins and other workers marched to fife and drum on the outskirts of town. These were depression years, however, and rather than trade union success, a shoe worker could expect wage cutbacks and convict labor. In 1877 a local "Workingmen's Party" endorsed William Marden as its candidate for state representative but received a meager ninety-five votes from Stoneham's workers. Some of the men involved in this party attempted to rejuvenate the moribund labor movement, but they also met with little success. There was simply not enough interest in Stoneham's working-class community.[33]

Yet Stoneham proved itself to be an unpredictable city. In September of the following year the glimmer of independent politics appeared again in the greenback agitation for Benjamin Butler, the perennial political favorite of the working class. In less than a year all three town selectmen were labor reformers or sympathizers, one a former Crispin, another the founder of the Workingmen's Party. In addition, as the economy improved the labor movement expanded. By 1883, at least 80 percent of the lasters had joined the Lasters' Protective Union, and though the Knights of Labor first appeared in Stoneham only in 1882, they had six local assemblies with a membership of 1,200 four years later.[34]

Meanwhile, the cooperators of Stoneham were also growing in numbers. The pioneer organizations, the Stoneham Cooperative Boot and Shoe Company and the Cooperative Union Store, both opened for business in 1873. In 1874 the local chapter of the Sovereigns of Industry started a dry goods purchasing cooperative and later opened a storefront. For two years a Stoneham resident, J. M. Winslow, edited and published the *National Sovereign*, a newspaper dedicated to the Sovereigns of Industry. In 1875 at least two of the original Stoneham Shoe cooperators helped form the Middlesex Cooperative Boot and Shoe Company, which was followed by the American Cooperative in 1882 and the Franklin Shoe Cooperative in 1883. Three years later, curriers organized a cooperative factory, and in 1887 a cooperative bank opened to assist working families interested in purchasing homes.[35]

Overall, these efforts were successful both in achieving their economic goals and in stabilizing working-class community life, and they did so democratically. All of Stoneham's cooperatives based their structure and operation on state laws governing cooperation. The laws, approved by the legislature in 1866 and 1870, limited stockholders to one vote and a maximum of $1000 of stock. Stoneham's shoe cooperatives issued stock at $250 a share, thus making the maximum holding for any one individual four shares. The law prescribed the structure of the business and required the stockholders to elect the board of directors and officers of the company at an annual meeting. In 1874 a change in the law required officers to be elected by the board of directors.[36] The only flaw in this democratic structure was its acceptance of nonmember employees. Rigorously democratic for stockholders, the cooperative could be just like any other employer for wage workers.

Yet this structure was remarkably successful in fulfilling the cooperatives' principle commitment to pay members the full value of their product. In the 1870s the Stoneham Cooperative set wage scales equal to or greater than those found in the other shops in town. By 1881 a laster's wage in this cooperative was 66 percent higher than what some Stoneham factories paid. The Middlesex Cooperative nearly matched these wages, and paid its other members and help 10 to 15 percent more than similarly skilled workers employed elsewhere in town. Unlike its sister factories, the Franklin Cooperative believed in distributing profits daily rather than yearly in order to pay the highest wages possible. Indeed, other shoe workers used the prices paid in these factories as a measure of what their employers were capable of paying. By the time the lasters' union established itself in Stoneham, all of the cooperative factories complied with their price lists. Ironically, the Stoneham Cooperative lowered more salaries than it raised by accepting the lasters' prices.[37]

If cooperatives paid wages equal to or higher than those found in other shoe factories, they did so by rejecting in part the marketing method then in vogue with other shoe manufacturers. Because of intense competition in the 1870s, shoe manufacturers produced on order only, a practice that accentuated seasonal fluctuations as companies hired and fired with the ebb and flow of demand. The level and consistency of production in the Stoneham Cooperative was also dependent upon seasonal demand and the agent's ability to drum up sales. Yet if sales were not forthcoming, as in the slow winter months, the company continued to produce in advance of orders. The directors did this quite self-consciously to keep the men and women consistently employed. In fact, all of the cooperatives were unique in remaining open virtually year-round.[38]

Despite these methods, the cooperatives succeeded admirably. The Stoneham Shoe Cooperative turned a small profit of only $857 after its first nine months of operation, but by the end of its second year it had earned a total of $4,444 over expenses. After putting aside 10 percent in a sinking fund as the law demanded, the firm declared a dividend of $100 a share.[39]

The Stoneham Shoe Cooperative's heyday, however, was in the first half of the 1880s, during which time the company increased its capital stock from $10,000 to $20,000, bought and occupied its own steam-powered factory, and paid yearly dividends ranging from fifteen to sixty-two dollars per share. The company put aside, as well, 25 to 66 percent of its yearly profits into sinking and reserve funds. During the depression year of 1877, the sinking fund enabled the cooperative to survive and to declare a small profit. In the early 1880s its annual sales peaked at $154,751 and the cooperative accumulated a substantial reserve of over $10,000. In 1885 it held property valued at $8,450 and machinery worth $6,514. R. G. Dun and Co. rated the Stoneham Shoe Cooperative as a reliable credit risk.[40]

Two of the other cooperatives, the Middlesex and the American, also paid dividends regularly and, along with the Franklin Shoe

Cooperative, set up their own steam-powered factories. They prospered so well in the early 1880s that one laster inaccurately proclaimed Stoneham "the only place in the world where cooperation has succeeded."[41]

Actually, the cooperators did much more than prosper. The shareholders, whether they were Irish-, Canadian-, or American-born, Protestant or Catholic, created through and around their places of work a rather close-knit social world undivided by ethnic differences. It was not uncommon to find after a day's work that a cooperative was serving dinner in its shop with other cooperators in attendance. On weekends they might go on outings and in the evenings stage musical entertainments. When baseball fever surged through the city, the Stoneham and Middlesex cooperatives formed teams and competed against one another. Some cooperators married the daughters of their fellow shareholders, and others lived with each other in the same houses or neighborhoods.[42] The integrity of the working-class community was reinforced by the relationships these shoe workers formed in and around their cooperative shops.

The members of this working-class community had matured through a variety of experiences. Many had settled in Stoneham after a period of geographic mobility and had married and acquired property. As residents they engaged their middle-class colleagues in voluntary associations and other local matters, and embraced trade unionism and labor reform. In the process they came to see their lives as wage laborers through the prism of democratic experience, artisanal culture, and local political power. The cooperative was the product of these influences and an attempt by shoe workers to adapt to and control the daily irregularities of industrial change that otherwise lay beyond their control.

It is apparent that much of what the cooperators did was motivated by or directed at stabilizing their family lives within the context of a larger community and market economy. As the workforce changed after the Civil War and women entered the factories, male shoe workers witnessed a breakdown in the sexual division of labor and a threat to their dominance in the production process. At the same time, women in Stoneham asserted themselves as wage workers and agitated for suffrage. As we have seen earlier in the July Fourth parade of 1873, male factory artisans were apparently disturbed by these changes, and they established cooperatives in part to oppose them and preserve community and family life. They tried to achieve this through the reaffirmation of male authority and the restoration of the sexual division of labor in their own factories.

The cooperative shops of Stoneham were never averse to hiring women. In its first year of operation the Stoneham factory employed ten women and twenty-nine men.[43] In 1885, when 15 percent of the 1,228 shoe workers of Stoneham worked in cooperatives, 39 percent of them were women. One-third of these women owned stock in their cooperatives. Yet, from the commencement of cooperation in 1873 to the end of the next decade, no woman ever occupied a position of authority in any cooperative in Stoneham. Moreover, the cooperators rigidly adhered to the sexual division of labor, which restricted women to the stitching room. They maintained a separation rooted in the prefactory family-based system of shoe production.[44]

The men who operated the cooperative store similarly intended to preserve the sexual status quo. An advertisement for the store in 1886 pictured a virtual cornucopia of produce and necessities. Emblazoned on a barrel and central to the ad was the motto: "The Family Peacemaker." This suggested that stress and conflict experienced by the family could be resolved through abundance, and that the essence of familial discord was not to be found in altered gender expectations but in material deprivation. Abundance provided through cooperation by men would stabilize the male-headed family.[45]

The shoe-working women of Stoneham supported these efforts, for a time, unreservedly. As Crispins, both women and men were instrumental in the formation of the Stoneham Boot and Shoe Company. The Knights invested one thousand dollars in the fledgling enterprise, while the Daughters donated a wax thread machine for the shop floor. Both men and women, it seems, recognized that the family was the cornerstone of stability, and women had as much of an interest in its defense as men.[46] However, there were women in the city who, over time, developed a different understanding of the cooperative's goals, though one that remained resolutely family-based. Rather than reinforcing the sexual status quo, cooperation could herald, in their minds, the formation of a radically egalitarian family life.

In the early 1880s, one resident of Stoneham, C. Fannie Allyn, spoke out eloquently for this position. Allyn was the daughter of a

Advertisement for the Stoneham Cooperative Union Store from the Stoneham City Directory, 1886–87. Courtesy of the State Library of Massachusetts.

shoe cutter, the widowed mother of one son, and had lived in Stoneham for years in the home of her parents. At one time she had worked in a match factory and was now a familiar figure at Stoneham's labor rallies. In these latter years she traveled widely to address Knights of Labor audiences and helped to launch the Fannie Allyn Local Assembly's cooperative fair in Cincinnati.[47]

Fannie Allyn was a labor feminist who saw in the Knights of Labor, suffrage, and cooperation the principal tools to achieve equality for women and the liberation of all working people. She based her analysis, as we saw earlier, on the family and the experience of self-supporting women. She argued, in effect, for the expanded participation of women in cooperation. The just wages guaranteed by cooperative production would not only give the worker his or her due but enable men and women to transform the family into an egalitarian institution.

As Fannie Allyn agitated for cooperation, women were buying stock in Stoneham's cooperatives. In 1881, four women acquired shares in the Stoneham Boot and Shoe Company, and five years later at least eleven women held shares in the American, six in the Franklin, and three in the Middlesex cooperatives. Though their numbers were small, the fact that women were allowed to purchase shares indicated an acceptance by men of their involvement. Women, however, used the position of stockholder to demand equal treatment and to expand their control in the workshop.[48] In 1886 the agent of one shoe cooperative in Stoneham complained bitterly of female stockholders in the cooperative's stitching room: "They are carried away, he said, by the idea that as stockholders they should be permitted to do as they please; and they are too independent. In the stitching room it is desirable, to economize machinery, to have stitchers change off, doing one kind of work a part of the day, and something else at other times. If they are stockholders young women object."[49] In other words, working women could act like skilled workingmen and refuse to allow a foreman to direct and speed up their labor. They acted with such confidence and independence because as shareholders they could justify their resistance, and they had the means to disregard standards of female propriety. In fact, in 1884 several women belonging to the order opened a cooperative shoe stitching shop, which they ran themselves.[50] The extension of democracy into the workplace had set a precedent for female participants that was difficult for male cooperators to contain.

The self-confidence of these female shoe workers coincided with the national and local resurgence of the labor movement. Beginning with a four-week strike of 160 workers in 1884, Stoneham's labor movement achieved unprecedented successes. Ironically, as the Knights of Labor and the cooperators realized their greatest strength, the cooperatives weakened and failed, one by one. The tumultuous events of the 1880s revealed the serious limitations of Stoneham's labor movement.

In April 1884, a young and aggressive firm, Sanborn & Mann, precipitated the first major labor confrontation in Stoneham in eight years. The firm reduced the wages of its employees by 20 percent and, according to the *Independent*, "thoroughly aroused" the entire city. Within a week a diverse group of townspeople met in the Grand Army of the Republic Hall to decide what action could be taken against the company.[51]

The women and men who crowded the hall listened eagerly to the invocations of a number of speakers, one of whom was John Best. Since 1880, Best had manufactured shoes in Stoneham in his own shop, and now, alongside labor leaders from Lynn and Stoneham, he addressed a large crowd of men and women, shoe workers and cooperators. He still commanded the respect of the working people of Stoneham and would represent them at the General Assembly of the Knights of Labor in 1886. Tellingly, the participants dubbed their new organization "the Citizens Protective Union" and, upon Best's suggestion, formed a committee to select a temporary list of officers. Of the seventeen men selected, seven worked in cooperative shops. Once again, John Best was among the leaders of a "citizens" union and a large number of cooperators. His participation spoke to the community of interests that lay deeply rooted in the town itself and the institutions that shoe workers had made and participated in. A small manufacturer, Best represented workers and cooperators because he respected these institutions (he was still an officer in the cooperative store) and understood the rights of citizenship shoe workers believed were their due. Similarly, the cooperators took leadership roles in the strike because they identified both as shoe workers and as citizens of Stoneham. In practical terms, any wage reduction could set a precedent and lower wages for all shoe workers, which would reduce the cooperators' earnings as the price of shoes dropped in the market. As citizens the cooperators had worked hard to create a stable democratic environment, and they allied themselves with those familiar men, whether manufacturers or workers, who would support their demands and preserve economic stability. The striking workers trusted them both and voted to follow the directives of the Citizens Protective Union.[52]

Before the strike at the factory of Sanborn and Mann began, a committee of three men canvassed the shops of Stoneham and gathered signatures of support from over two hundred workers and manufacturers. As the strike dragged on for four weeks, many of these and other workers joined the Knights of Labor. A number of women, led by Fannie Allyn, formed a local assembly of their own.

Mobilized, this coalition of shoe workers, cooperators, manufacturers, and even one farmer was a powerful enough force to defeat the firm of Sanborn and Mann.[53] The *Independent*, the voice of Stoneham's middle class, celebrated the victory with a paean to community harmony: "It was quite an interesting sight . . . when the 160 hands marched from the G. A. R. Hall, after cheering their B. of A.[board of arbitration], to the factory of Sanborn & Mann, then each dispersed to their places. Not a harsh word was uttered against the members of the firm, but each one cheerfully resumed his or her work, and so endeth the labor struggle."[54]

Four months later, the momentum from this "cheerful resumption of work" culminated in the People's Party campaign for presidential hopeful Benjamin Butler. The Knights, and now Daughters, of Labor spearheaded the campaign in Stoneham, and the party's active members made up a virtual roll call of cooperators, some drawn from the Democratic and Republican Parties, and many who had helped defeat Sanborn and Mann just months before. Party officers included members of the Stoneham, Middlesex, Franklin, and American shoe cooperatives.[55]

The results of the election of 1884 were a mixed blessing to the advocates of independent labor politics. Stoneham cast a clear majority of its ballots for the Republican presidential candidate Blaine. This was the first election Butler had ever lost in Stoneham. However, he had one consolation in defeat: he outpolled the national winner, Democrat Grover Cleveland, by sixty-one votes. The People's Party candidate for congress, Henry Lovering, fared much better and triumphed over his Republican opponent. Stoneham's incumbent Democrat and labor sympathizer George Cowdrey defeated both the Republican and People's Party candidates for a seat on the General Court.[56]

The inconsistencies in the election results pointed to something far more ominous then the defeat of Benjamin Butler. Stoneham's cooperators believed in the viability of an independent party, and such politics unified them. Yet the city's working-class community was less cohesive than the earlier victory over Sanborn and Mann indicated. Indeed, divisions within the Knights of Labor, founded in Stoneham by cooperators, provoked a crisis in the community.[57] A little more than a year after the election, the Knights locked horns with former allies of the labor movement, the directors of the American Cooperative Boot and Shoe Company.

In January 1886 the Knights of Labor approached every factory in Stoneham with a demand for the weekly rather than monthly payment of wages. All factories agreed to meet this demand except one, the American Cooperative Boot and Shoe Company. The directors refused to comply with an intransigence surprising and disturbing to their employees and townsmen. Consequently, both the company's stockholding and nonstockholding employees walked out of the factory. A reporter for the *Boston Globe*, perplexed by a cooperative on strike, asked an employee how worker-owners could strike against themselves. The shoe worker blamed the strike on two factors. First, he contended that too much stock was held outside of the shop; and second, that cooperation had certain structural inadequacies. If annually elected directors acted objectionably during their tenure, the workers had "no power to do much more than in the ordinary case of labor against capital." He was convinced, however, that a vote of the stockholders would support the demand for weekly pay.[58]

The striking shoe worker had uncovered some superficial truths. All of the cooperative shoe factories, of necessity, sold stock to individuals outside of their shops and thus paid dividends to nonworkers. The interests of these latter stockholders could diverge from those of member workers. In addition, none of the cooperatives functioned as direct democracies throughout the year. A lag time could exist between the formation of a majority position and the action of the board of directors. However, the unresponsiveness of the American's board of directors was unique among Stoneham's cooperatives. The other three factories never resisted the will of their member-workers.

One cause of the American's intransigence was the market economy that, acting with centrifugal force, tore at the unity of the working-class community. The competition that racked the shoe industry, and that became increasingly destructive as the decade wore on, could redirect the loyalty of workers to the progressively smaller locus of the firm, the family, or the individual. In the American Cooperative the survival of the firm took precedence over the union sympathies of the member-employees. In fact, by 1885 none of the working shareholders were union members. The directors, including one who was a former Crispin, resisted union interference in the operation of their factory because they actually came to believe that workers had "no right to ask it."[59] The interests of the cooperators, which were always rooted in community and family stability, could, under the right circumstances, cripple working-class solidarity by emphasizing the narrow interests of the firm's survival.

The ability of Stoneham's cooperators to resist this tendency to elevate business interests above those of the community of workers was put to the test during the late 1880s. This period was one of economic uncertainty, when the cooperators struggled continuously with the threat of failure. The Franklin Cooperative was the first to experience real hardship, and in April 1886 it fell into the hands of its creditors and soon closed. At the end of this year the situation seemed bleak for the Middlesex Cooperative as well. It registered a profit of only $545.[60] At the same time, the Stoneham factory had stabilized sales at its 1885 level but managed to earn a yearly profit of only $254, down from $4,260 the year before. Twelve months later the cooperative rebounded and earned $1,826 despite losses of over $2,000 and a cutback of one-third in production. Yet the losses it incurred in 1888 and the first half of 1889 crippled the business. With severely reduced production and a net loss of $2,800 for 1888, the firm could no longer remain open. Oddly enough, a $2,000 mortgage on the factory dating back to 1882 had never been repaid and the heirs of the recently deceased lender demanded repayment of the principal. This overwhelmed the cooperators, and in April of the next year the Board of Directors called in the salesmen, ended the retail trade, and did all they could to reduce expenses. By September a special stockholders committee recommended that the firm either close or the members organize a new company. After a long meeting where at first both suggestions were rejected, the stockholders finally decided to cut their losses and sell off the enterprise.[61]

This decline of cooperation in Stoneham came after years of success during the most trying economic times. Both the Stoneham and Middlesex Cooperatives survived the depression of the 1870s. The Franklin Cooperative was organized in what the *Boston Globe* called "one of the hardest years the shoe business has ever known." Yet, by the end of the 1880s two of the cooperatives had failed and the American had become a joint stock company. Of the four shoe factories, the Middlesex alone survived into the 1890s.[62]

The most obvious cause of these economic difficulties was a new industry procedure of selling goods on credit for periods of up to seven months. With little capital to spare, this made the cooperatives particularly vulnerable to the failure of their clients.[63] Both the Stoneham and Franklin Cooperatives appear to have suffered losses in this way.

Yet the failure of cooperation cannot be explained in these terms alone. The cooperators needed assistance to survive the vicissitudes of the market economy, and they should have looked in two places for it: the Knights of Labor and their own local organizations. Stoneham's cooperators, like many throughout the country, did, in fact, turn to the Knights' central organization for help. As their delegate to the General Assembly in 1886, John Best sat on the Committee of Cooperation and voted to implement a tax to fund cooperation. Most likely influenced by the failure of the Franklin Cooperative and the hard times experienced by all in Stoneham, he sought assistance from the most powerful source available to them. The Knights, however, failed to sustain their power. Their decision that year to set aside $40,000 annually for cooperation was never implemented, as the national organization began its rapid deterioration. District Assembly 30, under which Stoneham's six local assemblies functioned, experienced a similar pattern of decline. In 1884, the district claimed 6,112 members. In one year that figure grew to 7,536. By 1886, 81,191 men and women belonged to the district. This phenomenal growth then reversed itself dramatically. In 1887, the membership roles fell to 31,644, and by the next year only 9,179 knights claimed membership in District Assembly 30. The district, itself having proposed at least two plans for cooperation that were never implemented, could not provide a reliable alternative for the cooperators.[64] Stoneham's shoe workers must have looked on with decreasing confidence in the availability of any outside assistance.

The cooperators of Stoneham had only their own resources to depend upon. Yet, even in the face of increasing worker militancy, they never once turned to each other to join their productive or marketing efforts together. Three of the four shoe cooperatives sold their products in the Western states, and all four had drummers competing with one another for sales.[65] If they had jointly marketed their goods they would have saved money and effort. They never thought, though, in greater terms than their own businesses. When the Knights of Labor could not help them and the problems they faced could not be solved in their established modes of labor activism, the cooperators were stymied.

The cooperators of Stoneham developed an understanding of community as family members, factory artisans, wage workers, and trade unionists. Small-city life, through its voluntary and political associations, provided these shoe workers with a sense of power and an understanding of the democratic process. When they searched for alternatives to industrial instability they chose cooperation and applied their experience in democracy to their work lives. The male cooperators of Stoneham also acted to preserve their dominance in the family and on the shop floor by securing their role as providers and excluding women from positions of authority in the cooperatives. This began to change as the Knights of Labor organized and women rethought and tested the limits of their participation. However, the Knights' organization in Stoneham was just as volatile as elsewhere, and the alternatives it could provide locally were as limited as those of the district or national organizations.[66]

The cooperators were dependent upon their own community, a community of cross-class alliances that encouraged a familiarity with the middle class of Stoneham. Men like John Best, for example, crossed the boundaries of class. He was living proof that manufacturers were not all necessary enemies; that they, too, could be staunch supporters of labor. Certainly other manufacturers could be quite exploitative, but John Best's example showed that the will of the community could prevail over the willful behavior of individual men. The cooperators had established themselves as part of this world and achieved a real sense of power in it.

The power they had achieved, however, diminished their capacity to innovate and confront threats to their cooperative institutions. The very alliances that made their community viable narrowed their choices. Surely, the shopkeepers and professionals of the city would have looked askance at any "monopolistic" effort by cooperators to join their productive forces together, especially if those forces could threaten the position of other manufacturers in the city. In addition, their very success in local politics must have encouraged the cooperators' political ambitions, and even though their political agenda never included aid to cooperative enterprises, their failure to rally the city's workers around the People's Party campaign certainly discouraged their hope for unified action. So instead of threatening their fellow townsmen with a coordinated effort or an expansive cooperative vision, Stoneham's workers allowed their dream of cooperative control to lapse into a defensive trade unionism.[67] In the end, their integration into their city, and their actual power, immobilized them.

CHAPTER 5

COOPERATION AND COMMUNITY

The Coopers of Minneapolis

Storm clouds, wind, and rain made the last Sunday in May 1887 a typical spring day in the city of Minneapolis. The Knights of Labor had haplessly planned a parade for this Sunday, and the participants, as they gathered to march, met with intermittent showers and blustering high winds. The less courageous of the Knights' supporters took this as a sign to scurry home for protection. The bad weather, however, hardly dissuaded thousands of others who assembled in the industrial district just west of St. Anthony's Falls. By late morning an estimated four thousand people were set to march and, according to the *Minneapolis Tribune*, "the spectacle of the uniformed bodies, with numerous bands and hundreds of flags and lodge banners flying, was a grand and imposing one." The object of this public fanfare, the laying of the cornerstone for the Northwest's first Knights of Labor "temple," drew upward of sixteen thousand more people. In a crowded mass of humanity they converged at the intersection of Eighth Avenue and Fourth Street. A few celebrants even climbed up and straddled the shade trees lining the street, all eager to watch the dedication of organized labor's new home in the city.[1]

The parade was an impressive display of the labor movement's strength in 1887. It also suggested key differences between Stoneham and Minneapolis that would influence the course of the latter city's cooperative movement. The first and most obvious difference was that Minneapolis's population dwarfed Stoneham's. As a new western city, Minneapolis had grown rapidly from 2,555 residents in 1860 to 13,000 in 1870. By 1885 the city housed a staggering 130,000 people, an impressive 20,000 of whom could turn out for a labor parade.[2] Yet size and rapid growth were only two of the city's most obvious characteristics. The very nature of Minneapolis's political life also differed markedly from that found in the New England town of Stoneham. A variety of observers have characterized Minneapolis as New England-like during the nineteenth century, yet it clearly differed from Stoneham in significant ways. No town meeting brought Minneapolis's community together, and powerful industrialists and political machines clearly dominated its politics.[3] Conspicuously absent were the small-town cross-class alliances and familiarities that provided Stoneham's workers close access to power. Such an environment provided Minneapolis's labor reformers with unique possibilities. They found their will and imagination less constrained than their counterparts in Stoneham did. Indeed, the conditions of rapid growth and more distant political institutions in this western city would prove amenable to much working-class innovation.

Minneapolis's labor temple parade began early Sunday afternoon, guided by the well-known labor leader, cooper, and marshall-in-chief for the day, Chauncy W. Curtis. Curtis directed the procession through the city's streets, moving from Washington Avenue to Hennepin, down Hennepin to Nicollet, up Nicollet to Fifth Street, down Fifth to Eighth Avenue South, and ending at the Fourth Street intersection.[4] This man whom the Knights had chosen to lead their parade had long been among the city's most dynamic labor activists. As early as 1872, Curtis had helped the coopers in their pioneering attempts at trade unionism, and between 1868 and 1878 he had played an instrumental role in establishing four cooperative barrel factories, a cooperative publishing company, and a cooperative store. In 1878 he served as president of the Workingmen's Union, a political labor reform association, and in the early 1880s he turned his efforts to organizing the Knights of Labor.[5] His position in the day's events reflected the commitment the local Knights had made to the coopers' brand of cooperation and trade unionism.

Encouraged by Curtis, the coopers of Minneapolis were the first workers in the city to experiment with cooperative production. Beginning in 1868 with the establishment of one struggling and unsuccessful enterprise, barrel makers opened a series of shops over the next twenty years. By 1886 they operated seven successful factories and dominated the city's barrel industry. In the following year these cooperatives grossed over one million dollars worth of business and employed 368 journeymen-owners out of 593 working coopers in the city.[6] Their remarkable progress convinced many reformers both in Minneapolis and around the country that cooperative industry could provide a meaningful alternative to "competitive" capitalism.[7]

In the 1880s Minneapolis's cooperative movement expanded on the foundation of a reinvigorated labor movement. As the Knights of Labor grew in membership and power, they became the key players in the development of cooperative enterprises. Indeed, with the successful model of the coopers so convincingly close at hand, officials of the Knights had little trouble spreading their cooperative vision among the various organized workers in the city. District master workmen J. P. McGuaghey and T. W. Brosnan and district secretary John F. Cronin were particularly influential in spreading the cooperation gospel. Between 1868 and 1887, the city's workers established at least thirty-two cooperatives of various kinds, twenty-four of them after 1882, and ten of them during 1886 alone.[8]

In the labor press and other publications, reformers praised the coopers of Minneapolis for their achievements.[9] Yet as the barrel cooperatives flourished their success actually obscured a variety of intractable problems. First, all cooperators wanted to stabilize their work lives, end periods of unemployment, and increase wages. Despite their best efforts, however, the barrel makers in Minneapolis found the markets for their goods consistently volatile and difficult to control. They struggled time and again with rising costs, falling prices, mechanization, and fierce competition. Throughout the 1880s the coopers achieved only temporary stability and success. Second, despite the fact that cooperative members had a very close relationship with organized labor and had founded the Coopers' Assembly of the Knights in Minneapolis, their interests clashed at times with those of other organized barrel workers. In fact, their business decisions occasionally antagonized the nonmember journeymen and unskilled helpers employed in their own shops, as well as journeymen in the other company and cooperative shops. Moreover, in 1887 two cooperatives directly defied the Knights of Labor and flouted that union's efforts to stabilize barrel production. Within six months of the labor parade and its impressive display of solidarity, the Coopers' Assembly tried and expelled the members of one of the offending cooperatives, the most successful worker-owned enterprise in Minneapolis.

At the root of much of this conflict was an industry in competitive turmoil. Yet something far more revealing aggravated relations among the coopers. As the various parties struggled with the realities of market competition, they developed different expectations of what their utopian projects could and should accomplish. Cooperation, simply put, came to signify different things to different people. Defining community, solidarity, and cooperation differently, some coopers moved in more "collectivist" directions. Others opposed these efforts, remaining equally committed, so they believed, to their own ideals of cooperation. The parties to this conflict would never resolve the basic contradictions of cooperative production. Instead, their differences would contribute to the failure of the Knights of Labor and to their inability to provide stability and a living wage for barrel makers.

Minneapolis: Among The Mills, a Craftsman's Empire

When the first flour mills harnessed the energy of the Falls of St. Anthony, Minneapolis was hardly a city. Within a few short years the surrounding countryside attracted thousands of new settlers anxious to stake a claim to the land's rich agricultural potential. These settlers soon produced enough wheat to make Minneapolis the largest wheat market and processing center in the United States. In 1886 the city's twenty-six mills could produce thirty-five thousand barrels of flour a day. The mills, in turn, served as the industrial core of a dynamic new urban center.[10]

Within this dynamic economy the coopers quickly emerged as an essential element. The mills needed thousands of barrels, and the barrel factories needed highly skilled workers. This demand for coopers was fortuitous. It gave them considerable leverage in bargaining with their employers and, as with other skilled workers in this period, allowed for successful organizing. In 1868 Minneapolis coopers organized their first trade union, and then, in the early 1870s, they combined under the auspices of the International Workingmen's Association. They became major players in the labor movement's early years in the city, and they achieved steady work and good pay. Attractive conditions, however, brought many more coopers to the city than the labor market could absorb. In the early 1870s, the "boss" coopers, as the owners of the shops were called, took advantage of the overabundance of skilled labor to reduce wages and enfeeble the union.[11]

Under these conditions, Chauncy Curtis and a handful of coopers established the first two cooperative shops in Minneapolis. Both were informal businesses, unincorporated and transitory. The first shop lasted just a few months in 1868. The second, established in 1870, lasted two years, until one member assumed control of the shop's barrel contracts to begin his own factory.[12] Chastened by these experiences, Curtis, Francis Bachelder (a participant in the 1870 fiasco), and three other coopers incorporated a new barrel cooperative in 1874. Along with their new legal status, Curtis and Bachelder composed a set of by-laws designed to avert the organizational mistakes they had made in the past. These by-laws formed the basis for every subsequent cooperative barrel factory in Minneapolis.[13]

Curtis and Bachelder would become uniquely important activists in the local cooperative movement. Yet they resembled the typical cooperators of Stoneham in one very important way: their need for stability in employment and community life. Both coopers had experienced periods of geographic mobility. Curtis, originally from Massachusetts, made his way to Minnesota in the 1860s. Bachelder, born in Maine, had lived in New York for a time and then appeared in Minnesota in 1866. By 1874, Curtis and Bachelder, who had turned thirty-one and forty-five years old, respectively, had families and dependents to support.[14] At this point in their lives they turned to cooperative production for the stability regular employment as a barrel maker could not supply.

These two men worked together in labor reform for years, though they would follow very different paths into the 1880s and define their cooperative experiences in contrasting ways. Curtis, the quintessential activist, never stayed long in the cooperatives he established. He had a restive spirit, or perhaps an activist's impatience with day-to-day business decisions. His path would be unique—agitating, politicking, and above all organizing. Like many other coopers, though, he ultimately found little workplace stability. He eventually abandoned barrel making and the cooperatives altogether.[15] Bachelder, in contrast, actually achieved the stability most coopers found so elusive. He served as an officer for many years in one cooperative and represented the west side industrial district as a state legislator for two terms.[16] These accomplishments marked him as a leading spokesman for the coopers. Bachelder's success, however, was predicated on a conservatism that would isolate him at critical moments from the community of organized coopers. Indeed, his own cooperative directly defied the Knights of Labor in 1887. When faced with expulsion from the union, he and his workplace colleagues refused to back down from a confrontation with organized labor.

In the early 1870s, however, these differences had not yet surfaced. Curtis, Bachelder, and the others incorporated their business in late November 1874, and aptly named it the Cooperative Barrel Manufacturing Company. The small capital requirements of barrel making allowed them to start on a modest scale. Each of the sixteen original members put fifteen dollars down and agreed to pay five dollars weekly toward their share of $10,000 in capital stock. With enough money to start, they opened for business in early December and rented a building from "the widow Mayo" on Third Street between Ninth and Tenth Avenues South.[17]

Like Stoneham's cooperators, these men faced hostile opposition from a variety of sources. The other barrel companies, the "boss" shops, cared little for the cooperators' success. If their influence with the millers had prevailed, the cooperative would never have signed a single contract. The fact that the coopers' union had affiliated with the International Workingman's Association also won them few friends among their potential business associates. Yet the millers must have soon realized that a worker-owned business posed no immediate threat to the capitalist order. Surely they had nothing to fear from one small cooperative factory. Indeed, in the 1870s, liberal reformers waxed enthusiastic over the virtues of cooperatives. E. L. Godkin, for one, believed cooperatives would elicit sympathy for capital from their worker-owners. One of the leading new millers of Minneapolis, Charles A. Pillsbury, thought highly enough of the experiment to contract with it for the barrel needs of one entire mill. He stood by this contract over the years, and the Cooperative Barrel Manufacturing Company flourished.[18]

This cooperative actually thrived far beyond its members' expectations and soon outgrew its original location. The members then bought an old cooper shop and two quarter-acre lots at 1029 Sixth Street South, a propitious move, for rising property values would sustain their prosperity. Many of the original members bought land and homes in the immediate area and benefitted as well from the growth of the city and increasing land values. By the mid-1880s, the cooperative, now known as the Sixth Street Shop, would have as many as 120 working members, possess its own stave factory in Wisconsin, and hold assets worth $58,000.[19]

In order to survive, though, the Sixth Street cooperators would first have to make it through the depressed 1870s. They apparently did so with a deliberate and conservative business posture, remaining small and expanding slowly. Throughout this period their membership never exceeded a modest 25 or so men. By 1877, a faction of the members, which included Bachelder, grew dissatisfied. The exact nature of their dissatisfaction is not entirely clear, though they seemed unhappy with the shop's unwillingness to expand more rapidly. In late 1877 five members broke away to form the North Star Barrel Manufacturing Company. Curtis, who had left the Sixth Street shop and the city sometime earlier, returned and signed up with the new cooperative. The North Star would eventually become one of the largest cooperative barrel companies in Minneapolis.[20]

The appearance of the North Star initiated an era of rapid expansion in the industry and in the formation of cooperatives. Over the next eight years, nine new cooperative barrel factories opened for business. This growth resulted from a remarkable increase in flour production that began in 1878 and an almost equally remarkable increase in the city's population. During an eight-year period beginning in 1878, flour production increased over sixfold, from under one million to over six million barrels a year. In the same period the population of the city increased from under 47,000 to over 130,000 people.[21] Expansion, instability, and opportunity apparently encouraged the coopers to experiment with cooperative enterprises.

The coopers found cooperative production attractive for other, more important, reasons as well. They, unlike Stoneham's cooperators, still dominated the production process as individual craftsmen and exercised real independence in their work. By the 1870s, however, their work life was in turmoil. John D. Rockefeller had broken the power of the coopers in Ohio when he absorbed apprenticeship training into the Standard Oil empire. He succeeded in this by reducing the craft to several simple machine operations.[22] The coopers of Minneapolis also found

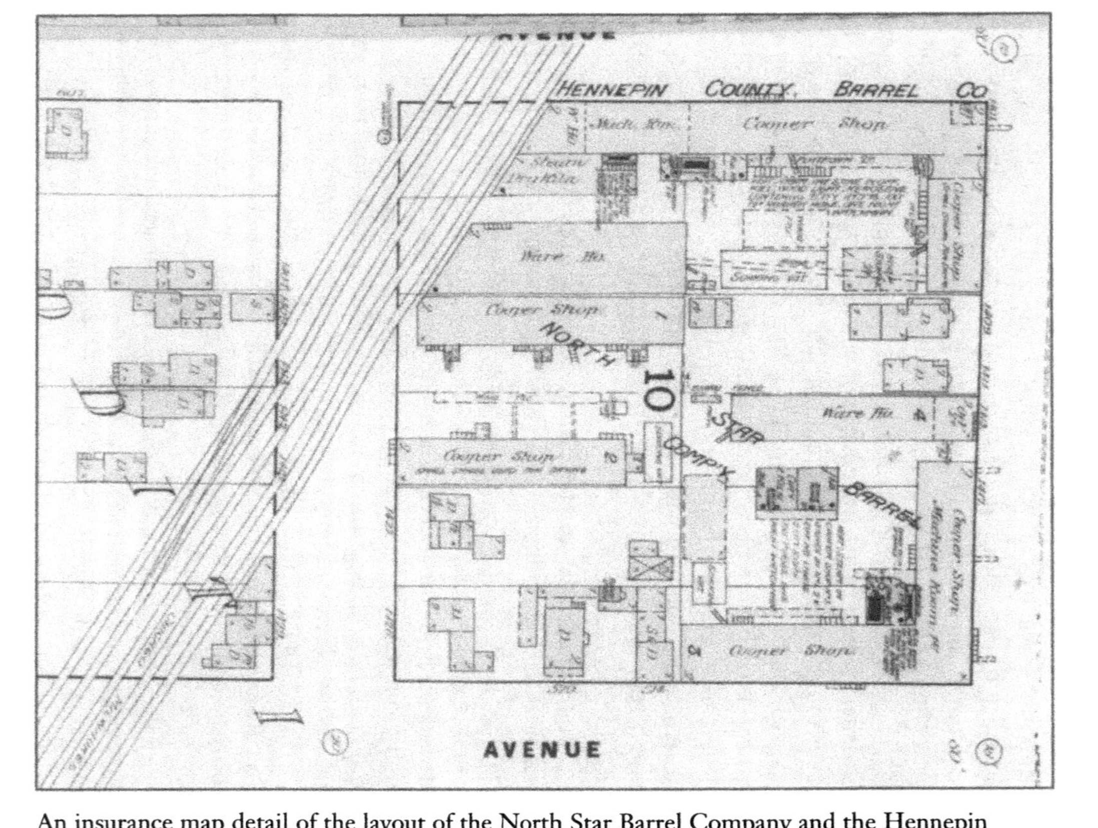

An insurance map detail of the layout of the North Star Barrel Company and the Hennepin County Barrel Company, 1885. From the collections of the Minnesota Historical Society.

themselves embattled by the machine, though no one manufacturer had monopoly control over the flour industry or the inclination to produce his own barrels. The boss coopers, however, did introduce machinery as early as 1874 and, perhaps in a more haphazard way than Rockefeller, transformed the craft of barrel making in their city. Cooperators contested the degradation of their skill by excluding machinery from their own shops for as long as possible.[23]

To these artisans, cooperation was a defense and a justifiable extension of their artisanal culture. Independence in the workplace and in spirit, the labor theory of value, the pride of craftsmanship, and a trade union tradition, all fused in the cooperative experience. When the secretary of the Phoenix Barrel Manufacturing Company, which was formed in 1881, listed the reasons why he and his compatriots started their cooperative, his words were permeated with artisanal sentiment:

> First. Believing that labor creates all dividends and that the cooperative system is the only avenue in business by which profits and dividends are placed in the hands of those to whom they rightly belong.
>
> Second. Because every man entering cooperation on this plan begins a practical business education which it is impossible to attain while working under the journeyman system.
>
> Third. We furnish ourselves nothing but first-class material from which to manufacture our goods, thereby avoiding the inconvenience placed upon journeymen who are often required to manufacture first-class goods from inferior material. . . .
>
> Fourth. The cooperative system relieves all who embrace it from the tyranny of unscrupulous bosses.[24]

For coopers the labor theory of value defined workers as the legitimate owners of profit and cooperation as the only means by which they could receive their rightful compensation. Moreover, these craftsmen took pride in their skill and believed that only through cooperative production could they consistently use the highest quality materials to produce a high-quality product. Yet more significantly, cooperation would free them, in the secretary's words, "from the tyranny of unscrupulous bosses" and provide the journeyman with an education in practical business enterprise. Central to the cooperative's appeal was this independence from a boss, and the business knowledge it provided. Central to the meaning of cooperation was how coopers interpreted this independence. Would these workers develop an expansive definition of cooperation, emphasizing the greater good of their community, or would they adhere to a more constricted notion of self-interest, possibly confined to the benefit of a particular firm at the expense of others? The answer to this question would indicate how class-oriented the cooperative experience would become.

Yet the one experience the cooperators of Minneapolis seemed to value universally was democratic process. The by-laws of the Sixth Street Shop, written by Curtis and Bachelder, created a rigorously democratic and egalitarian structure that was replicated in nearly every cooperative in the city. Each member was to purchase an equal share of stock and exercise but one vote. Meetings were to be held monthly to conduct the concern's business. In addition, members would work on a piece rate system and divide up their profits or losses in proportion to the wages earned by each individual.[25] On the shop floor itself, democratically adopted rules would govern daily operations and regulate the behavior of workers to insure equality and fairness. In the Hennepin County Barrel Company, for example, the coopers established a set of rules guaranteeing fair distribution of work. No cooper in this factory could hold an extra barrel in his berth if others were waiting for barrels to hoop. When business was slow, the men worked on a stint or a set quantity of work, and if someone failed to make his stint he had the privilege of completing it during the week. In addition, this shareholder had to work his "berth." The by-laws strictly prohibited him from contracting out his place in the factory. The cooperative existed to provide work for journeymen, and not, at least initially, for individuals to profit from the labor of others. Moreover, the foreman's power in the shop was severely limited. As inspector of finished barrels, he could theoretically make or break a member. He was, though, president of the company and as an elected official answered to his fellow members at each monthly meeting. If he believed a member should be fired because of inferior workmanship, he had first to show cause before the board of management and then to convince two-thirds of his fellow members at any monthly meeting to approve the dismissal.[26] The cooperative cooper was a respected and respectful king of his berth.

However, Minneapolis coopers, like the Stoneham cooperators, created something more than democratically organized individual shops. They created a community of cooperators. The barrel makers built their shops initially all on the west side of St. Anthony's Falls. The Sixth Street, North Star, Hennepin, Phoenix, and Union shops all functioned within a few blocks of one another along the Chicago, Milwaukee and St. Paul Railroad.[27] When westside land values rose beyond the coopers' means, they opened new shops in more remote areas and on the east side of the Falls.[28] Though these coopers initially owned no property, with striking consistency in shop after shop, they built homes around their factories. By 1886 the typical cooperator was married, owned his own home purchased through a cooperative building and loan association, and lived in the immediate vicinity of his workshop.[29]

The craft community in which they worked, and their interest in trade unionism and cooperative membership, elicited considerable loyalty from many of these men. Yearly parades and picnics, baseball games, and dances brought the men and their families together. The coopers even formed a band that performed at their various functions. At least one of the cooperatives established a type of mutual insurance program providing weekly cash payments when their members became too ill to work. At other times the cooperators would take up collections to aid sick members of their companies.[30]

The cohesiveness of the cooperative community counteracted what could have been a fractious admixture of ethnicities. Germans, Norwegians, Swedes, and Irish, along with a large number of Americans with native-born parents and a few Italians, predominated in the cooperative shops. In 1886 Albert Shaw studied the cooperatives and found this ethnic mix in most of them. Only in the North Star did Germans outnumber the others. In the Phoenix shop Americans formed the dominant group. Though many of the cooperators bought their homes through ethnically based building and loan associations, the cooperative experience seemed to soften the rough edges of ethnic difference. Barrel makers worked well together, and ethnic conflicts occurred rarely if at all.[31] Clearly the cooperators and the community life they spawned could directly counteract the forces of fragmentation so characteristic of American working-class life.

Cooperative factories were but one aspect of community life for the coopers. The very act of building and operating their businesses, of buying their homes and struggling to maintain stable lives encouraged them to try other cooperative forms. The idea, in fact, resonated with them beyond the workshop. In 1885 the coopers established their most significant community- rather than craft-based institution. During the summer a committee of the Coopers' Assembly met in the Sixth Street shop to consider opening a cooperative store. While the meeting drew about fifty coopers, the committee consisted largely of officers from five barrel cooperatives, all activists of one form or another in labor reform. The committee's chair, Steward Jensen, had been a member of the Sixth Street shop for years and had recently become treasurer of the Hennepin cooperative. He would run for alderman on the Union Labor Party ticket two years later and serve as recording secretary of the Coopers' Assembly in 1888. The secretary, George Clement, would soon be secretary of the Sixth Street shop. Michael Gill, soon to be elected president of the store, had been a member and officer of the Sixth Street shop as far back as 1877. He was presently master workman of the Coopers' Assembly. They all were aware of the cooperative movement in England, and they proposed to open their grocery on Rochdale principles.[32]

The coopers chose to locate their store within the vicinity of their shops in a "neat little brick building." Anyone was welcome to join, but the vast majority of members worked in the barrel trade. Members of the Sixth Street, Phoenix, Hennepin, and North Star shops all participated. They originally planned for members to make an initial investment of ten dollars for one share. Share-holders could hold a maximum of five but no less than three shares. However, their potential constituency found this requirement prohibitive, and they issued memberships for $1.25 down with not too rigorously enforced $.25 weekly assessments to follow. The store clearly was not a capital-intensive enterprise but one designed to serve this working-class community's needs. About 125 individuals joined, and the store flourished.[33]

Officially known as the Minneapolis Cooperative Mercantile Company, the store sold groceries and dry goods for cash only. In the Rochdale tradition it redistributed profits in proportion to purchases besides paying 6 percent dividends on all paid up shares. In an attempt to increase patronage, the cooperators decided a year after the store's founding to extend the sharing of profits to nonmember purchasers. They assisted friends in North Minneapolis in their efforts to open a store, talked of joining with a cooperative shoe store on Cedar Avenue, and acted as the official agent for the tobacco products of two cooperatives in Covington, Kentucky, and Raleigh, North Carolina. They also included in their own founding document a standard clause of the Rochdale constitution that called for the establishment of a "self-supporting home colony" to exemplify the ideals of cooperation.[34]

Albert Shaw, the nineteenth-century historian of the Minneapolis cooperators, described the wide net these businesses cast over workers' lives:

> In Minneapolis there are men who are earning their living in a cooperative cooper shop, paying for their home through a cooperative building and loan association, buying their groceries at a cooperative store, and having their washing done in a cooperative laundry. Some of them perchance enjoy the advantages of membership in a cooperative neighborhood improvement association, obtain books and magazines from a cooperative reading club or library association, and so on. Many of them belong to societies and orders which have as their most practical feature a system of cooperative life and accident insurance.[35]

The cooperators had devised a network of institutions for self-help to achieve steady work, permanence of place, and the preservation of their craft. They also considered transforming something far more elemental, their own habits and behavior. Barrel craftsmen had long-established reputations as boisterous and hard-drinking men. Traditionally they would nurse a "goose-egg" of liquor in their shops on Saturdays and, surely against the will of the boss coopers, lay waste to the entire workday. When their hard drinking on Saturday inevitably carried through the weekend, they would celebrate Blue Monday, starting work again on Tuesday. In the cooperative shops, however, the coopers enforced new behavioral norms. They banned alcohol from the workplace and at all meetings and restricted attendance at stockholders' meetings to the sober. No member was even allowed the privilege to smoke.[36] This discipline, utterly at odds with the coopers' past behavior, would have more than pleased the boss coopers. Yet the cooperators did not intend by this only to get more work out of the men. If a democratic business was to function they needed disciplined and committed members willing to bargain, negotiate, and compromise. After all, these ethnically diverse cooperatives could succeed only if all the members were willing to work together. As one cooper said, "there are a heap of things to put up with in cooperation."[37] Cooperation attempted to produce a more responsible and temperate "citizen."

Democracy and work, however, were far easier to compose in the by-laws of an organization then to integrate successfully in the workshop. One particularly difficult issue for any cooperative, in reality the sine qua non of any profitable business, had to do with the "right" to terminate worker-members. Given the nature of Minneapolis's cooperatives and the power of individual coopers within them, the firing of a member occurred only under the most unusual circumstances. Indeed, no cooperative seems to have fired a cooper until late 1884. In that year F. G. Grant, a member of the Union Cooperative Barrel Company, refused to trim one of his barrels when requested to by the president of the cooperative. He was charged with abusive behavior and violation of shop rules, and twenty-seven of the cooperative's thirty-two members voted to expel Grant. He refused, however, to abide by the order, and with the classic independence, not to say stubbornness, of a skilled artisan remained in his berth. This left the cooperative in a difficult situation. What could it do, in fact, to remove a recalcitrant member of its own organization? The cooperative resorted ultimately to the law and obtained a temporary restraining order from the county district court to forcibly remove Grant from the shop floor.[38]

Clearly in this episode all parties found themselves in unfamiliar territory. Grant argued that he had not violated the rules because the shop had no right to demand the reworking of a barrel already accepted as finished. He had completed his assigned work honestly, he believed, and no more should be demanded of him. In order to discipline Grant, the shop had no other recourse, short of physical expulsion, than to go to court for a legal remedy. Though the court decided in favor of the Union Barrel Company, it also found the cooperative frustratingly difficult to fathom. According to the millers' trade journal, the *Northwestern Miller*, the court understood the cooperative to be some kind of "association" whose by-laws it could not "properly inquire" into. The court also believed, however, that "the power to discharge employees must be vested in some one." In other words, workers by their very nature had to be dischargable even if they belonged to a cooperative. In this decision the subordinate status of any worker had prevailed over the owner status of a cooperative shareholder. The *Northwestern Miller* believed this resolved a long-running uncertainty about the legal right cooperatives had to fire their members. Yet even the *Miller* seemed unsure of how the cooperatives would behave. This decision, the journal reported, set a precedent the cooperatives would "probably" act on in the future.[39]

The Grant episode and its aftermath exposed the peculiar ambiguities of the cooperative experience. Though coopers had designed their businesses in the interests of skilled craftsmen, the fact that their business interests and their artisanal independence could conflict came to them as a surprise. Moreover, the interests of the group and its democratic expression could clearly come into direct conflict with the individual cooperator's perceived rights. In addition, the confusion of the court and its privileging of a shareholder's "worker" status paralleled the cooperators' ambivalence toward themselves as workers. Was it possible for them to blend the status of a worker with that of an owner unambiguously? If not, which status would prevail, and when? This ambivalence would bode ill for the industrial solidarity future conflicts would soon require of them.

The cooperators' attempt to fashion a democratic workplace created a complex human community, and they faced several other difficulties in blending democracy into everyday life. One of the most perplexing difficulties had to do with the nature of community life itself. It appears that the cooperative community was really very much like that of a small town, capable of embracing some members with generosity, but also quite capable of rejecting others with contempt. Among the coopers of Minneapolis, various ties of neighborhood, craft, and self-interest reinforced the cooperators' sense of unity. At the same time, conflicts could emerge when personalities, perhaps obnoxious, grated on the sensibilities of the majority. In addition, the cooperators' peculiar combination of independence and group loyalty could exacerbate potential conflicts between members. Rather than containing the boisterous behavior of the coopers, the cooperative could have the opposite effect. Indeed, an otherwise harmless event could accelerate into a more serious confrontation. All of this became evident in 1885 when a confrontation between two coopers in the Northwestern Cooperative ended in the death of one and the charge of murder for the other.

Custom had it in the Northwestern shop that when a cooper married he was expected to treat his shop mates to cigars. One member, Mark Norton, married in late November but refused to abide by the custom. Apparently tight-fisted and reserved, he became the object of considerable mischief. When no cigars were forthcoming, August Oys, a twenty-one-year-old German cooper, and a few others engaged in a series of pranks to either draw Norton out or simply antagonize him. First they emptied out the contents of his lunch pail and then hid it. Norton said little to this provocation and went home for his meal. The following day they placed an "effigy" of some kind in his berth. When Norton arrived in the morning the sight of the effigy apparently enraged him and he went straight to Oys, the alleged ringleader of the pranks. Norton accused him of hiding his lunch pail. When Oys denied this, Norton struck him in the face with his fist. Oys, backed up to a wall, grabbed a "chime maul" and struck out, hitting Norton twice, once on the arm and then on the back of the head. The latter blow fractured Norton's skull, and by evening he was dead. Oys immediately surrendered himself to the police.[40]

This unfortunate confrontation played itself out in an unexpected way. Rather than rallying around the fate of the thirty-five-year-old Norton, a charter member of the cooperative, and his ailing widow, the community of cooperators seemed to sympathize far more with August Oys. The young man's plight generated enormous sympathy from the coopers of his shop and elsewhere. Sympathetic coopers apparently made sure that Oys received proper legal assistance, and shortly before his trial members of his cooperative defended the young German for acting in self-defense. Their resolution to that effect appeared both in the *St. Paul Daily Globe* and in the *Northwestern Miller.* Large numbers of coopers attended the trial, which lasted little more than a day and a half. After the jury deliberated a total of ten minutes, it quickly found

August Oys as portrayed in the *St. Paul Daily Globe*, 1886. From the collections of the Minnesota Historical Society.

Oys not guilty. According to the *Miller*, the verdict was met with loud applause and seemed to satisfy the community of coopers.[41]

What was Mark Norton to his co-workers? Despite his "retiring disposition," why did he not elicit more of their sympathy? His fellow coopers surely would have known of his tragic personal circumstances. Less than a year before his own death, Norton's first wife had passed away, leaving him with a four-year-old son to care for. His brief second marriage was to a disabled woman who had lost her own family to a fire. The second wife was also addicted to opium, probably a consequence of her physical condition. Given these circumstances, Norton's withdrawn disposition and parsimony is hardly surprising. This did not seem to impress his colleagues, and his willful defiance of the cultural practices and expectations of the shop alienated him from his shop mates. His personal tragedies gained him no sympathy.[42]

It is possible that in another environment, such as in a "boss"-owned barrel factory, Norton would have backed down from the direct and violent confrontation he initiated with Oys. He could have left such a position with little sacrifice and found employment elsewhere. In the context of a cooperative, however, Norton had less mobility. In order to leave the shop it would have been necessary for him to sell his share, certainly a sacrifice and a chore that at times could be difficult. He probably would have resented the idea of having to leave. This was, after all, his own barrel shop, a place where his opinion and desires should have meaning. Surely he felt justified in standing his ground. Norton's death suggests that when an individual did not fit well into the community of coopers, the peculiar nature of the cooperative could exacerbate conflict. A cooperator's sense of ownership and subsequent unwillingness to compromise might collide with his shop mates' pressures to conform, and result in tragedy. This same pugnacious manly independence, when exercised by an entire cooperative shop, would have dire consequences for the movement as a whole.

Despite the unique problems faced by these cooperators, by the mid-1880s the Knights of Labor grew increasingly interested in cooperative enterprises of all kinds. In 1886, the master workman of Minnesota's District Assembly 79, J. P. McGaughey, assumed John Samuel's place as secretary to the Knights' National Cooperative Board. He, along with other local leaders, seriously encouraged cooperative activities and discussion in the city. Local assembly meetings debated the virtues of cooperation, and the issue was discussed at the weekly meetings of the city's Trade and Labor Assembly. McGuaghey, T. W. Brosnan, Jonathan Cronin, and another leading Knight, John Lamb, among others, propagandized or evangelized for cooperative principles on virtually any available occasion.[43]

Clearly, the Knights' leadership created an environment conducive to the spread of cooperative enterprises. In 1884, cigar makers opened a cooperative factory and printers organized two cooperative print shops. The Minneapolis Cooperative Mercantile Company opened the following year.[44] Cooperative products were popular enough that Brosnan Brothers shoe store advertised the sale of "the Stoneham Co-operative Co.'s shoes."[45] However, the banner year for cooperatives was unquestionably 1886. During that year, carpenters, laundresses, shirt makers, painters, and musi-

Labor activist and cooperator John P. McGaughey. From the collections of the Minnesota Historical Society.

cians all formed cooperatives. In addition, as a cooperative store opened in south Minneapolis, the Knights of Labor established their own cooperative building association and library. A dry goods cooperative opened for business as well.[46]

At the forefront of much of this activity was the aging printer and ideological torchbearer for cooperation in the city, James Rankin. Early chroniclers of Minneapolis' cooperatives characterized Rankin as the "father" and "patriarch" of the local movement.[47] Albert Shaw believed him to be the possible source of the idea in the city, and records do show his early role as a lecturer and promoter of cooperative enterprises. Most importantly, he edited two short-lived newspapers concerned with labor and cooperative reform, the *Minnesota Mirror* in 1883, and the *Christian Socialist* in 1886.[48] After nine months of agitating for cooperation through the *Mirror*'s pages, he handed the paper over to a group of local labor leaders who hoped to make of it an organ of the labor movement and "a nucleus for a workingmen's library and institute."[49]

Rankin gave up the newspaper but was soon busy with two other important local projects. Early in 1886 he published a forty-eight-page pamphlet, "Hard Times: Their Cause and Cure," an analysis of the labor problem and a prescription for change. The pamphlet was a local hit. According to the *St. Paul Daily Globe*, hundreds of copies sold at the newsstands, and the Knights of Labor (Rankin was a member of Local Assembly 805) sent the essay to numerous ministers and editors, among other interested parties. "Hard Times" chronicled Rankin's intellectual development as he grappled with the consequences of economic change and the declining status of craftsmen in the nineteenth century.[50]

Rankin had developed his basic ideas, he claimed, over a lifetime of study and labor.[51] He had already articulated some of the basic principles of "Hard Times" in the *Minnesota Mirror* two years before, ideas that were, however, neither original nor unfamiliar to the labor movement. What he offered that appeared unique was the influence and proximity of the singularly successful coopers' cooperatives. The coopers' efforts had proven to him that cooperation "is capable of doing all that is needed for the proper adjustment of social relations; that it is republican and Christian in its principles, methods and results." The cooperators had achieved industrial peace and sobriety, he exulted, while gaining the support and confidence of the millers and leading citizens of Minneapolis.[52] No less significantly, they had achieved personal pride and independence. In the "Jubilee" parade held in Minneapolis in 1883, Rankin saw the marching cooperators as men who

> looked and walked more like men proud of their good work . . . and of themselves as men and as masters of their own time and actions, than any other part of the great procession. Not one servant, not one boss among them—all equals and brothers in the successful prosecution of enterprises that give promise of influencing others to follow or to advance, and that will have a name in the history of the social redemption of the age. Such is our hope and prediction.[53]

Republican, Christian, and the source of independence, cooperation spoke to those fundamental if commonplace notions pervading the labor movement. What stood in the way of cooperation's success, according to Rankin, went to the very heart of the labor problem. To examining this fundamental problem he focused his energies and developed his ideas in the pamphlet "Hard Times."

The antithesis of cooperation, Rankin argued, was competition. Competition, in fact, had transformed a nation of villages, craftsmen, and farmers into an increasingly urbanized society typified by decreasing skill levels, long hours, and low pay. In "Hard Times," Rankin argued that legislation and the eight-hour movement could help rectify these problems. Ultimately, however, workers, he asserted, must control the labor market, and this could be accomplished only through "union" and "cooperation." Cooperation would be the means by which values opposed to competition's "mean war," that is, "temperance, economy, patience and forethought, and [a] tendency to promote the common welfare," could prevail.[54]

Rankin answered the objections to cooperation he expected to hear, such as the lack of business experience and capital among workers, by citing the coopers' achievements. Another, more fundamental, problem, however, had to be reckoned with. Wouldn't cooperatives, he imagined a critic suggesting, be subject to the same competitive pressures of any business and be forced to act "under the laws of competitive hostility?"[55] Here Rankin wavered from a more realistic assessment he had made earlier. Writing in the *Mirror*, he had recognized that the coopers did suffer from competition both as owners and as workers. As owners they were forced to underbid other shops to secure contracts with the flour mills. As workers they suffered from the ill-effects of an oversupplied labor market. Rankin believed a way had to be found to regulate this market, either by finding homes and work elsewhere for the coopers driving wages down or by establishing the cooperative guild advocated by Henry Sharpe.[56] In "Hard Times" he seemed to gloss over these problems. After all, he wrote, "the effect of cooperation on the character and habits of the members of the cooper shops carried on cooperatively, and on the whole trade, is so favorable as to delight those who take delight in seeing their fellow men improved mentally and morally."[57] Perhaps the phenomenal success of the coopers at this moment in time blinded him to the very real problems that would shortly debilitate the industry.

In the mid-1880s, Rankin was hardly alone in his optimism. The labor movement of Minneapolis seemed convinced that social change was imminent, and Rankin and the leaders of the Knights of Labor prepared, literally, to remake their work lives on a cooperative basis. In the words of District Master Workman T. W. Brosnan,

> Until the present system is abolished, man cannot be free. The competitive system means industrial slavery. What the world calls hire is only wages slavery. . . . We must endeavor to abolish this system and substitute for it the cooperative system—substitute peace for war and love for hate. Then will poverty be abolished and all its attending evils, intemperance, ignorance, prostitution, and all forms of crime.[58]

The district secretary-treasurer, Jonathan Cronin, argued in a similar vein: "Too much attention," he wrote, "cannot be given to the important subject of cooperation. We cannot hope to succeed in securing justice for the toiler, while the elements of industry remain under the control of a few; neither can we hope to ever get control of these elements ourselves in any other way than by cooperation."[59]

A few of the more outspoken leaders of the Minneapolis Knights had for years considered the merits of placing families in the countryside on an agricultural cooperative. At least since 1883 James Rankin had agitated for such a plan.[60] In early 1884 J. P. McGaughy and T. W. Brosnan, as well as John Lamb, organized the Cooperative Land Association and joined efforts with Rankin.[61] According to McGaughy and Rankin, such agricultural colonies had transcendent possibilities. They could be, in Rankin's words, "the solid rock basis of a new world, wherein shall dwell righteousness, peace and plenty."[62] T. W. Brosnan, who would become president of the Land Association in 1887, was no less enthusiastic: "If we can succeed in firmly establishing one colony, with home industries, established on home land, and protected by home exchange, with home money, under associated home government, we will have done more to solve the industrial question, than have the books of all the writers and talk of all the orators of the past hundred years."[63]

Though the stakes were high and the founders no doubt expected great results, their immediate plans were somewhat pedestrian. In March of 1886 the association bought 253 acres of land in Crow Wing County on Bay Lake, about 125 miles from Minneapolis. The officers had sold association shares for $10 primarily to fellow Knights, who then paid for them in small installments. The association apparently invested this money in Northern Pacific Railroad stock, with which they paid for the land. By October 1886, about 250 ten-dollar shares had been sold, netting $700.[64] This was enough to buy the initial acreage outright. Rankin, at the same time, organized the Pioneer Cooperative Company to settle the land, and in a written agreement with the association, eventually to buy it.[65]

On April 1, 1886, five families with their possessions headed off to Crow Wing County. Of the seventeen men, women, and children involved, seven were adult males, two of whom were coopers and former members of cooperatives. Within a short time they had planted corn, potatoes, beans, and other vegetables, processed sugar, and made operational a small abandoned saw mill already on the land. Though plagued by a chronic lack of capital, the cooperative colony persevered, and Rankin continued to promote the farm in the Twin Cities well into 1887. In England, the *Cooperative News* noted its existence, if not its triumphant success, and suggested the work be emulated by the cooperators and trade unionists of Great Britain.[66]

The Knights of Minneapolis had acted with unprecedented confidence in establishing their factories, stores, and colony. In addition, in 1887, leaders of District Assembly 79 laid plans for a central cooperative wholesale "depot," which they would establish, if only briefly, in 1888. Ideally this depot was to channel cooperatively produced goods to farmers and the farmers' produce to industrial cooperators.[67] The possibilities for labor reform in Minneapolis appeared almost limitless.

What made it possible for the Knights of Minneapolis to not only envision an alternative to "competition" but begin to implement it? After all, Stoneham's cooperators failed to develop any working alternative to their individual cooperatives. Deeply enmeshed in the political and social life of their small city, they found themselves and their imaginations constrained by their local affiliations. The coopers of Minneapolis, on the other hand, lived in a more polarized political and social environment than did

Stoneham's workers. The political system, in particular, was much more difficult to influence. In the 1870s and 1880s they participated in a number of political contests and succeeded in electing F. L. Bachelder to the state legislature.[68] Their connections with the machinations of government, however, were otherwise remote. In 1887 even John Lamb, appointed to head the State Bureau of Labor Statistics, recommended that workers maintain a safe distance from the state.[69] An advocate of cooperation, he advised wage earners to "not ask the state to do for us anything we can do for ourselves."[70] At the same time, the secretary-treasurer of the Knights' statewide District Assembly 79 criticized the "planting of political chestnuts" and argued that political reform could be accomplished only through social and industrial change.[71] In Minneapolis, the absence of the political and social integration of the working class created space for experimentation. The coopers and the Knights then turned to the reformative power of cooperative enterprise with great expectations and hope. That hope would translate into a extraordinary plan to reorganize the barrel industry in Minneapolis.

The coopers' cooperatives had, without question, succeeded admirably. Yet a number of problems continued to afflict the industry. The coopers faced a fundamental dilemma in the unstable nature of the market for barrels. James Rankin's earlier concerns with competition had proved farsighted. Barrel companies in Minneapolis routinely bid to supply an individual flour mill with a set number of barrels at a given price. This bidding was intensely competitive. Always suspicious that other companies might underbid them, the boss coopers, as well as cooperators, lowered prices again and again. Wage reductions inevitably followed.[72] The boss shops intensified this competition, having introduced barrel-making machinery as early as 1874 that increased production and created an oversupply of barrels.[73]

These pressures set the stage for a period of intensely volatile labor relations. In 1884, two major labor actions occurred. In the first, a strike, the coopers attempted but failed to increase their wages. They followed the strike with the formation of two new cooperative shops.[74] The second action occurred after "nearly all" the coopers in the city enrolled in the Knights of Labor and established their rather formidable Local Assembly 3363.[75] This near-universal enlistment in the Knights enabled the coopers to overcome some long-standing divisions between the cooperators

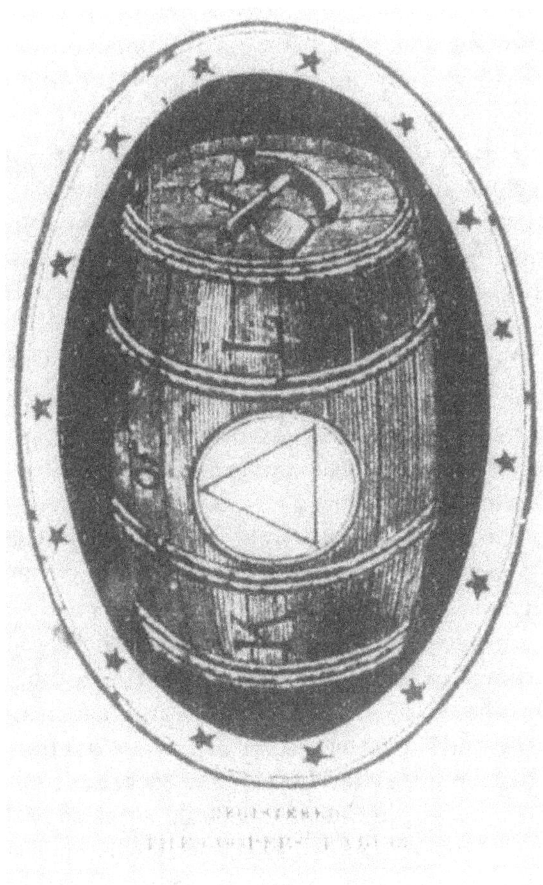

Registered trademark for Knights of Labor-made barrels from the *Journal of United Labor*, 1887. Wisconsin Historical Society.

and the "boss" shop journeymen and negotiate a mutually satisfactory strategy to improve wages. Together they demanded and received from the millers a seven to eight cent increase in the price of barrels.[76] The millers, displeased with this imposition, pressured the coopers to renegotiate and signed an agreement a few weeks later that reduced the price of hand-made barrels by two cents but guaranteed coopers a more than reasonable wage of sixteen cents per barrel until May 1, 1885.[77]

This solidarity between cooperators and journeymen was absolutely necessary for the coopers as a whole to increase their wages. They needed each other and acted together, in part, because they felt as one in the community of their craft—a feeling probably reinforced as coopers bought and sold shares in the cooperatives and moved back and forth among the various shops.[78] Yet when devising strategies for action, tensions emerged between the journeymen and cooperators from their very different relationships to the market. The journeymen coopers were wage workers who dealt directly with their bosses to negotiate wages or to strike. The cooperators' relationship with the boss shops was far more ambiguous. They faced the boss shops, not as workers, but as competitors. If the journeymen were to strike successfully they needed the cooperators to identify with them and see their interests as one. At a minimum they required the cooperators to refrain from taking their bosses' barrel contracts while any strike progressed. At most they could hope to receive the economic support of the cooperators who continued to work during a strike.

Immediate economic self-interest could readily push the cooperators, however, to act against the journeymen. Clearly they had no cause to strike against themselves and as competitors had an incentive to take the contracts of the struck boss shops for an immediate payoff. Yet they also had a long-term incentive to help the journeymen push up the costs of the boss shops and barrels in general. In this way they could force the millers, who were in effect their "bosses," to pay higher prices for barrels and increase their incomes. Alternatively, they and the boss shops could agree to end competition for contracts and demand a higher price from the millers. These convoluted relationships were complicated further when the cooperators hired journeyman and machine operators in their shops and became "bosses" themselves. What path the cooperators would follow depended upon their assessment of their varied interests and obligations at any given moment.

So despite the price agreement of 1884, which seemed to benefit the coopers handsomely, stability in the industry was by no means guaranteed. The relationships between the cooperatives and the boss shops, between cooperators and journeymen, and between barrel factories and the millers, remained volatile. Indeed, as early as December 1884, rumors circulated among the coopers that a few of the boss and cooperative shops had attempted to reduce prices. This strained relations among the shops and made continuation of the price agreement problematic. In addition, the unity of the Knights was tested when two cooperative shops laid off their "hired" men because of a decline in business. According to the *Miller*, many journeymen considered this "unjust and selfish" and spoke of opening a new cooperative of their own. The shops involved deflected this opprobrium and avoided the possible increase in competition by rehiring the laid-off men.[79]

From early 1885 until the end of the next year, the coopers rode an erratic market made all the more irregular by increased mechanization, growing exports of wheat, and aberrations in local conditions. The barrel market always fluctuated in tandem with the seasonal nature of wheat production and processing. In February 1885 the demand for barrels declined, and then, as expected, demand increased in April and May. However, the shops failed after May 1 to renew the contract they had established fixing the price of barrels. Two of the cooperatives cut prices by two cents and initiated the usual round of price and wage reductions. Now three of the cooperatives themselves complicated the picture by introducing their own machinery, practically doubling their capacity to make barrels. Over the next year two of these cooperatives would buy out members to reduce their workforces. The Cooperative Barrel Company reduced its membership from 120 to 90, while the North Star's enrollment decreased from 77 to 57. They would also now begin to hire machine operators as employees.[80]

The two-cent reduction by the cooperatives generated considerable ill will between the responsible parties and the journeymen coopers. Yet that was hardly the worst development of the year. During the summer months of July, August, and September, the mills shut down most operations while the power company, Minneapolis Mill, made improvements to the all-important canal. The cooper shops continued to operate and stored some 200,000 barrels in anticipation of the mills reopening in October. When the mills did reopen, the competitive pressure on prices was enormous. "Prices melted away," the *Miller* reported, "until there was no bottom at all."[81] Any attempt to control the price decline came to naught. Yet the only reported strike occurred in the Sixth Street shop, when twenty hired men walked off the job, demanding the cooperative discharge two Hungarian workmen. The Hungarians were accused of working at a slower pace than the other wage earners. Besides this rare display of ethnic intolerance, no other strikes occurred in 1885.[82]

The year 1886 began with more of the same. Excess barrel-making capacity and competition for contracts drove prices down. Barrels sold for as little as 33 cents, and wages bottomed out at

12 1/2 cents for handmade barrels, while the consensus among coopers held 16 cents to be a living wage. Adding to this tendency was an overall decline in demand for barrels. A large percentage of the flour produced in 1886 sold in foreign markets packaged in jute sacks. Some domestic flour made its way east in cotton sacks as well. The total output of flour for the year, though larger than in 1885, actually required fewer barrels.[83]

These factors led to renewed unrest among the coopers. In the middle of February as many as four hundred barrel makers met in the Coopers' Assembly to plan some response, and subsequently they developed a number of less-than-successful strategies. First, the assembly called for the various barrel shop managers, boss and cooperative, to meet and jointly raise wages. Nothing came of this because shops with contracts already in effect refused to renege on them. Next a committee consisting of one representative from each shop met with the Millers' Association to request that they increase the price paid for barrels voluntarily. This also came to naught, as did the intriguing offer by the Knights to purchase a large amount of flour in union-made barrels to sell in the manufacturing cities of Massachusetts. Finally, in April, the assembly's committee gave up and referred the matter to the board of the Knights District Assembly 79. At this point the district board managed to hammer out an agreement among the various barrel shops to raise barrel prices in all newly signed contracts. The new price guaranteed 15 cents per handmade barrel and 7 and 10 cents on machine work. The agreement was set to last for six months.[84]

As the months passed the overall barrel market deteriorated once again, and the price agreement began to fall apart as early as June. The coopers bickered among themselves, and their assembly voted to split, one group to represent journeymen and the other cooperators. However, this split proved to be temporary and suggested more confused dissatisfaction than any real desire to sunder the ties among barrel makers. At the same time coopers began to discuss the idea of combining their resources in a pool to divide the business among the various shops.[85] Before any agreement of this kind could be worked out, the coopers walked out in their first strike in two years. The cooperators and journeymen, rather than split apart, agreed to work together. The walkout was virtually universal, as the journeymen from the east side put down their tools and marched from shop to shop, calling out the men. They then crossed the Tenth Avenue bridge and, as the *Minneapolis Tribune* reported, "made the rounds to all the other shops being in every place successful, so that when evening came every shop in the city was closed and about 700 coopers had laid down their tools for some time to come."[86]

This unanimity of purpose made for a successful strike under less than ideal circumstances. Railroad switchmen in Minneapolis had struck their employers at the same time, and the mills, left without transportation, subsequently shut down. Yet within two weeks the six cooperative shops signed contracts to pay 15 cents per barrel until July 1, and then, with their members at work, gave financial support to the journeymen still out. Within a few days the boss coopers signed on and the strike ended.[87]

Despite the coopers' unity, any hope that this agreement would last longer than previous ones soon evaporated. At least two of the boss coopers attempted to break the agreement, one by locking out its workers and the other by simply reducing wages.[88] However, something was brewing among the cooperators and journeymen coopers. Perhaps it was a growing sense of power and new possibilities. The Knights had grown throughout the city and nearly all the coopers had joined. Printers, cigar makers, coopers, teamsters, shirt makers and laundresses, among others, had opened a variety of new cooperatives. A Union Labor Party emerged in 1887 and would make a reasonable if not victorious showing in city elections.[89] The Knights broke ground on their new "labor temple" and a group of intrepid reformers established a cooperative colony. Amidst all of these developments, an idea took hold of the coopers that would never have occurred to the cooperators of Stoneham. Unlike Stoneham's shoe workers, the coopers of Minneapolis had created independent communities with few apparent cross-class alliances. Apparently they had less fear of middle-class opprobrium. Community loyalties did not hold them back. The cooperators of Minneapolis were free to innovate.

At the same time, however, deep divisions emerged among the coopers that would ultimately tear their community apart. The troubles started in late December 1886, as barrel prices dropped and stock costs rose. All of the barrel shops soon found the $.15 per barrel wage quite difficult if not impossible to maintain. Some of the cooperatives assessed their members in order to meet payroll. The private shops attempted to reduce wages and the Hardwood

The Labor Temple of the Knights of Labor in Minneapolis, 1887. From the collections of the Minnesota Historical Society.

Storage and Parr Barrel companies locked out their workers. The Coopers' Assembly at first condemned the boss shops and paid the locked-out workers from its Assistance Fund and cooperative store. The North Star cooperative was unenthusiastic about providing this assistance, and dissension among the coopers mounted.[90]

With the cooperatives in effect reducing wages and the boss shops threatening their men, the contract, not to mention coopers' solidarity, was on the verge of disintegration. Faced once again with competition and price reductions, and now also with resistance from some cooperators, the assembly proposed something entirely different from its past strategies. The plan was a remarkable leap in what the Knights considered legitimate and feasible. In April, District Assembly 79 held daily meetings and devised a plan that would transform the cooperage business in Minneapolis; that is, they recognized the need to control the market for barrels and acted to divide up the business fairly among the various barrel makers of the city through a pool of cooper shops.[91]

The Knights of Labor and the coopers of Minneapolis formed an organization they called the "Coopers Association." In this organization the various cooper shops, both cooperative and boss, would effect, in the words of John Cronin, secretary of District Assembly 79,[92]

> a permanent settlement—one that could not be annulled at pleasure. . . . A fair division of trade was to be made between the various shops in proportion to the capacity of each. The number of men to be employed in each shop and the average number of barrels to be made by each man in a day were to be limited. A referee was to be selected to see that justice was done between the different companies, to further regulate the production of barrels by a reduction of the hours of labor per day, and, if necessary, to make a slight proportionate reduction in the number of men working in each shop, as it was thought probable that more coopers were working than were necessary to supply the demand, on the eight-hour basis. Contracts were not to be entered into, but a standard price was to be established for making barrels, which would enable those employed to earn fair wages. The selling price of barrels was to be governed by the market price of stock. Every person employed at the trade in the city was to become a member and retain good standing in the Cooopergl [*sic*] Local Assembly, K. of L., and the different shops were to use a K. of L. label on all barrels if the millers so desired. All serious difficulties were to be settled by the District Executive Board, or if necessary, by the General Executive Board, K of L., and, as a guarantee of good faith, each company was to bind itself to forfeit a certain sum for any violations of these provisions.[93]

This agreement gave the Coopers Association and the Knights of Labor the power to oversee the work of all shops, and to determine how much a shop was to produce, how many workers were to produce it, and at what price it was to be sold. The Knights of Minneapolis had gone far beyond the single cooperative as a solution to the labor problem.

The millers adamantly opposed this arrangement from its inception.[94] Charles Pillsbury, the erstwhile champion of the cooperators, made known his uncompromising opposition in a statement to the press. Pillsbury first assured the coopers that his firm was not responsible for the low wages paid in the industry. Moreover, he would willingly pay "as high a price as any miller in the city . . . [or] any other city in the United States." He refused, however, "to agree to a request to buy barrels from a consolidated monopoly who ask the millers to agree to buy barrels of them and from no one else." This, he stated frankly, would lead to "untold trouble" between the coopers and the millers. In addition, the pooling plan was not in the interests of the cooperative shops, who had nearly won the "battle in favor of cooperation," but in the interests, he claimed, of some unnamed parties. T. W. Brosnan of the Knights District Executive Board, after meeting with Pillsbury, reported the miller's willingness to spend "every cent he was worth" before buying barrels from the association.[95]

The opposition of the millers to the pool surprised no one. What did surprise the coopers was the opposition from within their own ranks. Three cooperatives, the Hennepin, Northwes-tern, and North Star, refused to abide by the scheme. The North Star members had little faith that such a plan could work and a majority of shareholders opposed it. In the Hennepin and Northwestern, however, the vote to not participate reportedly was "very close to a tie," and the Northwestern quickly compromised and entered the pool. The Hennepin remained outside of the agreement, but rather than challenge the association directly, took only its "fair" share of contracts. It therefore incurred little opprobrium from other coopers. The North Star, in contrast, took advantage of the millers' opposition to the pool to add to its regular contracts and vastly increase its business. The cooperative contracted with Pillsbury to make as many barrels as it could provide. This eliminated the yearly contract the flour maker traditionally signed with the Sixth Street shop. Apparently a large majority of the North Star members, including F. L. Bachelder, favored this policy, which generated untold bitterness among the other coopers.[96]

Despite the noncompliance of the North Star, five cooperative and two boss shops formed their association, elected officers, and posted a bond to guarantee their fealty. They then bargained with the reluctant millers, who would agree to pay only 38 cents per handmade barrel, a price that provided, under then-current costs, a wage of 15 cents per barrel. The agreement would last for one year.[97] The coopers clearly wanted more flexible control over the price of barrels, but they could get nothing better from the millers at this time.

Meanwhile, opposition to the North Star grew intensely bitter. Earlier in the year the cooperative had refused to pay assessments to support locked-out workers in the Hardwood shop. They claimed that for various reasons the Hardwood employees were not entitled to it. Now the North Star defied the entire community of coopers. Outraged members of the Coopers' Assembly wanted action taken against them immediately, and they discussed a possible boycott of the shop through the use of a special cooperative barrel label. Under this plan all barrels made by the association would be stamped with the label, and the Knights would declare a national boycott on unstamped flour barrels. The Knights' General Executive Board had already approved the use of such a label, and it had since been copyrighted.[98]

A boycott, though, presented the order with a peculiar problem. Virtually all the members of the North Star belonged to the Knights. In order to boycott the North Star's goods the organization would have to expel them. In early August this is precisely the course taken by the Coopers' Assembly, which expelled fourteen members of the North Star for violating their obligations as Knights. When this coercion failed, the Knights then called on all coopers working in the North Star shop, members and employees alike, to strike. Only four out of fifty-nine members, along with nine out of eighteen hired men, walked off the job. A stalemate now existed between the contending parties, with neither side willing to back down.[99]

The coopers managed to avoid an ongoing crisis when the Knights General Assembly met in Minneapolis in early November for its annual meeting. The Knights, who had accused Charles Pillsbury of colluding with the North Star, called Pillsbury and North Star president H. R. Burroughs before the General Executive Board. According to Brosnan, the threat that "the power of the Knights of labor would be brought against them" through a boycott forced the North Star to relent. Though it still refused to join the pool, the cooperative agreed to divide its Pillsbury contract with the Sixth Street shop. In addition, it agreed to buy out two of the strikers whom the cooperative had suspended in September.[100]

This agreement may have resolved the immediate crisis, but it did not allay the anger felt by many of the coopers. In December the local Knights summoned approximately forty members of the North Star to appear before a "judge" to answer to the charges of scabbing.[101] The North Star "scabs" denied any transgression. In their view they had remained good and loyal members of the Knights and had never violated their legitimate obligations to the order. At the same time the president of the cooperative explained, "The reason that our firm did not enter the coopers' organization recently formed was because we were doing well financially as a company. We did not feel like jeopardizing our business and taking the rates they proposed to give us."[102] According to the North Star, to act in the business's economic interest did not violate union principles. In what must have been a sign of contempt for the charges, only four of the men summoned appeared at the trial.[103]

In this environment of distrust and resentment the association tested its ability to control the vicissitudes of the barrel market. Over the next six months it made a concerted effort to distribute the work fairly among the various factories, but this proved difficult and, ultimately, unworkable. Some Knights and coopers attributed the failure of the pool solely to the opposition of the millers or to the behavior of the boss shops.[104] There certainly was some truth to these charges. The millers vehemently opposed the pool. They attempted to lure barrel manufacturers away with lucrative contracts and threats. Charles Pillsbury insisted on choosing his own barrels and refused to accept barrels from shops selected by the association.[105] That they failed for even a short while to lure companies away was a tribute to the power of the Knights in Minneapolis.[106]

Yet the actual reasons were far more complicated and have as much to do with the ideology of cooperation as they do with the power of the opposition. In Minneapolis, as in Stoneham the year before, a minority of cooperators seemed to divorce their interests from those of the labor movement. Rather than envision cooperation in its broadest terms, they would act with a destructive independence. This situation clearly exposed the limitations of working-class republicanism as a guide to cooperation. Cooperation offered members of the North Star Barrel Co. the opportunity for stability and democratic participation and an at times pugnacious manly independence. No rules, though, explicitly defined their obligations to other cooperative firms. So the members of the North Star chose to define their obligations narrowly. If joining the pool would force the North Star to share business, denying its members the maximum benefits of cooperation, then they would refuse to participate. They were acting, they argued, as any properly run business concern should act. To do otherwise would be a disservice to their own members. The barrel makers who refused to join the pool never admitted to betraying the principles of cooperation or their obligations as trade unionists. Even after the Knights expelled them from the local assembly, they insisted on their innocence and their good standing as union members.[107]

A final factor in the pool's demise concerned the strength of the labor movement. The Coopers' Assembly, and the Knights as a whole, began to lose membership in 1888. This was in no small way due to the inability of the Coopers' Assembly to resolve its various conflicts. In early 1887 Local Assembly 3363 had 441 members. By July 1888, this number had fallen to 113. Within six months they had a mere 28 left. The assembly never recovered. In this environment of distrust, opposition, and organizational weakness, the association could not survive. After July 1, 1888, the price of barrels fell to 34 cents and the wage for a handmade barrel to as low as 13 cents. The pool no longer had any power.[108]

The demise of the cooperative barrel shops in Minneapolis did not come so quickly as that of the pool. In fact, a few shops continued to function for many years, even though the millers' conversion to the use of bags eliminated any growth in demand for barrels. The last shop actually closed in 1931. Yet long before this time the cooperatives had abandoned their affiliations with the labor movement and any commitment to labor reform. The mechanization of barrel making played an important role in this development. When the cooperators introduced machinery into their own shops, they challenged the very nature of their enterprises. Market pressures convinced them to reduce their memberships, buy out shareholders, and hire nonmembers to run the machines. Undermining their own skill, the coopers eliminated one principle reason for their own cooperation, the maintenance of a craft tradition.[109]

As the decade came to a close, various other cooperative experiments proved evanescent. In early 1889 the coopers' store, after three years of successful operation, collapsed. The cooperative colony and depot disappeared shortly after their formation. Such failures, and the ongoing bickering among the coopers, surely disillusioned and disaffected the movement's erstwhile supporters. However, the single most important cause of the failure of cooperation in Minneapolis was the Knights' organizational decline after 1887. Without the Knights' power to bind working people together, Minneapolis' workers had little strength left to maintain a commitment to a broader cooperative community. Under such conditions the artisanal ethos that inspired the coopers to cooperate now constrained their imaginations. They continued to restrict membership to fully apprenticed craftsmen at a time when such artisans were a dying breed. Rather than admit machine operators as shareholders, the cooperators hired them only as wage laborers. As a consequence, some coopers achieved independence but did so as employers and their shops slowly lost their cooperative identities. In 1903 they would be expelled from the coopers' trade union.[110]

If Chauncy Curtis and Frances Bachelder had lived to see the century end, they would have looked back with very mixed emotions. For the two men, cooperation was both success and failure. Curtis, the activist cooperator, had probably participated in more cooperative experiments than any other worker in Minneapolis. When the opportunity arose, however, he abandoned the problems of barrel making and the cooperatives. In 1885 the city administration appointed him driver in the police department. Yet even after he lost the job in 1887, he did not return to his craft. He tried his hand at another useful skill, real estate sales.[111] Cooperation had failed to provide either stability or long-term opportunity for him. Bachelder remained a member of the North Star and saw it prosper for many years. In fact, in 1900 it was the most successful cooper shop in the city. However, by defying the Knights of Labor he had helped to define cooperation narrowly and defeat the collective tendency of the cooperative spirit. He surely was to blame, at least in part, for the movement's disintegration among the coopers.

Yet for a moment in the 1880s, the coopers of Minneapolis could justify their domination of an entire industry. As craft workers they carried with them an independence, pride, and trade union tradition that, combined with their desire for stability and community, sustained their cooperative activism. Yet it was as relatively isolated members of an expanding urban environment that they joined a broad-based labor movement and acted to transform their industry. The coopers understood their predicament through the lens of working-class republicanism provided by the leadership of the Knights of Labor. The Knights' power galvanized the coopers, and their leadership broadened the barrel makers' vision of feasible reform. However, they had no uniform cooperative vision, and under the pressures of the market the coopers bickered among themselves. When the labor movement collapsed in the late 1880s, they reverted to a strategy of craft exclusionism. For these craftsmen, cooperation lost its visionary appeal and became their last defense against the unskilled. They chose a path to independence that could not sustain cooperation.

Conclusion

Labor reformers of the Gilded Age believed in cooperation as a practical reform. Most workers, they maintained, could accumulate the resources required to establish a cooperative enterprise and satisfy their immediate needs either for necessities or for steady employment. Cooperation's ultimate goal to supersede the wage-system and competition, however, was not so easily defined or accomplished. As cooperators attempted to remake their communities, they drew upon a vision rooted in craft and trade union traditions that they often understood only in the vaguest moral terms. As they experimented with their own factories and stores, these practical utopians attempted to clarify their place as workers in an industrializing republic. They tested the boundaries of their republican vision and the meaning of democracy in a rapidly changing economic world. To what rights, they asked, did citizenship entitle them? What would a moral economic order in which equal rights prevailed look like? They found a range of answers as they organized in various cities and towns and attempted to make their cooperatives a success.

Success did not come easily, though, and cooperators understood that if they were to assert themselves and survive they needed the organized support of other workers. After experimenting within local and national labor unions and national reform organizations, men like Thomas Phillips and John Samuel looked to what Phillips called "the grandest conception of organized labor ever put into shape on this continent."[1] The Knights of Labor incorporated both trade unionism and labor reform in an attempt to organize whole communities of workers. The organization's power and seemingly limitless potential inspired many workers to believe that a cooperative future was possible.

The Knights, however, mistrusted centralized authority enough to undermine their own attempt to devise a workable national policy. While the General Assembly debated, the initiative fell to the local and district assemblies, who designed their own "centralized" strategies to find capital and develop markets. Nevertheless, the rapid decline of the Knights in the late 1880s made cooperation less plausible as a solution to the problems of wage labor. Without the order and its network of local assemblies to assist them, workers would never devise a centralized plan for cooperation, nor could they receive the support necessary to make a decentralized system work. Many knights who believed in the coming "emancipation of wage labor" now lost faith.

Some old stalwarts, however, continued to believe in the viability of cooperation. When after seventeen years Thomas Phillips quit the Knights, he became the first president of the Boot and Shoe Workers' International Union, an AFL affiliate, and an apparent convert to pure and simple trade unionism.[2] Yet, within a year he helped found a cooperative organization resembling both the Sovereigns of Industry and the Knights of Labor.

Phillips and a handful of reformers established a new organization in 1890 that they called the Industrial Republic. The "Republic" was part beneficial and building association and part cooperative society. In its basic design it resembled Henry Sharpe's Cooperative Guild. Sharpe, however, only outlined his plan as a proposal, while the Industrial Republic's constitution detailed precisely how the organization, its beneficial features, and cooperative societies would function.[3] Phillip's influence was obvious. He had learned from past mistakes and now proposed a very elaborate plan for a cooperative republic. Unfortunately, he now had no constituency to carry it out.

John Samuel similarly promoted cooperation and continued to believe in its practicality. In 1891, in a letter to J. C. Gray, the general secretary of England's Cooperative Union, Samuel explained why several efforts at cooperation in his city had failed. Even after initiating countless experiments, he could still find only one principal cause of failure, which was, he insisted, "[the] lack of patience and determination in meeting and overcoming first difficulties resulting from want of experience."[4] Meanwhile, he was involved in a new cooperative venture started by several Knights of Labor and he had faith in its future growth. "Should this weakling of ours survive," he wrote, "and acquire the strength and robustness of its great exemplar [Rochdale], it may prove to be a landmark in future cooperation in this western world."[5]

Samuel maintained his faith in cooperative reform though he concentrated his energy in a new direction and threw in his lot with Imogene Fales, the president of the American Sociologic Society. This society, unaffiliated with the labor movement, appealed to middle-class reformers and academics in its promotion of cooperative production and profit sharing. The future cooperative movement would, like this society, develop apart from the labor movement. Fales, in fact, was instrumental in bringing together delegates from cooperative stores in December 1889 in a national "Cooperative Congress." The congress included men such as James Rankin from Minneapolis and George Kuechler from Cincinnati. John Samuel became the Union's general secretary.[6] Samuel and his associates had found a new vehicle to promote their vision of reform as the labor movement narrowed its focus in the 1890s.

Other members of the Knights of Labor held on to their cooperative ideals and made their way into various socialist organizations. When a group of glass workers and miners bolted from the Knights in 1895 to form the Independent Order of the Knights of Labor, they made their ultimate aim the creation of a cooperative industrial system. In 1897, when they disbanded, the general officers recommended joining Eugene Debs's and Henry Demerast Lloyd's Brotherhood of the Cooperative Commonwealth. The Brotherhood and, under Debs's leadership, the Social Democracy of America advanced a program of cooperation and colonization in the western states. Long-time socialist cooperator Richard J. Hinton joined Debs and headed the colonization commission of the Social Democracy.[7]

Such was the compelling quality of the cooperative ideal. Nineteenth-century labor leaders were seduced by its practical and utopian appeal even as the labor movement that gave it substance collapsed. The notion that workers could exercise their rights as citizens, take fate into their own hands, and redeem the republic was a powerful intoxicant and, for a time, arguably realistic. If the Civil War, fought largely by the workingmen of the North, had transformed the slave system, why was the wage system any less vulnerable? Under certain circumstances, as in Minneapolis, cooperators could come close to eliminating that system. They combined the republican notions of independence and equal rights with their craft and trade union traditions and justified extraordinary powers as worker-citizens.

Yet this complex of ideas was riddled with contradictions. Profoundly democratic, the cooperators often fought to preserve their own advantages over women, nonwhites, and unskilled workers. Only under the influence of the Knights of Labor did cooperators recast their vision and widen the acceptable boundaries of democratic participation. Self-help, however, had its limitations. The Knights, of course, did not uniformly reject racial or sexual exclusivity, nor could their power stop the process of industrial change that made skills obsolete and some cooperatives outmoded. When the order disintegrated, it could no longer provide even the hope of assistance. The compelling, though ill-defined, vision of cooperation had the potential to support radical change. Yet, in its dependence upon the leadership and structural support of the Knights of Labor, it would ultimately fail. That failure surely disillusioned thousands of working men and women in the emancipatory potential of both cooperation and a labor movement built upon the ideals of republican independence.

To the leadership of the revived labor movement of the 1890s, the decline of cooperation was simply more evidence of the ill-conceived program of the Knights of Labor. Samuel Gompers led the American Federation of Labor toward a more conservative and practical trade unionism in which the "reformism" of the Knights had no place. However, in years to come, cooperation would continue to play a role among working-class Americans. The lure of building autonomous working-class institutions, harnessing capitalism for the benefit of workers as consumers and producers, and transforming America peacefully but fundamentally would draw working men and women again to the compelling vision of a cooperative future.[8]

Notes

Introduction

1. *The Attractions of North Adams and Vicinity, Its Drives, Rambles, Views, Places of Interest, Hotels, Manufactories, Business Houses, &c., By a Visitor* (North Adams, Mass.: Jas. C. Angell, Publisher, 1871), 20; Ron Takaki, *Strangers from a Different Shore: A History of Asian Americans* (New York: Penguin Books, 1989), 95–99; Richard B. Bennett, "Crispins, Calvin and the Chinese" (master's thesis, Wesleyan University, 1986); W. F. Spear, *History of North Adams, Mass. 1749–1885* (North Adams, Mass.: Hoosac Valley News Printing House, 1885), 104.

2. My account of the Chinese workers in North Adams is based on the following sources, though the sources contradict each other in some details: see *Massachusetts Bureau of the Statistics of Labor Annual Report of 1870*, microfiche edition, 98–116; Frederick Rudolph, "Chinamen in Yankeedom: Anti-Unionism in Massachusetts in 1870," *American Historical Review* 53, no. 1 (1947): 1–29; Marion Merril, "The Startling Tale of C. T. Sampson," *North Adams Transcript Supplement*, August 4, 1978; Bowen Chung, "Chinese in North Adams," unpublished paper in possession of author; Brent Filson, "Calvin Sampson's Chinese Experiment," *Yankee Magazine* 49 (February 1985): 93–97, 133–137; Bennett, "Crispins," 55–58; Takaki, *Strangers*, 95–99.

3. For biographical information on Sampson see "The Pioneers of North Adams," in *North Adams, Mass.* (Troy, N.Y.: *Troy Daily Times*, 1890), 61–63; and W. F. Spear, *History of North Adams*, 83–84; For the Knights of St. Crispin see Mary Blewett, *Men, Women and Work: Class, Gender, and Protest in the New England Shoe Industry, 1780–1910* (Urbana: University of Illinois Press, 1988); Alan Dawley, *Class and Community: The Industrial Revolution in Lynn* (Cambridge: Harvard University Press, 2000).

4. *Massachusetts Bureau of the Statistics of Labor Annual Report of 1870*, 98–102, 110.

5. Ibid., 98–102, 110–12, 114; Clare Horner, "Producers' Co-operatives in the United States, 1865–1890" (Ph.D. diss., University of Pittsburgh, 1978), 60–62; Bennett, "Crispins," 50–51.

6. *Hoosac Valley News*, August 4, 1869; *Massachusetts Bureau of the Statistics of Labor Annual Report of 1871*, microfiche edition, 115.

7. "Chinese Sampson's Imports," a one-page typed account from the vertical file of the North Adams Public Library, North Adams, Massachusetts.

8. *The Nation*, June 30 1870, 412–13; Bennett, "Crispins," 57–58, 61–62, 65, 70–73, 100, 103–6; Chung, "Chinese," 4–5, 11–14; Takaki, *Strangers*, 98.

9. Information on the cooperative factory in North Adams is limited. See Horner, "Producers' Co-operatives," 61; Bennett, "Crispins," 12, 95–96; *North Adams Transcript*, October 6, 1870, p. 2; and *Massachusetts Bureau of the Statistics of Labor Annual Report of 1871*, 455.

10. These issues will be discussed in chapter 2.

11. *Massachusetts Bureau of the Statistics of Labor Annual Report of 1871*, 113–14.

12. *North Adams Transcript*, October 6, 1870, p. 2.

13. *North Adams Transcript*, October 6, 1870, p. 2; For members of the cooperative, see ibid. and *Directory of North and South Adams, 1872*, 188; *Directory of North Adams (Massachusetts), 1874*, 31; and *Directory of North Adams, for 1875–76*, 37, 58, 81.

14. *Price, Lee & Co.'s Directory of North Adams for 1875–76*, 44, 81; Bennett, "Crispins," 95–96.

15. See chapter 1.

16. See David Roediger, *Wages of Whiteness: Race and the Making of the American Working Class* (New York: Verso, 1991); Matthew Frye Jacobson, *Whiteness of a Different Color: European Immigrants and the Alchemy of Race* (Cambridge: Harvard University Press, 1998); Eva Baron, *Work Engendered: Toward a New History of American Labor* (Ithaca, N.Y.: Cornell University Press, 1991).

17. A partial history of the cooperative movement can be found in Joseph G. Knapp, *The Rise of American Cooperative Enterprise: 1620–1920* (Danville, Ill.: Interstate Printers and Publishers, 1969); John R. Commons et al., *History of Labor in the United States*, 2 vols. (New York: Macmillan Company, 1918); John R. Commons, ed., *A Documentary History of American Industrial Society*, 11 vols. (Cleveland: A. H. Clark Co., 1910–11); Bruce Laurie, *Artisans into Workers: Labor in Nineteenth-Century America* (New York: Noonday Press, 1989); Horner, "Producers' Co-operatives"; Edwin Charles Rozwenc, "Cooperatives Come to America: The History of the Protective Union Store Movement, 1845–1867" (Ph.D. diss., Columbia University, 1941); Florence E. Parker, *The First 125 Years: A History of Distributive and Service Cooperation in the United States, 1829–1954* (Superior, Wis.: Cooperative Publishing Association, 1956); Norman Ware, *The Industrial Worker, 1840–1860: The Reaction of American Industrial Society to the Advance of the Industrial Revolution* (New York: Quadrangle/New York Times Book Company, 1964); Norman Ware, *The Labor Movement in the United States, 1860–1895* (New York: Houghton Mifflin Company, 1924); Gerald Grob, *Workers and Utopia* (Quadrangle/New York Times Book Company, 1969); Herbert B. Adams, ed., *History of Cooperation in the United States.* Johns Hopkins University. Studies in Historical and Political Science, vol. 6 (Baltimore: Johns Hopkins University Press, 1888); Philip Foner, *History of the Labor*

Movement in the United States, vol. 1 (New York: International Publishers, 1947); Howard Aldrich and Robert N. Stern, "Resource Mobilization and the Creation of U.S. Producer's Cooperatives, 1835–1935," unpublished paper, New York State School of Industrial and Labor Relations, Cornell University, January 1982; Derek C. Jones, "The Economics and Industrial Relations of Producer Cooperatives in the United States, 1791–1939," *Economic Analysis and Workers' Management* 11, no. 3–4 (1977): 295–316; Derek C. Jones, "American Producer Cooperatives and Employee-Owned Firms: A Historical Perspective," in *Worker Cooperatives in America*, ed. Robert Jackall and Henry M. Levin (Berkeley: University of California Press, 1984), 37–56; Frank Stockton, "Productive Cooperation in the Molders' Union," *American Economic Review* 21 (June 1931): 260–74; H. E. Hoagland, "The Rise of the Iron Molders' International Union," *American Economic Review* 3 (June 1913): 296–313; James Cebula, *The Glory and Despair of Challenge and Change: A History of the Iron Molders' Union* (Cincinnati: International Molders' and Allied Workers' Union, 1976); Jonathan Grossman, *William Sylvis, Pioneer of American Labor* (New York: Columbia University Press, 1945); and Franklin Henry Giddings, "Co-operation," in *The Labor Movement: The Problem of Today*, ed. George E. McNeill (New York: M. W. Hazen, 1886), 508–31.

18. John R. Commons et al., *History of Labor in the United States*, vol. 2 (New York: MacMillan Co., 1918), 430–38; Grob, *Workers and Utopia*, 39.

19. Laurie, *Artisans into Workers*, 90. In this instance Laurie is referring to the labor movement of the 1830s. Though he discusses cooperation with greater subtlety than most other historians, he still designates "cooperation" as a static ideology without examining the actual experience of the cooperators. See also, Robert E. Weir, *Beyond Labor's Veil: The Culture of the Knights of Labor* (University Park: Pennsylvania University Press, 1996), 62–63. For a variation on this view; Richard Oestreicher, "Terence Powderly, The Knights of Labor, and Artisanal Republicanism," in *Labor Leaders in America*, ed. Melvyn Dubofsky and Warren Van Tine (Urbana: University of Illinois Press, 1987), 42–43; and Kim Voss, *The Making of American Exceptionalism: The Knights of Labor and Class Formation in the Nineteenth Century* (Ithaca, N.Y.: Cornell University Press, 1993), 84–85.

20. Gary Gerstle, "Ideas of the American Labor Movement, 1880–1950," in *Ideas, Ideologies, and Social Movements: The United States Experience Since 1800*, ed. Peter A. Coclanis and Stuart Bruchey (Columbia: University of South Carolina Press, 1999), 72–76.

21. See chapter 5.

22. Voss, *American Exceptionalism*, 72–89, 231–49.

23. For relevant treatments of the rise of the AFL see ibid.; Laurie, *Artisans into Workers*, 176–210; Philip Foner, *The History of the Labor Movement in the United States*, vol. 2 (New York: International Publishers, 1955), 174–77; John H. M. Laslette, "Samuel Gompers and the Rise of American Business Unionism," in *Labor Leaders in America*, ed. Melvyn Dubofsky and Warren Van Tine (Urbana: University of Illinois Press, 1987), 62–88.

24. Timothy Messer-Kruse, *The Yankee International: Marxism and the American Reform Tradition, 1848–1876* (Chapel Hill: University of North Carolina Press, 1998); Craig Phelan, *Grand Master Workman: Terence Pow-*

derly and the Knights of Labor (Westport, Conn.: Greenwood Press, 2000). Robert Weir, in his book *Knights Unhorsed: Internal Conflict in a Gilded Age Social Movement* (Detroit: Wayne State University Press, 2000), depicts Drury as more complex than either Messer-Kruse or Phelan but also as a sectarian.

Chapter 1

1. "Co-operative Tract, No. 1," *Pamphlets in American History*, Cooperative Societies #20 (Sanford, N.C.: Microfilming Corp. of America, 1979–84), microform.

2. Clare Horner, "Producers' Co-operatives in the United States, 1865–1890" (Ph.D. diss., University of Pittsburgh, 1978), 2 and chapters 2 and 3. For the estimated number of consumer cooperatives see the following discussion.

3. Bruce Laurie, *Artisans into Workers: Labor in Nineteenth-Century America* (New York: Noonday Press, 1989), 89–91; Joseph G. Knapp, *The Rise of American Cooperative Enterprise: 1620–1920* (Danville, Ill.: Interstate Printers and Publishers, 1969), 10; John R. Commons, ed., *A Documentary History of American Industrial Society* (Cleveland: A. H. Clark Co., 1910–11), 5:58–59, 328, 368; Horner, "Producers' Co-operatives," 22–26; Edwin Charles Rozwenc, "Cooperatives Come to America: The History of the Protective Union Store Movement, 1845–67" (Ph.D. diss., Columbia University, 1941), 27–29, 33, 39, 116; Norman Ware, *The Industrial Worker, 1840–1860: The Reaction of American Industrial Society to the Advance of the Industrial Revolution* (New York: Quadrangle/New York Times Book Company, 1964), 187–92; George McNeill, ed., *The Labor Movement: The Problem of To-day* (New York: M. W. Hazen Co., 1887), 99–101.

4. Horner, "Producers' Co-operatives," 26–30; Ware, *Industrial Worker*, 194; Sean Wilentz, *Chants Democratic: New York City and the Rise of the American Working Class, 1788–1850* (New York: Oxford University Press, 1984), 366–69.

5. Laurie, *Artisans into Workers*, 89–91; Horner, "Producers' Co-operatives," 22, 29–30; Rozwenc, "Cooperatives Come to America," 98–104.

6. For the membership of the Union Cooperative Association see Union Cooperative Association-Committee of Management Minutes, vol.1, December 1, 1864, to May 2, 1865; vol. 2, April 10, 1866, to October 18, 1866, Cooperative Associations Papers, Box 1, Folder 10, Wisconsin State Historical Society, Madison (hereafter cited as UCA Minutes); "Good News From Delaware," *Fincher's Trades' Review*, December 10, 1864, 6; "Cooperation in Philadelphia," *Fincher's Trades' Review*, January 27, 1866, 68. The location and date of the first Rochdale cooperative in the United States is unknown. Thomas Phillips of the Union Cooperative Association and Thomas Sellers of the Lawrence (Massachusetts) Cooperative Association each claimed their respective institutions as the first American cooperatives to base their operations on the Rochdale model. See Clifton K. Yearley Jr., "Thomas Phillips: A Yorkshire Shoemaker in Philadelphia," *Pennsylvania Magazine of History and Biography* 79 (April 1955): 178–79. See also,

"Philadelphia Union Co-operation, No.1," *Fincher's Trades' Review*, May 6, 1865, 91, and "Reply to 'Worker,'" *Fincher's Trades' Review*, May 20, 1865, 99. This is also discussed in Irwin Yellowitz, *Industrialization and the American Labor Movement, 1850–1900* (Port Washington, N.Y.: Kennikat Press, 1977).

7. See George Jacob Holyoake, *Self-help by the People: History of Co-operation in Rochdale* (London: Holyoake & Co., 1858), 16, 46; G. D. H. Cole, *A Short History of the British Working Class Movement, 1789–1947* (London: George Allen & Unwin, 1948), 156; Sidney and Beatrice Webb, *The Consumers' Cooperative Movement* (London: Longmans, Green and Co., 1921), 4–16; and Johnston Birchall, *Co-op: The People's Business* (Manchester, UK: Manchester University Press, 1994).

8. See, for example, H. L. to Editor, *Fincher's Trades' Review*, December 2, 1865, 3, and, "Co-operation. Massachusetts Co-operative Stores," newspaper unknown, January 18, 1870, John Samuel Papers, newspaper clippings, Box 4, Wisconsin State Historical Society, Madison (hereafter cited as John Samuel Papers); manuscript headed, "Written while in Fincher's office between 1865–6," notebooks, vols. 13–16, Notes on Cooperation, John Samuel Papers, microfilm reel no. 3, p. 848. See also Massachusetts Bureau of the Statistics of Labor, "Cooperation," *Annual Report of 1875*, part 5, 55–61, microfiche; "Statements of Co-operative Associations, Certified to Secretary of Commonwealth as Organized under Chapter 290, Acts of 1866," *Pamphlets in American History*, Cooperative Societies #134 (Sanford, N.C.: Microfilming Corp. of America, 1979–84), microfiche; Edward Bemis, "Cooperation in New England," in *History of Cooperation in the United States*, ed. Herbert Adams. Johns Hopkins University Studies in Historical and Political Science, vol. 6 (Baltimore: Johns Hopkins University, 1888), 26–32, 53, 66, 78–79, 127, 128.

According to John Andrews (see John Commons et al., *History of Labor in the United States* [New York: Macmillan Company, 1918], 2:39), runaway wartime inflation generated this resurgence of distributive reform. Inflation, however, influenced workers only to the extent that it contributed to economic instability. Indeed, cooperative stores appeared in greater numbers during deflationary periods following the war. According to David Montgomery, prices declined steadily from the severe inflation of the Civil War to 1857 levels by 1876 and then to a much lower level by 1879. See *Fall of the House of Labor: The Workplace, the State, and American Labor Activism, 1865–1925* (Cambridge: Cambridge University Press, 1987), 47–48. In the mid-1870s, cooperative stores associated with the Sovereigns of Industry multiplied in eighteen states. According to James Ford (*Co-operation in New England, Urban and Rural* [Philadelphia: Press of Wm. F. Fell Co., 1913], 22), the Sovereigns had as many as 280 local councils in New England and 170 in the middle and central states, each with its own purchasing club or store. Unstable conditions alone, of course, cannot explain why the labor movement embraced this particular form of collective action.

9. *New York Tribune*, October 11, 1858; Thomas Phillips, "Biography of Thomas Phillips," Cooperative Associations Papers, Box 1, Folder 4a, Wisconsin State Historical Society, Madison (hereafter cited as Cooperative Associations Papers); Clifton K. Yearley Jr., *Britons in American Labor: A His-*

tory of the Influence of the United Kingdom Immigrants on American Labor, 1820–1914. Johns Hopkins University Studies in Historical and Political Science, series 75, no. 1 (Baltimore: Johns Hopkins Press, 1957), 202–3, 266–76; Peter Gurney, "George Jacob Holyoake: Socialism, Association and Co-operation in Nineteenth-Century England," in *New Views of Co-operation*, ed. Stephen Yeo (London: Routledge, 1988), 52–72. See, for example, *Fincher's Trades' Review*, November 28, 1863, 104; November 5, 1864, 90, 91; November 19, 1864, 99; *K.O.S.C. Monthly Journal*, January 1873, 105–14, Knights of St. Crispin Papers, Miscellaneous Holdings, Wisconsin State Historical Society, Madison. The Rochdale experience was mentioned often in *Fincher's Trades' Review, The Daily Evening Voice, The Sovereigns of Industry Bulletin, and the Iron Molders' International Journal*. See "Co-operation in Federal Street," *Fincher's Trades' Review*, December 3, 1864, 3.

10. Holyoake, *Self-help by the People*, 57.

11. Barbara Blaszak, *George Jacob Holyoake (1817–1906) and the Development of the British Cooperative Movement* (Lewiston, N.Y.: Edwin Mellen Press, 1988), 65–68; Cole, *A Short History*, 155–61. For a short period (from the late 1860s to the mid-1870s) of trade union involvement in productive cooperation, see Cole, *A Short History*, 219. See also Bill Lancaster, *Radicalism, Cooperation and Socialism: Leicester Working-Class Politics 1860–1906* (Leicester, UK: Leicester University Press, 1987), 134–49, for trade union and socialist involvement in cooperation.

12. Scattered evidence suggests that the Machinists and Blacksmiths and the Carpenters and Joiners Unions were the most active in establishing cooperative stores in the mid-1860s; see *Fincher's Trades' Review*, January 23, 1864, April 16, 1864, January 14, 1865, February 18, 1865, April 29, 1865, February 24, 1866. When Trades' Assemblies organized stores, however, a wide range of unions participated; see *Fincher's Trades' Review*, November 26, 1864, on Cincinnati and the following discussion of Charlestown, Massachusetts, and Philadelphia. According to the statistics provided by Horner ("Producers' Co-operatives," 229–42), the trades most active in cooperative industries between 1865 and 1875 were (from most to least active) shoe making, iron molding, clothing manufacturing, machine shops, cigar making, and printing. Workers established at least five hundred producers' cooperatives in the twenty-five years after the Civil War; see Commons et al., *History of Labor in the United States*, 2: 111; Knapp, *American Cooperative Enterprise*, 32.

13. Steven J. Ross, *Workers on the Edge: Work, Leisure, and Politics in Industrializing Cincinnati, 1788–1890* (New York: Columbia University Press, 1985), 97–100, 112–13, 118–20; Alan Dawley, *Class and Community: The Industrial Revolution in Lynn* (Cambridge: Harvard University Press, 2000), 92–94; Victor Clark, *History of Manufactures in the United States*, vol. 2 (New York: McGraw-Hill Book Company, 1929), 468–71.

14. Ross, *Workers on the Edge*, 116–17; James E. Cebula, *The Glory and Despair of Challenge and Change: A History of the Iron Molders' Union* (Cincinnati: International Molders' & Allied Workers' Union, 1976), 5; Jonathan Grossman, *William Sylvis, Pioneer of American Labor* (New York: Columbia University Press, 1945), 132–42.

15. See discussion of shoe cooperatives in Stoneham, Massachusetts, in

chapter 4 of this volume. The cooperators in Troy, New York, in the 1860s kept their union shop committees in their factory; see Steven Leikin, "The Practical Utopians: Cooperation and the American Labor Movement, 1860–1890" (Ph.D diss., University of California, Berkeley, 1992), chapter 2. William Sylvis, president of the Iron Molders' Union, wrote in 1864, "Such a shop would . . . become a regulator in the trade, as to prices, the hours of labor, and the rules of the shops. . . . It would be a tremendous lever to assist in securing legislation . . . on the apprentice question . . . [and] the eight-hour system." *Fincher's Trades' Review*, September 24, 1864, 67.

16. Martin Shefter, "Trade Unions and Political Machines: The Organization and Disorganization of the American Working Class in the Late Nineteenth Century," in *Working-Class Formation: Nineteenth-Century Patterns in Western Europe and the United States*, ed. Ira Katznelson and Aristide R. Zolberg (Princeton, N.J.: Princeton University Press, 1986), 199–202; Montgomery, *Fall of the House of Labor*, 44–57; Bruce Laurie and Mark Schmitz, "Manufacture and Productivity: The Making of an Industrial Base, Philadelphia, 1850–1880," in *Philadelphia: Work, Space, Family, and Group Experience in the 19th Century*, ed. Theodore Hershberg (Oxford: Oxford University Press, 1981), 47–53.

17. Laurie and Schmitz, "Manufacture and Productivity," 86–88.

18. For an estimate of fifty operating stores at the end of 1869, see "Co-operation. Massachusetts Co-operative Stores," newspaper unknown, January 18, 1870, John Samuel Papers, newspaper clippings, Box 4. I counted a minimum of fifty-five formed from 1864 through 1869 from the following sources: "Statements of Co-operative Associations, Certified to Secretary of Commonwealth as Organized under Chapter 290, Acts of 1866" (Boston: Wright & Potter, State Printers, 1868); *Pamphlets in American History*, Cooperative Societies #134 (Sanford, N.C.: Microfilming Corp. of America, 1979–84), microfiche; *Fincher's Trades' Review:* "Editorial Correspondence," November 5, 1864, 90; "Editorial Correspondence," November 12, 1864, 94; "Auditor," January 14, 1865, 27; "Our Boston Letter, July 15, 1865, 53; *Daily Evening Voice:* "Cooperative Convention," April 7, 1865, n.p.; "Uncle Sam," August 9, 1865, n.p.; "Mechanics' Co-operative Association," April 2, 1866, n.p.; and "Crispin Co-operative Aims and Enterprises, *American Workman*, October 2, 1869, 5.

19. "Editorial Correspondence," *Fincher's Trades' Review*, November 12, 1864, 94; "Our Boston Letter," *Fincher's Trades' Review*, January 13, 1866. On Simpson, see *Daily Evening Voice*, April 17, July 8, October 2, 1865, n.pp. On Spaulding, see Iron Molders' Union, *Synopsis of the Proceedings of the Annual Convention of the Eighth Session of the Iron Molders' Union*, 1867, 52.

20. *Fincher's Trades' Review:* "Editorial Correspondence," November 12, 1864, 94; "A Voice from the Old Bay State," April 1, 1865, 71; "Our Boston Letter," July 15, 1865, 53; and "Workingmen's Charitable Co-operative Association of Charlestown and Vicinity," *Daily Evening Voice*, April 5, 1865, n.p.

21. "Republican Caucus in Charlestown. A Spicy Discussion. A Radical Change in the Management of the Party," *Daily Evening Voice*, October 2,

1865, n.p.; "Our Boston Letter," *Fincher's Trades' Review*, December 30, 1865, 37; "Co-operation," *Daily Evening Voice*, February 15, 1866, n.p.; Annual Register of Executive and Legislative Departments of the Government of Massachusetts, 1866, Appendix of Journal, 467; David Montgomery, *Beyond Equality: Labor and the Radical Republicans, 1862–1872* (Urbana: University of Illinois Press, 1981), 265, 266–77. The Republican Party's receptiveness to labor reform quickly waned in 1866.

22. *Journal of the House of Representatives of Massachusetts* (Boston: Wright & Potter, State Printers, 1866), 125, 250, 239, 252, 313, 327, 403, 418, 421, 445, 449. For the bills introduced and amended, see Massachusetts House Bills Nos. 212 (March 1866), 319 (April 1866), and 404 (May 1866); Edwin G. Nourse, *The Legal Status of Agricultural Co-operation* (New York: MacMillan Company, 1927), 39–43.

23. "Co-operative Convention," *Daily Evening Voice*, April 7, 1865, n.p. Representatives from Charlestown, Lawrence, Lowell, and Waltham, Massachusetts, and Woonsocket, Rhode Island, attended the convention. They decided that their cooperatives were not yet stable enough to support a wholesale store.

24. "Our Boston Letter," *Fincher's Trades' Review*, March 24, 1866, 132; Report of the Committee on Cooperation, Iron Molders' Union, *Synopsis of the Proceedings of Eighth Session of the Iron Molders' Union*, 1867, 50–51.

25. Clifton Yearley, in *Britons in American Labor*, gives a detailed account of British immigrants involved in the cooperative movement and the Americans they influenced, including Thomas Phillips, John Samuel, Johathan Fincher, William Sylvis, and John Shedden. For a recent study dealing with Phillips and Shedden, see Timothy Messer-Kruse, *The Yankee International: Marxism and the American Reform Tradition, 1848–1876* (Chapel Hill: University of North Carolina Press, 2000), 135–38, 240.

26. In 1851 tailors and bookbinders both had functioning cooperatives in Philadelphia. In 1860 a joint stock shoe manufacturing company was formed by organized shoemakers. See Edgar Barclay Cale, "The Organization of Labor in Philadelphia, 1850–1870" (Ph.D. diss., University of Pennsylvania, 1940), 28, 31, 37; and Bruce Laurie, *Working People of Philadelphia, 1800–1850* (Philadelphia: Temple University Press, 1980), 184. For biographical information on Phillips and an illuminating discussion of his life see, Yearley, "Thomas Phillips," and Commons et al., *History of Labor in the United States*, 2:39–40. It was a member of the UCA who wrote, "I often think of the first 'shilling' pamphlet we had from Mr. Holyoke [*sic*], as I watch the proceedings at the store."

27. "Origin of 1st Co-op," Union Cooperative Association, Cooperative Associations Papers, Box 1, Folder 9, Wisconsin State Historical Society, Madison (hereafter cited as Cooperative Associations Papers); "Co-operation in Federal Street," *Fincher's Trades' Review*, December 3, 1864, 3; "Communications," *Fincher's Trades' Review*, November 7, 1863, 91; UCA Minutes, vol. 1, 1864–65, Cooperative Associations Papers, Box 1, Folder 10; Questor, "Co-operation in Federal Street," *Fincher's Trades' Review*, November 25, 1864, 3; Worker, *Fincher's Trades' Review*, August 13, 1864, 43.

28. UCA Minutes, vol. 1; The occupations of thirty-five of the fifty-six

members could be determined. See Cale, "Labor in Philadelphia," 76; "Trades' Assembly Ball," *Fincher's Trades' Review*, November 12, 1864, 94. John Samuel, William Sylvis, and J. C. Fincher were all members of the UCA and founders of the Trades' Assembly. Thomas Phillips was an active member of the Trades' Assembly. For evidence that they were all members of the UCA, see UCA Minutes, vol 1.

29. Account Book: Union Cooperative Association, Philadelphia, October 13, 1863 to May 31, 1866, vols. 1–3, Cooperative Associations Papers, Box 1, Folder 11; Worker, *Fincher's Trades' Review*, August 13, 1864, 43.

30. UCA Minutes, vol.1, December 1, 1864, May 2, 1865; UCA Minutes, vol. 2, April 10, 1866, October 18, 1866; "Good News From Delaware," *Fincher's Trades' Review*, December 10, 1864, 6; "Cooperation in Philadelphia," *Fincher's Trades' Review*, January 27, 1866, 68. James Penrose, an organizer of the pre–Civil War Iron Machinery Molders' Union in Philadelphia, and Nathaniel Thayer, a machinist who assumed the editorship of *Fincher's Trades' Review* for a short time in 1865, were also members. See UCA Minutes, vol. 2, February 6, 1866 and March 6, 1866, and Cale, "Labor in Philadelphia," 21, 97. Sylvis and Fincher appeared together often at union rallies, and Sylvis's letters and articles appeared regularly in the *Review*. According to Jonathan Grossman (*William Sylvis*, 221), Sylvis "made a warm friend of Jonathan Fincher . . . [which] expanded into a harmonious relationship between their respective unions. . . . A picture of Sylvis and Fincher together adorned the walls of several meeting halls." In 1868, when Sylvis entered into a partnership with A. C. Cameron to publish the *Workingmen's Advocate*, he took over Fincher's newspaper office (where he published the *Welcome Workman* after the *Review* folded), making it a branch of the *Advocate*; see Cale, "Labor in Philadelphia," 95, 102–3. John Samuel was a member of the editorial staff of the *Review*; see Commons et al., *History of Labor in the United States*, 2:25. Sheddon was associated with Fincher as early as 1863; see "Co-operation in Our City: An Appeal to the Employees, both Male and Female, of the City of Philadelphia," *Fincher's Trades' Review*, October 31, 1863, 85. Thomas Phillips "was well acquainted with the Review people being a frequent visitor at the office." (Thomas Phillips to U. S. Stephens, October 12, 1879, Thomas Phillips Papers, Box 1, Folder 5). Sylvis died in 1869. See also David Montgomery, "William H. Sylvis and the Search for Working-Class Citizenship," in *Labor Leaders in America*, ed. Melvyn Dubofsky and Warren Van Tine (Urbana: University of Illinois Press, 1987), 27–28.

31. "Letter to the Officers of Sub. M. and B. Unions . . . Gents . . . ," *Fincher's Trades' Review*, May 21, 1864, 99; "Lawrence Co-operative Association," *Fincher's Trades' Review*, April 22, 1865, 83. On Charlestown, see *Fincher's Trades' Review*, August 20, 1864, 47; January 14, 1865, 27; January 6, 1866, 45.

32. For biographical information on Sylvis see Montgomery, "William H. Sylvis," 3–29; Grossman, *William Sylvis*; *The Iron Molders' International Journal*, July 1866, 111–12, August 1867, 120–21, February 1868, 196–97; *Fincher's Trades' Review*, October 31, 1863, January 16, 1864, September 3, 1864, September 24, 1864; *Synopsis of the Proceedings of the International Iron Molders' Union Convention of 1868*, Research Collections in Labor Studies,

Labor Union Periodicals. Part 1, Metal Trades (Bethesda, Maryland: University Publications of America, 1990), microfilm reel no. 1, pp. 23–27. In the molders' journal a regular column appeared in 1866 entitled "Cooperation Abroad." Information about Rochdale and other European cooperative movements appeared there. See, *Iron Molders' International Journal*, March, May, June, July, October, November, and December 1866 issues; and Grossman, *William Sylvis*, 195, 201–4. Grossman mistakenly argues that Sylvis, using Rochdale as a model for both consumer and producer cooperatives, did not know the difference between these two forms of cooperation. Americans in the 1860s, however, knew of Rochdale through George Jacob Holyoake's work, in which he described the payment of a dividend to labor in Rochdale's early experiment with production. That Rochdale abandoned the labor dividend in 1862 was probably not known to Americans in the 1860s. On the termination of the labor dividend, see Sidney Pollard, "Nineteenth-Century Co-operation: From Community Building to Shopkeeping," in *Essays in Labour History*, ed. Asa Briggs and John Saville (London: MacMillan & Co., 1960), 97; and Horner, "Producers' Co-operatives," 174–81.

33. Ray Boston, *British Chartists in America, 1839–1900* (Totowa, New Jersey: Rowman and Littlefield, 1971), 94; Commons et al., *History of Labor*, 2: 25; Yearley, *Britons in American Labor*, 230–43, 263–65, 280–94, 294–302; UCA Minutes, vol. 2, October 18, 1866; Samuel was associate editor of *Coleman's* from 1873 to 1875. See John Samuel to Richard Ely, January 9, 1912, Richard Ely Papers, Box 40, Folder 5, Wisconsin State Historical Society, Madison; H. Miller, *Description of John Samuel Papers*, John Samuel Papers, Wisconsin State Historical Society, Madison; J. Samuel to J. Butterfield, *Sovereigns of Industry Bulletin!*, November 1875, 2; W. H. Earle to Bro. Samuel, January 20, 1877, John Samuel Papers, Box 1, Folder 2; J. Butterfield to Bro. Samuel, January 30, 1878, ibid.; Union Cooperative Printing Company, Minutes, November 25, 1880 to June 13, 1881, Cooperative Associations Papers, Box 1, Folder 13; John Samuel to L. E. Lockwood, June 2, 1886, John Samuel Papers, Box 1, Folder 6, Correspondence, Jan.–May 1886; "An Experiment Which May Be Tried in Any Local Assembly," *Journal of United Labor*, July 1886, 2139; Membership List and Minutes of the Missouri Co-operative Coal Association, 1883, John Samuel Papers, Microfilm edition, reel 3, Notebooks, vols. 17–18, Wisconsin State Historical Society, Madison; Norman Ware, *The Labor Movement in the United States* (New York: Vintage Books, 1929), 328.

34. Laurie, *Working People*, 180; John Shedden is listed as president of Section 26 of the International Workingmen's Association on Thomas Phillips's membership card in Thomas Phillips Papers, Box 1, Folder 5, Wisconsin State Historical Society, Madison (hereafter cited as Thomas Phillips Papers). See also Sovereigns of Industry Circular, "State Council of Pennsylvania," Sovereigns of Industry Papers, Box 2, Folder: Pioneer Council #1, Wisconsin State Historical Society, Madison (hereafter cited as Sovereigns of Industry Papers); Bemis, "Cooperation in New England," 52; Yearley, *Britons in American Labor*, 210, 262; Messer-Kruse, *Yankee International*, 136, 224, 240.

35. UCA Minutes, vol. 2, September 7, 1865; Account Book: Union

Cooperative Association, Philadelphia, October 13, 1863–May 31, 1866, vol. 1, Cooperative Associations Papers, Box 1, Folder 11, December 1865; Commons et al., *History of Labor*, 2:40; "Wholesale Prices of Groceries," *Fincher's Trades' Review*, April 7, 1866, 148; All of the following letters from box 1, folder 5, Thomas Phillips Papers: W. B. Lemmon, New Brighton, Pa., to Thomas Phillips, March 2, 1866; Andrew J. Carney, Westernport, Allegheny County, Md., to Thomas Phillips, April 9, 1866; J. H. Harrison, Washington, Government Printing Office, to Thomas Phillips, April 13, 1866; J. P. Couch, sec. Union Co-operative Association No. 1 of Beaver Falls, New Brighton, Pa. to Thomas Phillips, April 19, 1866; Jones, Reading, Pa., to Thomas Phillips, May 8, 1866; R. H. Harrison, pres. Machinists and Blacksmiths Union, Fort Wayne, Ind., Pittsburgh, Fort Wayne and Chicago Railway Co. to Thomas Phillips, May 8, 1866; Geo. H. Spaulding, pres. W. C. Cooperative Association, Charlestown, Mass., to Thomas Phillips, June 8, 1866; Andrew J. Carney, Westernport, Allegheny Co., Md., Franklin Mines to Thomas Phillips, June 17, 1866; George Ellison, Erie, Pa., to Thomas Phillips, June 18, 1866; J. H. Binder, Royers Ford, Pa., to Thomas Phillips, June 26, 1866; Charles Bowman, Mineral Ridge, Mahoning County, Ohio, to Thomas Phillips, June 28, 1866; St. Clair, Schuylkill County, Pa., to Thomas Phillips, September 15, 1866; John Harms to Jonathan Fincher, August 27, 1866; G. S. Rowbotham to Mr. J. C. Fincher, *Fincher's Trades' Review*, May 21, 1864, 99.

36. UCA Minutes, vols. 1 and 2. The UCA admitted members regularly at various meetings. The association had approximately 160 members during its lifetime. See *Fincher's Trades' Review:* Worker, "Co-operation in Philadelphia," March 24, 1866, 133; North-West, "Co-Operation in Twentieth Ward, Phila," February 3, 1866, 80; Energy, "Co-operation in Philadelphia," March 17, 1866, 125; "Signs of the Times," March 24, 1866, 132.

37. "Co-operative Tract, No. 1," *Pamphlets in American History*, Cooperative Societies, # 20, n.d.

38. *Fincher's Trades' Review:* "Co-operative Store Anniversary," December 24, 1864, 14; "Co-operative Associations," September 19, 1863, 62.

39. "Origin of 1st Coop," December 16, 1862, Cooperative Associations Papers, Box 1, Folder 9.

40. Thomas Phillips, "Grumblers," 1865, *Pamphlets in American History*, Cooperative Societies #31 (Sanford, N.C.: Microfilming Corp. of America, 1979–84), microfiche.

41. *Fincher's Trades' Review:* "Co-operation in Federal Street," December 3, 1864; Worker, August 13, 1864, 43.

42. "Answer to Correspondent on Cooperation," *Fincher's Trades' Review*, May 19, 1866, 195.

43. Worker, *Fincher's Trades' Review*, April 30, 1864, 85.

44. Phillips, "Grumblers."

45. Edward W. Bemis, "Cooperation in the Middle States," in *History of Cooperation in the United States*, ed. Herbert Adams, Johns Hopkins University Studies in Historical and Political Science, vol. 6 (Baltimore: Johns Hopkins University, 1888), 141–42.

46. UCA Minutes, vol. 2, July 3, 12, 18, 26, 1866.

47. UCA Minutes, vol. 2, September 10, 1866.

48. In 1867 Sylvis formulated plans for an International Foundry funded and controlled by the Molders' Union. The foundry was built in Pittsburgh but folded due to a lack of capital. During this time the name of the union was changed to the Iron Molders' International Co-operative and Protective Union upon Sylvis's initiative. See Grossman, *William Sylvis*, 200–204, 206–9; Montgomery, "William H. Sylvis," 12–26. See also Horner, "Producers' Co-operatives," 174–81, 233; Frank Stockton, "Productive Cooperation in the Molders' Union," *American Economic Review* 21 (1931): 260–74; and Cebula, *Glory and Despair*, 13–14. The Knights of Labor will be dealt with in detail in chapter three of this volume.

49. Don D. Lescohier, *The Knights of St. Crispin, 1867–1874: A Study in the Industrial Causes of Trade Unionism*, Bulletin of the University of Wisconsin, no. 355, Economics and Political Science Series (Madison, Wis., 1910) vol. 7, no. 1:49–55; Knights of St. Crispin, *Proceedings of Third Annual Meeting of the International Grand Lodge of the Order of Knights of St. Crispin, Held in Boston, Massachusetts* (Milwaukee: Evening Wisconsin Book and Job Printing House, 1870), 27, 34. See also convention proceedings from 1869 and 1872. Thomas Phillips was a member of the committee on cooperation which recommended central funding in 1870; see Phillips, "Biography of Thomas Phillips." On the Crispins, see Dawley, *Class and Community;* Mary Blewett, *Men, Women, and Work: Class, Gender, and Protest in the New England Shoe Industry, 1780–1910* (Urbana: University of Illinois Press, 1988); "Crispin Co-operative Aims and Enterprises," *American Workman*, October 2, 1869, 5; and Horner, "Producers' Co-operatives," 229–42. One of the first cooperative factories was in Painesville, Ohio; see "Constitution and By-Laws of the Painesville Co-operative Boot and Shoe Manufacturing Association," 1869, *Pamphlets in American History*, Cooperative Societies #155 (Sanford, N.C.: Microfilming Corp. of America, 1979–84), microfiche; and Office Of the American Workman, W. Gass & Co. to Thomas Phillips, April 7, 1869, Cooperative Associations, Thomas Phillips Papers, Box 1, Folder 5. See also, Knights of St. Crispin, *Report of the Special Committee on Co-operation to the International Grand Lodge, K.O.S.C., Adopted April 26th, 1871* (Lowell, Mass: Stone & Huse Book Printers, 1871), appendix.

50. Thomas Phillips to Mr. Andrews, June 21, 1908, John Commons Papers, Box 1, Folder 3, Correspondence, Wisconsin State Historical Society, Madison (hereafter cited as John Commons Papers). See also Lescohier, *Knights*, 42–43. The first strike in the early months of 1870 is discussed in Lescohier. The first shoe workers' cooperative in postwar Philadelphia opened during this strike and is mentioned in Cale, "Labor in Philadelphia," 66. It is not clear, though, if this first factory was sponsored by the Crispins. Phillips was Grand Sir Knight of the state lodge; the second lockout affected Friendship Lodge, No. 219, Thomas Phillips's local. See K.O.S.C. Office of the Grand Lodge of Pa. handbill, November 14, 1870, Knights of St. Crispin Papers, Miscellaneous Holdings, Wisconsin State Historical Society, Madison (hereafter cited as Knights of St. Crispin Papers); "Biography of Thomas Phillips"; K.O.S.C. Pennsylvania handbill; Friendship Lodge, No. 219 handbill, Knights of St. Crispin Papers, Miscellaneous Holdings.

51. Cale, "Labor in Philadelphia," 67; Thomas Phillips to Mr. Andrews, March 28, 1908, John Commons Papers, Box 1, Folder 3, correspondence; Phillips, "Biography of Thomas Phillips." See letter of agreement between the Grand Lodge and the cooperative factory signing over the assets to a committee from the factory consisting of Thomas Phillips and two other shoe workers, Knights of St. Crispin Cooperative Association, Cooperative Associations Papers, Box 1, Folder 1.

52. Cooperation Balance Sheets, 1872–1873, Philadelphia Cooperative Shoe Manufacturing Association, Cooperative Associations Papers, Box 1, Folder 3, June 1872 and November 1873. The number employed is my estimate based on daily wages for twelve men calculated on a sheet inserted in the account book. See also Thomas Phillips to John Commons, September 24, 1910, John Commons Papers, Box 1, Folder 5, correspondence; Phillips, "Biography of Thomas Phillips."

53. Phillips, "Biography of Thomas Phillips."

54. Philadelphia Local Section #26 Membership List, International Workingmen's Association Papers, microfilm edition, reel 2, Wisconsin State Historical Society; Minutes of Meetings of the Philadelphia Section of the International Workingmen's Association, October 9, 1871 to March 10, 1873, International Workingmen's Association Papers, microfilm edition, reel 2, Wisconsin State Historical Society, 7, 11–12, 16, 19, 39, 67, 71–73. For the proposed bank and newspaper, see "'International.' The Philadelphia Sections," Thomas Phillips Papers, Box 1, Folder 8; Judith Lazarus Goldberg, "Strikes, Organizing, and Change: The Knights of Labor in Philadelphia, 1869–1890" (Ph.D. diss., New York University, 1985), 77–79. A copy of the first and only issue of their cooperative newspaper, the *Free and Independent Labor Champion*, is in the Thomas Phillips Papers, Box 1, Folder 7. Section #26 is thoroughly examined in Messer-Kruse, *Yankee International.*

55. Minutes of Meetings of the Philadelphia Section, 62, 71–72; Philadelphia Local Section #26 Membership List. Compare to list of members in UCA Minutes. Out of frustration, one member brought an inventor with him to a meeting who had developed a new type of window shade. The inventor offered to split the profits in half with a cooperative society willing to produce it. The member, one Citizen Kilgore, "thought that we had talk enough on this floor during the past year, he wanted something practical." Minutes of Meetings of the Philadelphia Section, 209–10.

56. A complete history of the Sovereigns of Industry has yet to be written, though some details of its development can be found in Messer-Cruse, *Yankee International*, 239–44; Commons et al., *History of Labor*, 2:171–75; Edwin M. Chamberlin, *The Sovereigns of Industry* (1875; reprint, Westport, Conn.: Hyperion Press, 1976), 123–60; Bemis, "Cooperation in New England," 37–47; Franklin Henry Giddings, "Co-operation," in *The Labor Movement: The Problem of Today*, ed. George E. McNeill (New York: M. W. Hazen, 1886), 515; Ford, *Co-operation in New England*, 21–28; Philip Foner, *History of the Labor Movement in the United States*, vol. 1 (New York: International Publishers, 1978), 475–76; and Horner, "Producers' Co-operatives," 32–34.

57. Commons et al., *History of Labor*, 2:173; Horner, "Producers' Co-operatives," 32; *Sovereigns of Industry Bulletin!*, July 1876, 6; September 1876,

2; Phillips, "Biography of Thomas Phillips"; Thomas Phillips to J. Butterfield, Sec. of National Council, Sovereigns of Industry, October 10, 1874, Philadelphia, Pa., Thomas Phillips Papers, Box 1, Folder 5; Goldberg, "Knights of Labor," 80. Compare membership list of Section #26 with Sovereigns of Industry of Pennsylvania-Pioneer Council, Philadelphia. List of members, 1874–1877, Sovereigns of Industry Papers, Box 1, Wisconsin State Historical Society, Madison (hereafter cited as Sovereigns of Industry Papers). Of the 225 men and women who enlisted in the Pioneer Council, approximately 56 percent were skilled workers, 16 percent were professional and white-collar workers, 9 percent were housekeepers, 8 percent were dealers of various commodities, and 6 percent were manufacturers.

58. "Declaration of Purposes," *Sovereigns of Industry Bulletin!*, 1, no. 12, November 1875, 1.

59. Ibid., "Confidential Circular. Office of the National Council," August 1, 1874, Sovereigns of Industry Papers, Box 2, Folder: Pioneer Council #1; State Council of Pennsylvania order list for bulk groceries, Sovereigns of Industry Papers, Box 2, Folder: Pioneer Council #1; *Sovereigns of Industry Bulletin!:* W. H. H. B., July 1876, 6, and W. H. H. B., November 1875, 1; S.G., November 1875, 2; "Connecticut," January 1875, 3; "Pennsylvania," January 1875, 4; "Cooperation and Small Councils," March 1875, 3; July 1875, 1, 3–4. The Sovereigns Executive Council officially endorsed the Rochdale system in 1877; see *Sovereigns of Industry Bulletin!*, November 1877, 4–5. James Ford maintains, with some justification, that the Sovereigns was the first organization to effectively disseminate the Rochdale system of cooperation in America (*Cooperation in New England*, 27). The competing scheme was known as the Springfield plan, upon which the Sovereigns' most successful store was based. Like the Protective Union stores, the store in Springfield, Massachusetts, sold goods slightly above cost. Stock was purchased by councils, who borrowed the money from individual members, but directors were elected by the councils at large, not by individual contributors. This, Bemis disapprovingly noted in his "Cooperation in New England," was "very much the state of things . . . advocated by some socialists, viz: An industry managed by the votes of a democracy" (44). The low prices attracted a large membership and a huge volume of sales. Unfortunately, this also engendered a ruinous bout of competition with other retailers and caused the store to eventually fail. In 1878, after four years of operation, the store attempted to convert to the Rochdale plan, but poor management and possible malfeasance led to its collapse. See Bemis, "Cooperation in New England," 40–46; Proposal for Sovereigns' Wholesale and Retail Central Store and Board of Trade, Sovereigns of Industry Papers, Box 1, Pamphlets; "By-Laws of the New England S. of I. Co-operative Board of Trade," Sovereigns of Industry Papers, Box 2, Folder: Pioneer Council #1; *Sovereigns of Industry Bulletin!:* "Wholesale Grocery," June 1876, 1; "Sovereigns' Boards of Trade," June 1876, 5–6; "Annual Meeting of the National Council of the Sovereigns of Industry," February 1875, 1–3; "Meeting of the Penn'a State Council, S. of I." September 1876, 2–3.

60. Commons et al., *History of Labor*, 2:174–75. Robert Schilling, a founder of the Industrial Brotherhood and former president of the Coopers'

Union, joined the Sovereigns of Industry. He advocated state sponsorship of cooperatives while the organization opposed state involvement of any kind. See Ware, *The Labor Movement*, 16–18; Robert Schilling, "Third Annual Session of the National Council, S. I.," *Sovereigns of Industry Bulletin!*, May 1877, 2. George McNeill, a leading labor reformer and eight-hour activist, was secretary of Massachusetts' State Council; see *Sovereigns of Industry Bulletin!*, November 1875, 2. John Orvis, a former Brook Farm resident, Fourierist, and supporter of the prewar Working Men's Protective Union, was national lecturer for the organization. Orvis at first actually opposed the plan to open cooperative stores. In an argument reminiscent of the Jacksonian era, he maintained that the incorporation of cooperative stores was a violation of equal rights. He later became a vocal supporter of Rochdale cooperation. See Commons et al., *History of Labor*, 2:173; Rozwenc, "Cooperatives," 47, 52. See the exchange between Orvis and the compilers of the Burton Plan in *Sovereigns of Industry Bulletin!*, July 1875, 3–4 and "The Rochdale Co-operative Store," May 1876, 5. On relations between labor and capital, and anti-trade unionism, see "Annual Meeting" [President Earle's address], *Sovereigns of Industry Bulletin!*, February 1875, 1–2; For a different position on trade unions, see discussion of the Pioneer Council in the following. For different positions on labor and capital, see "Meeting," *Sovereigns of Industry Bulletin!*, September 1876, 2.

61. Thomas Phillips to editors, n.d., Thomas Phillips, Papers, Box 1, Folder 5; "Meeting of the Penn'a State Council, S. of I.," *Sovereigns of Industry Bulletin!*, September 1876, 2; Sovereigns of Industry of Pennsylvania, Pioneer Council, Philadelphia, Minutes, July 25, 1877, Sovereigns of Industry Papers, Wisconsin State Historical Society, Madison.

62. Letter from W. H. H. B to Bro. Butterfield, *Sovereigns of Industry Bulletin!:* July 1876, 6 and "Notes and Clippings," July 1876, 8. See Circular from State Council of Pennsylvania, Sovereigns of Industry, listing a variety of goods available in bulk, and Confidential Circular, August 1, 1874 in Sovereigns of Industry Papers, Box 2, Folder: Pioneer Council #1: John Sheddon, "Pennsylvania," *Sovereigns of Industry Bulletin!*, January 1875, 4.

63. Address on the Sovereigns of Industry by Thomas Phillips, Thomas Phillips Papers, Box 1, Folder 5; "S. I." Address by Thomas Phillips, Sovereigns of Industry Papers, Box 2, Folder: Pioneer Council #1 Philadelphia.

64. Sovereigns of Industry of Pennsylvania, Pioneer Council, Philadelphia Minutes, February 29, 1878, August 28, 1878. Sovereigns of Industry Papers.

65. The representatives of the fifty to sixty Knights' assemblies comprising District Assembly No. 1 in Philadelphia met in the mid-1870s in the Sovereigns' meeting hall. They, along with a number of councils of the Sovereigns of Industry, unanimously chose Thomas Phillips to write a labor column in the *Public Record*, a Philadelphia newspaper. Phillips wrote the column, committed primarily to the propagation of cooperative ideals, for fourteen months. By Phillips's account, neither organization ever objected to his column, "so that its contents may farily [*sic*] be take[n] as representing the sentiments of the organized laborers of that date." See Phillips, *Biography of Thomas Phillips;* Goldberg, "Knights of Labor," 82; Note from Thomas Phillips, November 7, 1905, John Commons Papers, Box 1, Folder 1, Corre-

spondence.

66. Goldberg, "Knights of Labor," chapters 2 and 3. For a general overview of the Knights, see Laurie, *Artisans into Workers*, chapter 5.

67. "Laws of the Pennsylvania Co-operative General Trading and Manufacturing Association, Incorporated March 1st, 1876," *Pamphlets in American History*, Cooperative Societies No. 168, 2; Goldberg, "Knights of Labor," 47, 68, 90–92.

68. Commons et al., *History of Labor*, 2:40; Ware, *The Labor Movement*, 30, 111–15. On Samuel, Wright, Phillips, Drury, and Turner, see Goldberg, "Knights of Labor"; Messer-Kruse, *Yankee International;* Craig Phelan, *Grand Master Workman: Terence Powderly and the Knights of Labor* (Westport, Conn.: Greenwood Press, 2000); and Weir, *Knights Unhorsed.*

Chapter 2

1. Knights of Labor, District Assenbly 79, *Record of Proceedings of the Twentieth Regular Meeting of D.A. 79, K. of L. held at St. Paul, Minnesota, July 17, 1887*, John P. McGauhey Papers, Minnesota Historical Society, St. Paul, 8.

2. David Montgomery, "William H. Sylvis and the Search for Working-Class Citizenship," in *Labor Leaders in America*, ed. Melvyn Dubofsky and Warren Van Tine (Urbana: University of Illinois Press, 1987), 28; Jonathan Grossman, *William Sylvis: Pioneer of American Labor*, Columbia University Studies in History, Economics, and Public Law, no. 516 (New York: Columbia University Press, 1945).

3. "Workingwoman's Association. Meeting at 'The Revolution' Office," *The Revolution*, October 1, 1868, 196–98. Typescript of Original Newspaper Article, Excerpts from Books, Magazines, and Newspapers Concerning Labor Unions, 1827–1879, Wisconsin State Historical Society, Madison. See also Ellen Carol DuBois, *Feminism and Suffrage: The Emergence of an Independent Women's Movement in America, 1848–1869* (Ithaca, N.Y.: Cornell University Press, 1978), 126–61.

4. "Workingwoman's Association. Meeting at 'The Revolution" Office," 196–98.

5. Women's support of the patriarchal family is discussed in Ava Baron, "Gender and Labor History: Learning from the Past, Looking to the Future," in *Work Engendered: Toward a New History of American Labor*, ed. Ava Baron (Ithaca, N.Y.: Cornell University Press, 1991), 27–32; see also Mary Blewett, *Men, Women, and Work: Class, Gender, and Protest in the New England Shoe Industry, 1780–1910* (Urbana: University of Illinois Press, 1988), 116–41.

6. My own approach to this has been influenced most heavily by Leon Fink, "The New Labor History and the Powers of Historical Pessimism: Consensus, Hegemony, and the Case of the Knights of Labor," *Journal of American History* 75, no. 1 (1988): 115–36; idem, "Looking Backward: Reflections on Workers' Culture and Certain Conceptual Dilemmas within Labor History," in *Perspectives on American Labor History: The Problems of Synthesis*, ed. J. Carroll Moody and Alice Kessler-Harris (DeKalb: Northern Illinois University Press, 1989), 5–29; idem, *Workingmen's Democracy: The Knights of*

Labor and American Politics (Urbana: University of Illinois Press, 1983); Kim Voss, *The Making of American Exceptionalism: The Knights of Labor and Class Formation in the Nineteenth Century* (Ithaca, N.Y.: Cornell University Press, 1993); Sean Wilentz, *Chants Democratic: New York City and the Rise of the American Working Class, 1788–1850* (New York: Oxford University Press, 1984); David Montgomery, *Citizen Worker: The Experience of Workers in the United States with Democracy and the Free Market during the Nineteenth Century* (Cambridge: Cambridge University Press, 1993); Ava Baron, *Work Engendered;* and Blewett, *Men, Women, and Work.*

7. Member of No. 2 to Editor, *Iron Molders' International Journal*, May 1868, 246.

8. Dry Sand to Editor, January 7, 1865, 23 and M. M., "Special Matters in New York," July 1, 1865, 40 in *Fincher's Trades' Review;* John Samuel, Untitled Cooperative Address, ca. 1866, John Samuel Papers, reel 3, microfilm, Wisconsin State Historical Society, Madison (hereafter cited as John Samuel Papers).

9. A. D. T., "A Molder's Dream," *Iron Molders' International Journal*, December 10, 1876, 170–71.

10. David Montgomery, *The Fall of the House of Labor: The Workplace, the State, and American Labor Activism, 1865–1925* (Cambridge: Cambridge University Press, 1987), chapter 1.

11. Dugald Campbell to Editor, *Iron Molders' International Journal*, March 1866, 24–25. Dugald Campbell was well known as a poet among his fellow iron molders; see Daniel Walkowitz, *Worker City, Company Town: Iron and Cotton-Worker Protest in Troy and Cohoes, New York, 1855–1884* (Urbana: University of Illinois Press, 1981.)

12. C. J. C. to Editor, *Iron Molders' International Journal*, August 1867, 134.

13. W. F. Troughton to Editor, May 1866, 55–56 and F. L. Stevens to Editor, July 1866, 120, *Iron Molders' International Journal;* William Sylvis to Editor, *Fincher's Trades' Review*, September 24, 1864, 67.

14. Iron Molders' Union, *Synopsis of the Proceedings of the 13th Session of the Iron Molders' International Union*, July 1876, 18. Research Collections in Labor Studies, Labor Union Periodicals. Part 1, Metal Trades (Bethesda, Md.: University Publications of America, 1990), microfilm, reel no. 1.

15. Ibid.

16. P. C. Forrester, "A Challenge from Chicago," *Fincher's Trades' Review*, December 5, 1863, 3.

17. As discussed in chapter 1, under the Rochdale system a cooperative store would sell shares but allow the stockholder only one vote regardless of the number of shares held. The shares would entitle him or her to a fixed dividend of no more than 5 percent on the investment. Stores sold all goods for cash at market prices, with the profits returned to members in proportion to their purchases; "Constitution and By-Laws of the Troy Workingmen's Cooperative Association," *Pamphlets in American History*, Cooperative Societies #213 (Sanford, N.C.: Microfilming Corp. of America, 1979–84), microform.

18. See Wilentz, *Chants Democratic*, 157–68; Fink, *Workingmen's Democracy*, 6–7.

19. Advocates of cooperation advanced the one member-one vote rule but this was not always the case in practice. See Clare Horner, "Producers' Cooperatives in the United States, 1865–1890" (Ph.D. diss., New York University, 1985), 152–54.

20. Samuel, Untitled Cooperative Address, John Samuel Papers, reel 3, microform.

21. Fink, *Workingmen's Democracy*, 6–7; Bruce Laurie, *Artisans into Workers: Labor in Nineteenth-Century America* (New York: Noonday Press, 1989), 87, 151–53; Lawrence Glickman, *A Living Wage: American Workers and the Making of Consumer Society* (Ithaca, N.Y.: Cornell University Press, 1997), 17–29. See David Roediger, *The Wages of Whiteness: Race and the Making of the American Working Class* (New York: Verso, 1991), for a critical reading of the racial nature of the concept of wage slavery.

22. For another example, see "The Labor Movement of 1878 in Chicago," typescript of a *Chicago Tribune* article, June 30, 1878, Labor Collection: Miscellaneous Biographies and Papers, Box 1, Wisconsin State Historical Society, Madison.

23. Hugh Cameron, "Co-operation," *Journal of United Labor*, December 10, 1886, 2217; "The Quaker City Co-operative Carpet Company," *Journal of United Labor*, November 10, 1886, 2199.

24. The literature on republicanism and the American working class has burgeoned in recent years. The most relevant works for my purposes are: Wilentz, *Chants Democratic;* Fink, *Workingmen's Democracy;* idem, "Looking Backward"; idem, "The New Labor History"; Richard Oestreicher, "Terence V. Powderly, the Knights of Labor, and Artisanal Republicanism," in *Labor Leaders in America*, ed. Melvyn Dubofsky and Warren Van Tine (Urbana: University of Illinois Press, 1987); William E. Forbath, "The Ambiguities of Free Labor: Labor and the Law in the Gilded Age," *Wisconsin Law Review* (July/August 1985): 767–817; Voss, *American Exceptionalism;* "Prospectus of the *Daily Evening Voice*," *Daily Evening Voice*, December 12, 1864, n.p.

25. See William Sylvis, "Address delivered by William Sylvis President Iron Molders' International Union of North America, Before the Convention Now in Session in Buffalo, N.Y.," *Fincher's Trades' Review*, January 16, 1864, 25.

26. Massachusetts Bureau of the Statistics of Labor, *Annual Report*, 1870, microfiche edition, 345; Cameron, "Co-operation," 2217; Forbath, "Ambiguities of Free Labor," 767–817.

27. For a good example of this see Sylvis, "Address," 25. The power they sought to exercise was largely outside the purview of the state. Though cooperators participated enthusiastically in the democratic process, and within the Knights of Labor called for state ownership of the communication and transportation systems, they actually viewed state power with profound mistrust. They did not expect the state to take an active role in organizing civil society by sponsoring individual cooperatives, and instead looked to education, self-help, and voluntary action—the actions of independent citizens—as the appropriate tools to accomplish much of their reform agenda. In fact, by the 1880s cooperators often defined their position vis-à-vis the state in direct

opposition to that of the state control advocates, the so-called state-socialists. Even after the collapse of the Knights of Labor, a longtime cooperator could be found organizing an association designed to transform the entire economy through self-help. In the 1890s, Thomas Phillips, a labor leader and cooperator from Philadelphia, established a voluntary organization dedicated to comprehensive cooperative reform called the Industrial Republic. See conclusion following; see also Fink, *Workingmen's Democracy*, 18–35.

28. Roediger, *Wages of Whiteness*, esp. chapters 3, 4, 7; Noel Ignatiev, *How the Irish Became White* (New York: Routledge, 1995). For two recent discussions of white working-class identity and its import for labor history, see Alan Dawley, preface to *Class and Community: The Industrial Revolution in Lynn* (Cambridge: Harvard University Press, 2000), and Bruce Nelson, *Divided We Stand: American Workers and the Struggle for Black Equality* (Princeton, N.J.: Princeton University Press, 2001), xix–xliv.

29. For examples see this chapter following, and chapters 3 and 4.

30. Montgomery, "William H. Sylvis," 22–24; Craig Phelan, *Grand Master Workman: Terence Powderly and the Knights of Labor* (Westport, Conn.: Greenwood Press, 2000), 151–54; Peter Rachleff, *Black Labor in Richmond, 1865–1890* (Urbana: University of Illinois Press, 1989), 117–20; Philip Foner, *History of the Labor Movement in the United States*, vol. 2 (New York: International Publishers, 1947), 58–60; Robert Weir, *Knights Unhorsed: Internal Conflict in a Gilded Age Social Movement* (Detroit: Wayne State University Press, 2000), 37.

31. Philip Foner, *History of the Labor Movement in the United States: From Colonial Times to the Founding of the American Federation of Labor*, vol. 1 (New York: International Publishers, 1978), 398–406; Montgomery, "William H. Sylvis," 22, 24; Harold McDougall, *Black Baltimore: A New Theory of Community* (Philadelphia: Temple University Press, 1993), 32–33; Juliet E. K. Walker, *The History of Black Business in America: Capitalism, Race, Entrepreneurship* (New York: Simon & Schuster Macmillan, 1998), 169; Laurie, *Artisans into Workers*, 159.

32. Producerism is discussed in Fink, *Workingmen's Democracy*, 9; Laurie, *Artisans into Workers*, 68–71, 150; and especially Voss, *American Exceptionalism*, 34–35, 86–87, 224–25.

33. "Constitution and By-Laws of the Troy Workingmen's Co-operative Association"; "Constitution and By-lays of the Trenton Cooperative Benefit Society, No. 1," *Pamphlets in American History*, Cooperative Societies #214 (Sanford, N.C.: Microfilming Corp. of America, 1979–84), microform.

34. Earnest to Editor, *Fincher's Trades' Review*, February 18, 1865, 47.

35. John A. Curran, *Iron Molders' International Journal*, November 1867, 165.

36. Isaac Rhen, "Defects of the Wages System," *Second Annual Report of the Bureau of Statistics of Pennsylvania, For the Years 1873–74* (Harrisburg, Pa.: B. F. Myers, State Printer, 1875), 590.

37. Ibid.

38. Voss, *American Exceptionalism*, 87. For a profile of John Best, see chapter 4 of this volume.

39. S. L. Gault Jr. FS LA 3396 to John Samuel, September 14, 1886,

John Samuel Papers, Box 1, Folder 7, Correspondence, June–Dec. 1886.

40. Jonathan Garlock, *Guide to the Local Assemblies of the Knights of Labor* (Westport, Conn.: Greenwood Press, 1982), 210, 662.

41. John Samuel to S. L. Gault, September 25, 1886, John Samuel Papers, Box 1, Folder 7, Correspondence, June–Dec. 1886.

42. Ibid.

43. For middle-class and community support of strikes, see Herbert G. Gutman, "The Workers' Search for Power: Labor in the Gilded Age," and "Labor in the Land of Lincoln: Coal Miners on the Prairie," in *Power and Culture: Essays on the American Working Class* (New York: Pantheon Books, 1987), 76–77, 136–38. For a view challenging the "Gutman thesis," see Faye Dudden, "Small Town Knights: The Knights of Labor in Homer, New York," *Labor History* 28 (summer 1987): 307–27.

44. For example see "Co-operation," *Daily Evening Voice*, January 24, 1866; Hiram Lord, "Union Co-operative Association," *Fincher's Trades' Review*, May 6, 1866, 184; "Co-operative Societies in France," *Workingman's Advocate*, May 12, 1866; "Banquet in Honor of the Machinists' & Blacksmiths' International Union," *Fincher's Trades' Review*, October 8, 1864, 74; Old Hunphrey, "To the Workingmen of Cleveland," *Fincher's Trades' Review*, December 2, 1865, 5; Sylvis "Address"; Jno. Orvis, "The Question," *American Workman*, June 26, 1869, 5; Iron Molders' Union, "President's Address," *Synopsis of the Proceedings of the Seventh Session of the Iron Molders' Union*, 1866, 14; idem, "Report of the Committee on Co-operation," *Synopsis of the Proceedings of the Eighth Session of the Iron Molders' Union*, 1867, 50.

45. Worker, "Why Not Manufacture? No. IV," *American Workman*, June 5, 1869, 6.

46. A Reader of the Review to the Editor, *Fincher's Trades' Review*, January 23, 1864, 31.

47. Earnest to Editor, *Fincher's Trades' Review*, February 18, 1865, 47.

48. "Journeymen Shoemakers' Co-operative Shoe Company," *Pamphlets in American History*, Cooperative Societies #252 (Sanford, N.C.: Microfilming Corp. of America, 1979–84), microform.

49. "The Moral Tendency of Co-operation," *Fincher's Trades' Review*, August 13, 1864, 42.

50. J. B., "Co-operation—The Marriage of Capital and Labor—A Workingman's Appeal," *American Workman*, June 26, 1869, 4.

51. For example, see Robert Curley to Editor, *Journal of United Labor*, June 15, 1880, 27.

52. For example, see the proposed charter for the Co-operative Store of Philadelphia, ca. 1865, which restricted membership to heads of families, "Charter: Cooperative Store of Philadelphia," *Pamphlets in American History*, Cooperative Societies #122 (Sanford, N.C.: Microfilming Corp. of America, 1979–84), microform. See chapter 4 of this volume for the exclusion of women from positions of authority in the cooperative shoe factories of Stoneham, Massachusetts.

53. "Co-operative Tract, No. 1," *Pamphlets in American History*, Cooperative Societies #20 (Sanford, N.C.: Microfilming Corp. of America, 1979–84), microform.

54. Free and Independent Labor Champion, Thomas Phillips Papers, Box 1, Folder 7, Wisconsin State Historical Society, Madison (hereafter cited as Thomas Phillips Papers).

55. This idea is developed for a later period in Dana Frank, "Gender, Consumer Organizing, and the Seattle Labor Movement, 1919–1929," in *Work Engendered: Towards a New History of American Labor*, ed. Ava Baron (Ithaca, N.Y.: Cornell University Press, 1991), 273–96; idem, *Purchasing Power: Consumer Organizing, Gender, and the Seattle Labor Movement, 1919–1929* (Cambridge: Cambridge University Press, 1994); and Ellen Furlough, "French Consumer Cooperation 1885–1930: From the 'Third Pillar' of Socialism to 'A Movement for all Consumers'" (paper presented at the International Conference on Consumer Cooperation in the Western World, 1840–1950: An Alternative to Capitalist Consumerism?, University of Kansas, Lawrence, April 7, 1990).

56. See Montgomery, "William H. Sylvis," 26–27; Susan Levine, "Labor's True Woman: Domesticity and Equal Rights in the Knights of Labor," *Journal of American History* 70 (September 1983): 323–39. See also Blewett, *Men, Women, and Work*, 246–52.

57. Women workers did establish cooperatives of their own, such as the collar workers of Troy, New York, in the 1860s. In the 1880s women founded the Our Girls' Cooperative Clothing Company of Chicago and the Martha Washington K. of L. Co-operative Overall Association of Indianapolis. Both of these cooperatives made a special point of inserting in their constitutions either "she or he," in the case of Our Girls,' or simply "she," in the case of Martha Washington, for every "he" mentioned in the standard constitution. See "Our Girls' Co-operative Clothing Mfg. Co. of Chicago Illinois," *Pamphlets in American History*, Cooperative Societies #161 (Sanford, N.C.: Microfilming Corp. of America, 1979–84), microform; "Rules and Regulations of the Jewel Co-operative Knitting Co. of St. Louis, Mo.," *Pamphlets in American History*, Cooperative Societies #111 (Sanford, N.C.: Microfilming Corp. of America, 1979–84), microform; "By-Laws of M.W.C.A.," *Pamphlets in American History*, Cooperative Societies #140 (Sanford, N.C.: Microfilming Corp. of America, 1979–84), microform; Horner, "Producers' Co-operatives," 91–92; and Carole Turbin, *Working Women of Collar City: Gender, Class, and Community in Troy, New York, 1864–1886* (Urbana: University of Illinois Press, 1992), 163–64. In Minneapolis during the 1880s, cooperative coopers assisted women laundry workers in starting a cooperative laundry. See Albert Shaw, "Cooperation in the Northwest," in *History of Cooperation in the United States*, ed. Herbert Adams (Baltimore: Johns Hopkins University Press, 1888), 269.

58. "To the Officers and Members of Local Assembly—Members of Hancock Assembly no 6272 K. of L.," June 23, 1887, John Samuel Papers. Box 2, Folder 1, Correspondence, 1887.

59. This parallels to some degree the argument made by Susan Levine in *Labor's True Woman: Carpet Weavers, Industrialization, and Labor Reform in the Gilded Age* (Philadelphia: Temple University Press, 1984).

60. For information about Allyn, see "Letter from C. Fannie Allyn," February 12, 1887, and "Death of a Graduate," November 1, 1879, *Stone-*

ham Independent; United States Ninth Census, 1870, vol. 21, Middlesex County, Massachusetts, 661; United States Tenth Census, 1880, vol. 17, Middlesex County, Massachusetts, 349; Geo. C. Kuechler, Secretary Co-operative Board, Cincinnati, Ohio, "Co-operative Fair," *Journal of United Labor,* May 10, 1886, 2065; "Co-operative Fair [Flyer]," February 21, 1886, John Samuel Papers, Box 1, Folder 6, Correspondence, Jan.–May 1886; and Martha Coons, "Section Two: Factories and Workers in the Nineteenth Century," in *Stoneham Massachusetts: A Shoe Town* (Stoneham: Stoneham Historical Commission, 1981), 96. See also chapters 3 and 4 of this volume.

61. "Butler and Lovering: A Flag Raising and Rally," *Stoneham Independent,* October 11, 1884.

62. "A Spicy Letter from C. Fannie Allyn," *Stoneham Independent,* August 8, 1885.

63. *Stoneham Independent:* "Why Workingmen Should Organize," January 15, 1881; "Letter from Fannie Allyn," June 26, 1886; "Lecture by C. Fannie Allyn," November 6, 1886.

64. The guild and its significance is considered in greater detail in chapter 3 of this volume. The Minneapolis Knights had such plans as well; see chapter 5 of this volume; *Journal of United Labor:* Henry E. Sharpe, May 25, 1884, 706–7; "Article III," July 10, 1884, 742; Henry E. Sharpe, September 10, 1884, 790.

65. J. Milton Putnam to Editor, *Journal of United Labor,* July 10, 1884, 743.

66. J. K. N., LA 2776, "Co-operation 'Boiled Down' by a Woman—Our M. A.," *Journal of United Labor,* November 25, 1884, 850.

67. Hugh Cameron, "What Co-operation Is," *Journal of United Labor,* October 10, 1884, 814.

68. H. C. "Cooperation," *Journal of United Labor,* December 10, 1884, 860.

69. See chapters 4 and 5 of this volume.

70. C. J. C. to Editor, Louisville, Ky., *Iron Molders' International Journal,* August 1867, 134.

71. "Journeymen Shoemakers' Co-operative Shoe Company."

72. George S. Blauvelt, RSLA 2892, Nyack, N.Y., December 13, 1885, John Samuel Papers, Box 1, Folder 5, Correspondence, June–Dec. 1885. See also Horner, "Producers' Cooperatives," 151.

73. Duncan McPhail, "Peoria Co-operative Coal Association," *Journal of United Labor,* May 25, 1885, 989.

74. Ibid.; see Horner, "Producers' Cooperatives," 148–49 for a somewhat different view on the Peoria miners.

75. Austin City, Texas, to John Samuel, August 23, 1885, John Samuel Papers, Box 1, Folder 5, Correspondence, June–Dec. 1885.

76. Bruce Laurie and Mark Schmitz, "Manufacture and Productivity: The Making of an Industrial Base, Philadelphia, 1850–1880," in *Philadelphia: Work, Space, Family, and Group Experience in the 19th Century,* ed. Theodore Hershberg (Oxford: Oxford University Press, 1981), 43–92.

77. William Sylvis, Editorial, *Iron Molders' International Journal,* August

1867, 119–21.

78. "Our True Policy," *Iron Molders' International Journal*, July 1866, 111–12, an unsigned editorial in the *Journal* that in all likelihood was written by Sylvis; for another cooperator's confidence, see A. H. Prager, "Co-operation," *Journal of United Labor*, October 10, 1886, 2183–84. During the depression of the 1870s, the failure of numerous molders' cooperatives and the members' willingness to pursue their own good over that of the union discouraged then president of the Molders' Union, William Saffin. See *Iron Molders' International Journal:* "Co-operation," December 1872, 7; "Co-operation," December 10, 1875, 518.

79. "Compact of the Equitable Co-operative Machine Manufacturing Association," *Fincher's Trades' Review*, February 24, 1866, 104.

80. For a discussion of Phillips's Christian roots, see Clifton K. Yearley Jr., "Thomas Phillips: A Yorkshire Shoemaker in Philadelphia," *Pennsylvania Magazine of History and Biography* 79 (April 1995): 167–96; and idem, *Britons in American Labor: A History of the Influence of the United Kingdom Immigrants on American Labor, 1820–1914*, Johns Hopkins University Studies in Historical and Political Science, series 75, no. 1 (Baltimore: Johns Hopkins University Press, 1957); Worker (Thomas Phillips), "The Labor Cause. Why Not Manufacture? No. III," *American Workman*, May 1869, 5; Worker, "Why not Manufacture? No. VIII," *American Workman*, October 2, 1869, 8.

81. The influence of religion on the labor movement in this period has been dealt with by Herbert G. Gutman, "Protestantism and the American Labor Movement: The Christian Spirit in the Gilded Age," in *Work, Culture and Society in Industrializing America* (Oxford: Basil Blackwell, 1966), 79–118, and Ken Fones-Wolf, *Trade Union Gospel: Christianity and Labor in Industrial Philadelphia, 1865–1915* (Philadelphia: Temple University Press, 1989).

82. Thomas Phillips, "Cooperation, the Remedy for the Evils of Society," ca. 1869, Cooperative Associations, Thomas Phillips Papers, Box 1, Folder 6.

83. Examples of this can be found throughout the period under study. For example, see C. M. Talmage to Editor, *Fincher's Trades' Review*, November 5, 1864, 91.

84. Phillips, "Cooperation, the Remedy," an insert between pages 12 and 13 and 39.

Chapter 3

1. Leonard Wheeler to J. P. McGaughey, Gilbertville, Mass., May 24, 1886, John Samuel Papers, Box 1, Folder 6, Correspondence, Jan.–May 1886, Wisconsin State Historical Society, Madison (hereafter cited as John Samuel Papers).

2. The Knights of Labor was an awkwardly structured and cumbersome organization. As historians have recently argued, it was institutionally susceptible to internecine conflict. Craig Phelan characterizes the Knights as challenged by a "multiplicity of goals" advocated by distinct and conflicting constituencies. I believe, however, that he overemphasizes the distinctiveness

of various constituencies within the order and their exclusive demand of one strategy over another. Craig Phelan, *Grand Master Workman: Terence Powderly and the Knights of Labor* (Westport, Conn.: Greenwood Press, 2000), 129–70.

3. Knights of Labor, *Record of the Proceedings of the General Assembly of the Knights of Labor of America. Eleventh Regular Session, Held at Minneapolis, Minnesota, October 4 to 19, 1887*, 1594, Terence Powderly Papers, Catholic University of America, Washington, D.C., microfilm, reel 67 (hereafter cited as Terence Powderly Papers).

4. The declaration of support for cooperation was adopted wholesale, according to Powderly, from the Preamble of the Industrial Brotherhood. See Terence V. Powderly, *Thirty Years of Labor, 1859–1889* (New York: Augustus M. Kelley Publishers, 1967), 230.

5. Knights of Labor, "Annual Report of the Grand Master Workman-Uriah S. Stevens," in *Record of the Proceedings of the Second Regular Session of the General Assembly of the ********* Held at St. Louis, Mo., January 14–17, 1879*, 55–56, Terence Powderly Papers, reel 67.

6. Knights of Labor, *Record of the Proceedings of the Third Regular Session of the General Assembly Held at Chicago, Ill., Sept. 2–6, 1879*, Terence V. Powderly Papers, 149, reel 67.

7. Knights of Labor, *Record of the Proceedings of the Fourth Regular Session of the General Assembly Held at Pittsburgh, Pa., Sept. 7–11, 1880*, Terence Powderly Papers, 169–72, reel 67.

8. Ibid.

9. Craig Phelan, in his biography of Powderly, portrays the labor leader as knowing "almost nothing about cooperation." This claim is unsupported by the evidence. See Phelan, *Grand Master Workman*, 138.

10. Clare Horner, "Producers' Cooperatives in the United States, 1865–1890" (Ph.D. diss., New York University, 1978), 188–89.

11. Ibid., 190, 204; Norman Ware, *The Labor Movement in the United States* (New York: Vintage Books, 1929), 327; Knights of Labor, *Record of the Proceedings of the Eighth Regular Session of the General Assembly, Held at Philadelphia, PA, Sept, 1–10, 1884*, 679–80, Terence Powderly Papers, reel 67. In July 1883 the total fund held by local assemblies equaled $2,292.35.

12. Knights of Labor, *Record of the Proceedings of the Seventh Regular Session of the General Assembly, Held at Cincinnati, Ohio, Sept. 4–11, 1883*, 462, 491, Terence Powderly Papers, Reel 67.

13. Horner, "Producers' Cooperatives," 190–91.

14. "The Industrial Co-operator," October 1880, vol. 1, no. 1, *Pamphlets in American History*, Cooperative Societies #242 (Sanford, N.C.: Microfilming Corp. of America, 1979–84), microform; Horner, "Producers' Cooperatives," 192; Knights of Labor, *Proceedings of the Eighth Regular Session*, 643–50. For the most recent survey of communitarian experiments in the nineteenth-century United States, see Edward K. Spann, *Brotherly Tomorrows: Movements for a Cooperative Society in America, 1820–1920* (New York: Columbia University Press, 1989), and Carl J. Guarneri, *The Utopian Alternative: Fourierism in Nineteenth-Century America* (Ithaca, N.Y.: Cornell University Press, 1991). For a standard work, see Arthur Bestor, *Backwoods*

Utopias: The Sectarian Origins and the Owenite Phase of Communitarian Socialism in America: 1663–1829 (Philadelphia: University of Pennsylvania Press, 1950, 1970).

15. Henry E. Sharpe, ed., "Co-operation," *Journal of United Labor,* October 1883, 580–81. I have assumed that as editor of this column, Henry Sharpe is also the author of unsigned editorials.

16. See Knights of Labor, *Proceedings of the Eighth Regular Session,* 646–50; see also "The Industrial Co-operator."

17. Horner, "Producers' Cooperatives," 192; Knights of Labor, *Proceedings of the Eighth Regular Session,* 643–49. Sharpe was accused of kidnapping, "selling wife's printing press," "brutal and systematic ill-treatment of brothers and sisters," "refusing even an egg to a sick brother," and "compelling a sister to rise from her meals to feed his dog," among other charges; see Robert Weir, *Knights Unhorsed: Internal Conflict in a Gilded Age Social Movement* (Detroit: Wayne State University Press, 2000), 118–25.

18. Henry E. Sharpe, ed., "Co-operation," *Journal of United Labor,* January 1884, 628.

19. Henry E. Sharpe, ed., "Co-operation," *Journal of United Labor,* March 1884, 664.

20. Henry E. Sharpe, ed., "Co-operation," *Journal of United Labor,* January 1884, 628.

21. Ibid.; Henry E. Sharpe, ed., "Co-operation," *Journal of United Labor,* November 1883, 598–99.

22. Henry E. Sharpe, ed., "The Fatality of the Wage System," *Journal of United Labor,* April 25, 1884, 706–7.

23. Horner, "Producers' Cooperatives," 192. As president of the Cooperative Board, Sharpe edited a regular column in the *Journal of United Labor* entitled "Co-operation."

24. Horner, "Producers' Cooperatives," 191–93. The guild plan was first proposed in the June 1884 issue of the *Journal of United Labor* and later presented in substantially the same form at the General Assembly in Philadelphia. Henry E. Sharpe, ed., "Article I," *Journal of United Labor,* June 10, 1884, 716; Henry E. Sharpe, ed., "Article II," *Journal of United Labor,* June 25, 1884, 728; Knights of Labor, *Proceedings of the Eighth Regular Session,* 604; Henry E. Sharpe, ed., "Co-operation," *Journal of United Labor,* August 25, 1884, 776–77.

25. Sharpe, "Article I," 716; Sharpe, "Article II," 728.

26. Knights of Labor, *Proceedings of the Eighth Regular Session,* 604.

27. Ibid., 600.

28. Ibid., 600–603.

29. Ibid., 603.

30. J. Samuels, *Journal of United Labor,* July 25, 1884, 754; Richard J. Hinton, 2020, *Journal of United Labor,* July 25, 1884, 754; "Biographical sketch of Richard J. Hinton," *Official Historical Handbook Independent Order Knights of Labor,* Knights of Labor Papers, Box 1, Wisconsin State Historical Society Madison (thanks to an anonymous manuscript reader for this citation); Timothy Messer-Kruse, *The Yankee International: Marxism and the*

American Reform Tradition, 1848–1876 (Chapel Hill: University of North Carolina Press, 1998), 115; Knights of Labor, *Proceedings of the Eighth Regular Session*, 752–54. Beaumont was a current and Rockwood a former grand officer of the Knights; See *Journal of United Labor:* "Addresses of Grand Officers," June 1883, 512, and "Addresses of Grand Officers," May 10, 1884, 696; Henry Sharpe to John Samuel, June 19, 1884, John Samuel Papers, Box 1, Folder 3, Correspondence, 1882–84. Fecker and Fayram were both advocates of cooperation; see Henry Fecker, "Make the Co-operation Fund Imperative," *Journal of United Labor*, May 1884, 695, and Amos Fayram to John Samuel, December 13, 1881, John Samuel Papers, Box 1, Folder 2, Correspondence, 1873–81. For Rankin see chapter 5 of this volume. Foster and Barry were both grand officers; see "Addresses of Grand Officers," *Journal of United Labor*, March 1884, 668. Victory Drury and the Home Club of New York opposed the Integral plan, but whether that opposition was to the plan or to Sharpe himself, historians disagree. See Phelan, *Grand Master Workman*, 140, and Weir, *Knights Unhorsed*, 121, 125.

31. Knights of Labor, *Proceedings of the Eighth Regular Session*, 755.

32. Ibid., 752; Henry E. Sharpe, *Journal of United Labor*, September 10, 1884, 790. Gerald Grob cited the order's rejection of Sharpe's plan as evidence of a membership disinterested in cooperation itself. The unanimous approval of cooperation by the General Assembly, however, discredits that judgment. See Gerald Grob, *Workers and Utopia* (New York: Quadrangle/New York Times Book Company, 1961), 45.

33. Henry E. Sharpe, *Journal of United Labor*, September 10, 1884, 790.

34. *Journal of United Labor:* Henry E. Sharpe, "Comments by the Editor," August 10, 1884, 766–68; Robert Graham and Henry Ringemann to Editor, August 25, 1884, 777–78; John Watford and Arthur Peters to Editor, August 25, 1884, 778.

35. Oscar H. Bowman, R.S.L.A., 2112 to Editor, *Journal of United Labor*, August 10, 1884, 766.

36. Quoted in Horner, "Producers' Cooperatives," 194.

37. Weir, *Knights Unhorsed*, 121–24.

38. Henry Sharpe recommended that the Executive Board take up the Cannelburg mine as a cooperative. See Phelan, *Grand Master Workman*, 141.

39. The story of the Cannelburg mine has been told in a number of places. This summary is culled from Horner, "Producers' Cooperatives," 194–204, esp. 196–97; see also Ware, *Labor Movement in the United States*, 329–33. This glassworkers' assembly had recently won a significant five-month struggle against their employers' association with aid from the Knights. Phelan tells a detailed story of the mine and its failure; see *Grand Master Workman*, 141–46.

40. "The Cannelburg Miners," *Journal of United Labor*, April 1884, 676; Horner, "Producers' Cooperatives," 197.

41. Frederick Turner to John Samuel, December 18, 1884, John Samuel Papers, Box 1, Folder 3, Correspondence, 1882–84; Knights of Labor, "Report of the General Secretary Treasurer," in *Record of the Proceedings of the Ninth Regular Session of the General Assembly, Held at Hamilton, Ontario, Oct. 5–13, 1885, 38,* Terence Powderly Papers, Reel 67.

42. Quoted in Horner, "Producers' Cooperatives," 196.

43. Circular from Secretary McClelland, May 28, 1884, John Samuel Papers, Box 1, Folder 3, Correspondence, 1882–84.

44. John Samuel to Wm. Lewis, Supt. Cannelburg Mine, May 23, 1885, John Samuel Papers, Box 1, Folder 4, Correspondence, Jan.–May 1885.

45. Craig Phelan argues that the Knights' Executive Board supported the mine at first in order to appease disappointed cooperators in the order; see Phelan, *Grand Master Workman*, 141. The difficulties facing the mine are well documented in Horner, "Producers' Cooperatives," 200–204.

46. For the limitations of the board, see Horner, "Producers' Cooperatives," 205–9; See also Hugh Cameron to John Samuel, July 14, 1885, John Samuel Papers, Box 1, Folder 5, Correspondence, June–Dec. 1885.

47. J. P. McGaughey, Sec. Coop Board, Minneapolis, to John Samuel, March 28, 1886, John Samuel Papers, Box 1, Folder 6, Correspondence, Jan.–May 1886; Knights of Labor, *Proceedings of the Eleventh Regular Session*, 1593.

48. Samuel proposed this in countless places. For two examples, see Letter to Editor from John Samuel, *Journal of United Labor*, August 15, 1880, 50, and John Samuel to Joseph Ferris, Recording Secretary of LA 271, May 30, 1885, John Samuel Papers, Box 1, Folder 4, Correspondence, Jan.–May 1885. He also corresponded with leading English cooperators, such as E. V. Neale, general secretary of the Central Cooperative Board. See John Samuel to L. Stefflre, Manistee, Mich., February 6, 1882, John Samuel Papers, Box 1, Folder 3, Correspondence, 1882–84.

49. John Samuel to Editor, *Journal of United Labor*, July 15, 1881, 133.

50. John Samuel to James Beck, West Belleville, Ill., August 15, 1883, John Samuel Papers, Box 1, Folder 3, Correspondence, 1882–84.

51. John Samuel, "Co-operation. The Revised Constitution," *Journal of United Labor*, September 1882, 297; Peter D. Cattanoch, Troy, N.Y. to John Samuel, December 5, 1884, John Samuel Papers, Box 1, Folder 3, Correspondence, 1882–84. For McGaughey, see Knights of Labor, *Record of the Proceedings of the Special Session of the General Assembly, Held at Cleveland, O., May 25 to June 3, 1886*, 71, Terence Powderly Papers, Reel 67; Knights of Labor, *Proceedings of Eleventh Regular Session*, 1593; Frederick Turner, Gen Sec Treasurer, Philadelphia, Pa. to John Samuel, December 18, 1884, John Samuel Papers, Box 1, Folder 3, Correspondence, 1882–84; John Samuel to Joseph Ferris, May 30, 1885, John Samuel Papers, Box 1, Folder 4, Correspondence, Jan.–May. 1885; John Samuel to R. S. Cruikshank, July 10, 1885, John Samuel Papers, Box 1, Folder 5, Correspondence, June–Dec. 1885. Bruce Laurie, in *Artisans into Workers*, mistakenly argues that "Samuel resisted using funds in the national coffers for local projects, which threw assemblies back on their own resources" (155).

52. Faye Dudden, "Small Town Knights: The Knights of Labor in Homer, New York," *Labor History* 28 (summer 1987): 313–15; Knights of Labor, *Record of the Proceedings of the Tenth Regular Session of the General Assembly, Held at Richmond, Va., Oct 4–20, 1886*, 77, 98, Terence Powderly Papers, Reel 67; Knights of Labor, *Proceedings of the Eleventh Regular Session*, 1398.

53. Horner, "Producers' Cooperatives," 200–204; A variety of factors

have been cited to explain the mine's failure, none satisfactorily. See Ware, *Labor Movement in the United States*, 332–33; Phelan, *Grand Master Workman*, 141–46. After the Knights gave up on the mine, some of the original miners leased it back and ran it successfully for a few years. See Grob, *Workers and Utopia*, 46.

54. The story of the Homer Wagon Works as told by Dudden differs from that of the two reports in the Knights *Proceedings*, which she does not cite. She suggests that their failure to sell enough stock caused them to close their original cooperative factory, through which they were to produce a patented wagon. They then reopened another one with the financial help of the Knights. The reports mention a problem with financing but nothing of the closing and reopening of the factory. See Dudden, "Small Town Knights," 319, 323–24. See also, Knights of Labor, *Proceedings of the Eleventh Regular Session*, 1318–19, 1397–98.

55. Dudden argues that the conflict over moving the factory led to its demise in 1887. There is evidence, however, that the factory was run by the Knights up to 1894. See Knights of Labor, *Proceedings of the Thirteenth Regular Session of the General Assembly Held at Atlanta, Ga., 1889*, 12–13, Terence Powderly Papers, reel 67; and "Address to the Independent Order of Knights of Labor," in *Official Historical Hand-Book Independent Order Knights of Labor*, 1898, Knights of Labor Papers, Box 1, Folder 1887–1902.

56. Horner makes a similar argument. See "Producers' Cooperatives," 202–3, 222–25.

57. Knights of Labor, *Proceedings of the Tenth Regular Session*, 292; Grob, *Workers and Utopia*, 45; Horner, "Producers' Cooperatives," 208–9; John R. Commons et al., *History of Labor in the United States* (New York: Macmillan Company, 1918), 2:436; Knights of Labor, *Proceedings of the Eleventh Regular Session*, 1806.

58. Laurie, *Artisans into Workers*, 156–57. For an illuminating discussion of this period, see Richard Schneirov, *Labor and Urban Politics: Class Conflict and the Origins of Modern Liberalism in Chicago, 1864–97* (Urbana: University of Illinois Press, 1998), 183–210; the exact number of cooperatives is impossible to determine, though Clare Horner has compiled a fairly comprehensive list of producer cooperatives. Between 1884 and 1888, 290 producer cooperatives were established. In 1886 alone, workers established at least ninety-six cooperative factories and workshops. Horner, "Producers' Cooperatives," appendix 1, 229–42. There were probably a few hundred cooperative stores opened in the mid-1880s.

59. Meridian, Miss. to John Samuel, January 11, 1885, John Samuel Papers, Box 1, Folder 4, Correspondence, Jan.–May 1885.

60. Horner, "Producers' Cooperatives," 42; *Journal of United Labor*: Thos. Dinan, DMW, "Reports of District Master Workmen," April 15, 1885, 969; M. E. Frost to Editor, "Reports of the DMW," June 1883, 495; L. V. Moulton to Editor, "Reports of District Master Workmen," April 25, 1885, 969–70; "Self-Help," December 25, 1884, 870.

61. The eight trades most frequently engaged in cooperative production during these years were: coal mining, printing and publishing, boot and shoe making, cigarmaking, coopering, glass making, clothing manufacturing, and

iron molding, in descending order; see Horner, "Producers' Cooperatives," 104–9, 243. For the experience of coal miners in the nineteenth century, see Herbert G. Gutman, "Labor in the Land of Lincoln: Coal Miners on the Prairie," in *Power and Culture: Essays on the American Working Class* (New York: Pantheon Books, 1987), 117–212; Anthony F. C. Wallace, *St. Clair: A Nineteenth-Century Coal Town's Experience with a Disaster-Prone Industry* (Ithaca, N.Y.: Cornell University Press, 1987); John McBride, "Coal Miners," in *The Labor Movement: The Problem of Today*, ed. George McNeil (Boston: A. M. Bridgman & Co., 1886) 241–67.

62. WHA to John Samuel, November 15, 1880, John Samuel Papers, Box 1, Folder 2, Correspondence, 1873–81; *Journal of United Labor:* Wm. Block of L.A. No. 849, Osage City, Kan. to Brother Litchman, May 15, 1881, 119; "Local Co-operative Enterprise," November 1882, 337; "Local Co-operative Enterprise," February 1883, 405; Roy Pat Oneil, L.A. 1868, Gillespie, Ill. to John Samuel, June 12, 1885 [date letter answered], John Samuel Papers, Box 1, Folder 5, Correspondence, June–Dec. 1885.

63. Wm. H. Smith, Org, McHenry, Ky. to John Samuel, August 6, 1885, John Samuel Papers, Box 1, Folder 5, Correspondence, June–Dec. 1885.

64. Wm. H. Smith, Organizer, L.A. 3688, McHenry, Kentucky to John Samuel, July 6, 1885, John Samuel Papers, Box 1, Folder 5, Correspondence, June–Dec. 1885.

65. *Membership List and Minutes of the Missouri Co-operative Coal Association*, 1883, John Samuel Papers, microfilm, reel 3, Notebooks, vols. 17–18.

66. John H. Abernathy Jr., "The Knights of Labor in Alabama" (master's thesis, University of Alabama-Tuscaloosa, 1960), 65–67.

67. Ibid., 68–69; Melton McLaurin, *The Knights of Labor in the South* (Westport, Conn.: Greenwood Press, 1978), 125–26.

68. For a different argument, see Horner, "Producers' Cooperatives," 170–218. She draws the distinction between localists and centralizers quite clearly.

69. *Membership List and Minutes of the Missouri Co-operative Coal Association;* James Beck to Adolph Madera, August 13, 1883, John Samuel Papers, Box 1, Folder 3, Correspondence, 1882–84.

70. Emil Lesser, Sec and treas. Mutual Land and Improvement Company, to John Samuel, August 3, 1888, John Samuel Papers, Box 2, Folder 2, Correspondence, 1888.

71. Abernathy, "Knights of Labor in Alabama," 69. This appropriation was never made.

72. L. V. Moulton to Editor, *Journal of United Labor,* April 25, 1885, 969–70. For a discussion of marketing cooperative products, see Horner, "Producers' Cooperatives," 159–69.

73. See also Timothy T. O'Mally, District Recording Secretary, District Assembly 38, to Editor, "Correspondence," *Journal of United Labor,* January 1883, 384; "To the Knights of Labor Wherever Found" [a circular], May 22, 1886, John Samuel Papers, Box 1, Folder 6, Correspondence, Jan.–May 1886; [Circular from] Office of Exec. Com., C.L.P. Co. [Cooperative Lawrence Piano Co.], April 19, 1884, John Samuel Papers, Box 1, Folder 3, Correspondence, 1882–84; J. R. Ray, sec. National K. of L. Co-operative

Tobacco Company, Raleigh, N.C., to John Samuel, August 19, 1885, John Samuel Papers, Box 1, Folder 5, Correspondence, June–Dec. 1885; "To the Knights of Labor of America" [a circular from Local Assembly 4865, Waterford, N.Y.], April 29, 1886, John Samuel Papers, Box 1, Folder 6, Correspondence, Jan.–May 1886; Knights of Labor, *Proceedings of the Eleventh Regular Session*, 1611.

74. Horner, "Producers' Cooperatives," 159–69; W. L. Sculli, MW L.A. 8197, Gibson City, Ford Co, Ill., to John Samuel, September 28, 1886, John Samuel Papers, Box 1, Folder 7, Correspondence, June–Dec. 1886; Thos. Clark, RS LA 2945 Canton, Kansas to John Samuel, November 30, 1887, John Samuel Papers, Box 2, Folder 1, Correspondence, 1887; L. H. Sexton, *Journal of United Labor*, April 25, 1885, 963; "Reasons Why You Should Use Co-operative-Made Goods in Preference to All Others," ca. 1887, Toledo, Ohio, John Samuel Papers. Box 2, Folder 1, Correspondence, 1887; Knights of Labor, *Proceedings of the Eleventh Regular Session*, 1698; DA 148, Olean, New York, to Editor, *Journal of United Labor*, April 23, 1887, 2362.

75. Geo. C. Kuechler, Secretary Cooperative Committee, Fannie Allyn LA 4457, Cincinnati, Ohio, February 21, 1886, John Samuel Papers, Box 1, Folder 6, Correspondence, Jan.–May 1886; Geo. C. Kuechler, LA 4457, Cooperative Board, Cincinnati, Ohio, to John Samuel, April 15, 1886, John Samuel Papers, Box 1, Folder 6, Correspondence, Jan.–May 1886; Geo. C. Kuechler, "Co-operative Fair," *Journal of United Labor*, May 10, 1886, 2065; Amos Warner, "Three Phases of Co-operation in the West," in *History of Cooperation in the United States*, ed. Herbert Adams, Johns Hopkins University Studies in Historical and Political Science, vol. 6 (Baltimore: Johns Hopkins University, 1888), 403–5; Horner, "Producers' Cooperatives," 164–65.

76. "Cooperative Fair Business Circular," 1886, John Samuel Papers, Box 1, Folder 7, Correspondence, June–Dec. 1886; Circular for "Co-operative Fair," February 21, 1886, John Samuel Papers, Box 1, Folder 6, Correspondence, Jan.–May 1886; Letters from Geo. C. Kuechler, Secretary Cooperative Committee, Fannie Allyn LA 4457, Cincinnati, Ohio, February 21, 1886 and April 15, 1886, John Samuel Papers, Box 1, Folder 6, Correspondence, Jan.–May 1886.

77. Knights of Labor, *Proceedings of the Eleventh Regular Session*, 1582.

78. Both of these cooperatives made a special point of inserting in their constitutions either "she or he," in the case of Our Girls', or simply "she," in the case of Martha Washington, for every "he" mentioned in the standard constitution. "Our Girls' Co-operative Clothing Mfg. Co. of Chicago Illinois," *Pamphlets in American History*, Cooperative Societies #161 (Sanford, N.C.: Microfilming Corp. of America, 1979–84), microform; "Rules and Regulations of the Jewel Co-operative Knitting Co. of St. Louis, Mo.," *Pamphlets in American History*, Cooperative Societies #111 (Sanford, N.C.: Microfilming Corp. of America, 1979–84), microform; "By-Laws of M.W.C.A.," *Pamphlets in American History*, Cooperative Societies #140 (Sanford, N.C.: Microfilming Corp. of America, 1979–84), microform; Horner, "Producers' Cooperatives," 91–92.

79. Horner, "Producers' Cooperatives," 216–17.

80. The Watch-Case cooperative was formed before the district estab-

lished the association. The company allowed shareholders one vote, as was customary in most cooperatives, and paid interest on its stock. It operated outside of the district's authority, but how far and to what effect is impossible to determine. Horner suggests that its "incentives to stockholders" accounted for the cooperative's success. See Horner, "Producers' Cooperatives," 217–18; *District Assembly Forty-Nine, Knights of Labor. New York and Vicinity* (New York: Concord Co-operative Printing Company, 1888), Knights of Labor, Miscellaneous, Catherwood Library Cornell Labor Documentation Center, Ithaca, N.Y.

81. See chapters 4 and 5 of this volume for examples of this in both Stoneham, Mass., and Minneapolis, Minn.; see also Horner, "Producers' Cooperatives," 215. In 1888, thirty-four producer cooperatives were formed; only a handful opened in 1889. See Horner, "Producers' Cooperatives," appendix 1.

82. Knights of Labor, *Proceedings of Sixth Regular Session*, 291; Ralph Beaumont to Editor, *Journal of United Labor*, January 1883, 383–84; "To Whom it May Concern!" [a circular from the Coopers' Co-operative Association], April 3, 1883, John Samuel Papers, Box 1, Folder 3, Correspondence, 1882–84; *Journal of United Labor:* "Causes of the Failure of Co-operative Enterprises," January 1884, 626; "Causes of the Failure of Co-operative Enterprises," February 1884, 640–41; and Hugh Cameron, "Cameron on Co-operation," October 25, 1884, 826–27; J. H. H. Hamer, Recording Secretary LA 852 to John Samuel, May 12, 1887, John Samuel Papers, Box 2, Folder 1, Correspondence, 1887; Knights of Labor, *Proceedings of the Eleventh Regular Session*, 1558–59.

83. "To the members of the K. of L., wherever found" [from] P. F. Gannon, MWLA 2085, Jas. Hanley, MWLA 3323, Jos. Normandy, MWLA 3597, John O'Keefe, DMWDA 99, Providence, R.I., September 21, 1885, John Samuel Papers, Box 1, Folder 5, Correspondence, June–Dec. 1885; John Samuel to Henry Mente, February 8, 1886, John Samuel Papers, Box 1, Folder 6, Correspondence, Jan.–May 1886; Geo. C. Kuechler, Sec. Fair Committee on Co-operation Fannie Allyn Assembly, 4457 to John Samuel, February 26, 1886, John Samuel Papers, Box 1, Folder 6, Correspondence, Jan.–May 1886; John Samuel to Louis Werner, Bonne Terre, Mo. LA 4180, May 17, 1886, John Samuel Papers, Box 1, Folder 6, Correspondence, Jan.–May 1886; Knights of Labor, *Proceedings of the Ninth Regular Session*, 36.

84. J. H. H. Hamer to John Samuel, September 27, 1887, John Samuel Papers, Box 2, Folder 1, Correspondence, 1887.

85. The significance of how social movements frame defeat is discussed by Kim Voss, *The Making of American Exceptionalism: The Knights of Labor and Class Formation in the Nineteenth Century* (Ithaca, N.Y.: Cornell University Press, 1993), 224–28, 240–45; and idem, "Claim Making and the Framing of Defeats: The Interpretation of Losses by American and British Labor Activists, 1886–1895," in *Challenging Authority: The Historical Study of Contentious Politics*, ed. Michael P. Hanagan et al. (Minneapolis: University of Minnesota Press, 1998), 136–48.

86. Knights of Labor, "Report of the General Master Workman," in *Record of the Proceedings of the General Assembly of the Knights of Labor of Amer-*

ica Twelfth Regular Session, Held at Indianapolis, Indiana, November 13 to 27, 1888, 8–9, Terence Powderly Papers, reel 67.

87. Beckmeyer was recording secretary for District Assembly 51 of Newark, New Jersey, in 1887. Henry Beckmeyer to Terence Powderly, January 21, 1887, Terence Powderly Papers. Thanks to Kim Voss for this reference; Henry A. Beckmeyer, "Our Co-operative Column," *Journal of United Labor*, February 28, 1889, 2794; idem, "Our Co-operative Column," *Journal of United Labor*, December 20, 1888, 2754.

88. Beckmeyer, "Our Co-operative Column," February 28, 1889, 2794.

89. Beckmeyer, "Our Co-operative Column," *Journal of United Labor*, January 3, 1889, 271.

90. The Cooperative Board ceased to exist in 1890, though it was ineffectively revived in 1893. See Weir, *Knights Unhorsed*, 124.

Chapter 4

1. "People's Column," *Stoneham Independent*, September 5, 1874 (letter from Grumbler indicates that Farm Hill was populated mostly by poll tax payers); "The Fourth of July in Stoneham," *Stoneham Amateur*, July 12, 1873; Susan Davis, *Parades and Power: Street Theatre in Nineteenth-Century Philadelphia* (Philadelphia: Temple University Press, 1986).

2. "The Fourth of July," *Stoneham Amateur*, July 12, 1873.

3. Ibid.

4. Ibid.; on Marden see *Stoneham Independent*, January 22, 1887; "The Fourth of July" *Stoneham Amateur*, July 12, 1873. General Neverready was Robert Strickland, whose personal property holdings in 1873 indicate that he was a small tradesmen; see *Valuation of the Town of Stoneham, and State, County and Town Tax for the Year 1873* (Stoneham: Gray & Metcalf, Printers, Sentinel Office, 1873), 48; William B. Stevens, *History of Stoneham Massachusetts with Biographical Sketches of Many of its Pioneers and Prominent Men* (Stoneham, Mass.: F. L. & W. E. Whittier, 1891) 247; "Oration," Stoneham Amateur, July 12, 1873.

5. "Oration," *Stoneham Amateur*, July 12, 1873; *Record of Service of Stoneham Soldiers in the Civil War, 1861–1865* (Stoneham, Mass.: Press of F. L. & W. E. Whittier, 1891), 10, 21; *Stoneham City Directory*, 1869, 92, State Library of Massachusetts, Boston; "Stoneham Cooperative Shoe Factory," *Stoneham Amateur*, January 10, 1874; "Records of the Stoneham Co-operative Shoe Company, from 1872 to 1889," 16, Stoneham Historical Society, Stoneham; Martha Coons, "Section Two: Factories and Workers in the Nineteenth Century," in *Stoneham Massachusetts: A Shoe Town* (Stoneham, Mass.: Stoneham Historical Commission, 1981), 91; Stevens, *History of Stoneham*, 132, 279.

6. Coons, "Factories and Workers," 80–85; Stevens, *History of Stoneham*, 91–92. See also Alan Dawley, *Class and Community: The Industrial Revolution in Lynn* (Cambridge: Harvard University Press, 2000); Mary Blewett, *Men, Women, and Work: Class, Gender, and Protest in the New England Shoe Industry, 1780–1910* (Urbana: University of Illinois Press, 1988).

7. Coons, "Factories and Workers," 84–85. See Dawley, *Class and Com-*

munity, 90–96, for a description of the factory system's growth in Lynn, Massachusetts. See also Stevens, *History of Stoneham*, 91, 346; Francis A. Walker, *Ninth Census—Vol. 1, The Statistics of the Population of the United States* (Washington, D.C.: Government Printing Office, 1872), 167. In 1875 there were more women than men living in Stoneham; see Carroll D. Wright, *Compendium of the Census of Massachusetts: 1875* (Boston: Albert J. Wright, State Printer, 1877), 24.

8. For biographical information on John Best, see Stevens, *History of Stoneham*, 304–6. On Samuel Trull, see *Stoneham Soldiers*, 10, and United States Ninth Census, 1870, manuscripts, vol. 21, Middlesex County, Mass., 639. For his early activities in town politics, see *Stoneham Amateur:* "Labor Reform Caucus," October 22, 1870; October 29, 1870; "Caucus," March 7, 1874. On William Marden, see *Stoneham Independent*, January 22, 1887.

9. Coons, "Factories and Workers," 91; *Stoneham City Directory*, 1869, 92; Blewett, *Men, Women, and Work*, 168–69, 187–88; see also *Stoneham Amateur:* July 23, 1870; Bob to Editor, August 13, 1870; "Calico Ball," February 25, 1871; March 2, 1872.

10. Coons, "Factories and Workers," 91; *Stoneham Amateur:* October 29, 1870; March 2, 1872; October 22, 1870, supplement no. 23.

11. Don Lescohier, *The Knights of St. Crispin, 1867–1874: A Study in the Industrial Causes of Trade Unionism*, Bulletin of the University of Wisconsin, no. 355, Economics and Political Science Series (Madison, Wis., 1910) vol. 7, no. 1:38–40; Dawley, *Class and Community*, 186–87; Coons, "Factories and Workers," 91.

12. Blewett, *Men, Women, and Work*, 151–52, 168–69, 183, 187–88, 189–90; Coons, "Factories and Workers," 91; "Independence Day," *Stoneham Independent*, July 11, 1874.

13. See "Records of the Stoneham Co-operative," 1, for a list of the original members. See also "Stoneham Co-operative Shoe Manufactory," *Stoneham Amateur*, January 10, 1874. Eighteen of the twenty-five men were listed as "works in shoe factory" in the United States Ninth Census, 1870, 589, 591, 597, 605, 612, 613, 622, 625, 630, 631, 636, 638, 644, 656, 658, 674, 681. Coons, "Factories and Workers," 92, writes that in the 1869 directory, ten of these men were listed as shoemakers, two as finishers, two as sole cutters, two as shoe cutters, one as a pegger, and one as an engineer. This suggests that many of the men may have been broadly trained shoe workers who could no longer find employment using all of their skills. In their cooperative they worked only as factory artisans, not as shoemakers, and did not attempt to recreate antiquated methods of production. See Steven J. Ross, *Workers on the Edge: Work, Leisure, and Politics in Industrializing Cincinnati, 1788–1890* (New York: Columbia University Press, 1985), 98, 112–15, for a description of changes in the shoe industry in the 1870s. For places of birth, see United States Ninth Census, 1870, 589, 591, 597, 605, 612, 613, 622, 624, 625, 626, 630, 631, 636, 638, 644, 656, 658, 674, 681 (for birthplace of A. B. Jones, see *Stoneham Soldiers*, 7). See Coons, "Factories and Workers," 99, for birthplaces of shoe workers.

14. United States Ninth Census, 1870, 636; *Stoneham Soldiers*, 38; *Valuation of the Town of Stoneham, and State, County, and Town Tax for the Year 1867*

(Woburn, Mass.: James M. Cooms, Printer, 1867); *Valuation of the Town of Stoneham, and State, County, and Town Tax for the Year 1873*, 11; *Stoneham Amateur:* "Stoneham Co-operative Shoe Manufactory," January 10, 1874; February 14, 1874; *Stoneham Independent:* "Town Officers," August 8, 1874; "Town Meeting," March 13, 1875.

15. This analysis is based on data found on forty-seven members of the Stoneham Cooperative Boot and Shoe Company (there were approximately sixty members in all). The data come from the federal census from Middlesex County, 1870 and 1880, the *Valuation of the Town of Stoneham and State, County, and Town Tax* from 1867 to 1889, and from information gathered from the *Stoneham Amateur* and *Stoneham Independent.* These figures on all shoe workers in Stoneham have been tabulated from the 1870 federal manuscript census for Stoneham, Middlesex County, except for the figure from 1885, which was calculated from the *Census of Massachusetts: Population and Social Statistics, Part II* (Boston: State Printers, 1887), 266–68.

16. Property holdings information was collected from the various editions of the *Valuation of the Town of Stoneham and State, County, and Town Tax* from 1867 to 1889. See also Coons, "Factories and Workers," 99.

17. At least four of the cooperators were born in Stoneham: Orin A. Green, Ephraim Perry, Calvin H. Conant, and John F. Marston; see *Stoneham Soldiers*, 14, 16, 21, 33; Massachusetts Bureau of the Statistics of Labor, *Annual Report*, 1886, 220, microfiche.

18. *Stoneham City Directory*, 1869, 91–93; *Stoneham City Directory*, 1886–87, 230, 232–34, State Library of Massachusetts, Boston; *Stoneham City Directory*, 1888–89, 238–39, 241–44, State Library of Massachusetts, Boston. See the following articles in the *Stoneham Amateur:* "Labor Reform Caucus," October 22, 1870, October 29, 1870, March 2, 1872; "Caucus," March 7, 1874. See also the following articles in the *Stoneham Independent:* "Local," September 12, 1874; "Caucus," October 3, 1874; "Republican Caucus," October 24, 1874; "Town Meeting," March 13, 1875; "Town Meeting," August 21, 1875; "Workingmen's Party," September 29, 1877; "Town of Stoneham," January 29, 1876; "Town Meeting," March 18, 1876; "The Strike at Mann & Brackett's," July 22, 1876; "Visit of the Two Murphy Lieutenants," March 30, 1878; "St. Patrick's Church Fair," September 6, 1879; "Local," July 28, 1883; "Installation," July 18, 1874; "Local," August 22, 1874; "C.T.A.S.," February 10, 1877; "Town Meeting," March 13, 1880; "Officers of the Fire Companies," May 8, 1880; "Lodge Officers," June 19, 1880; "Town Meeting and Election," November 6, 1880; "St. Patrick's T.A. Society," July 16, 1881; "Local," November 19, 1881; "Town Meeting," November 12, 1881; "Town Meeting," March 17, 1883; "Elections and Town Meeting in Stoneham," November 10, 1883; "Town Meeting," April 15, 1884; "Stoneham Shoe Employe[e]s Aroused," April 12, 1884; "The People's Party," September 13, 1884; "Butler and Lovering: A Flag Raising and Rally," October 11, 1884; "Local," July 11, 1874; "Fire Department," May 8, 1875. See also Stevens, *History of Stoneham*, 98–105, 177–82; Grand Army of the Republic, Post 75, J. P. Gould, List of Officers and Members, Stoneham Historical Society, Stoneham, Mass.

19. In 1875 only eight of Stoneham's thirty-one shoe factories produced

$100,000 worth, or more, of shoes. "The Decennial Census," *Stoneham Independent*, September 11, 1875.

20. "The Strike at Mann & Brackett's," *Stoneham Independent*, July 29, 1876.

21. "Stoneham Shoe Employe[e]s Aroused," *Stoneham Independent*, April 12, 1884.

22. *Stoneham Independent*, January 3, 1885.

23. "Does Co-operation Pay?" *Stoneham Amateur*, September 9, 1873; "Local," *Stoneham Amateur*, May 3, 1873; Massachusetts Bureau of the Statistics of Labor, *Annual Report*, 1886, 219; Coons, "Factories and Workers," 92.

24. "Records of the Stoneham Co-operative Shoe Company," January 9, 1873, 17; *Stoneham Independent:* "Installation," July 18, 1874; "Installation," January 9, 1875; "C.T.A.S.," February 10, 1877. I have assumed that the installation of officers in the Grand Army of the Republic local involved the election of officers, as it did in 1874 and after. See also "Adjourned Town Meeting," *Stoneham Independent*, March 3, 1875. Although the recorded town meeting cited here is from 1875, the town meeting procedures had varied little over the years. See Stevens, *History of Stoneham*, 38: "[In 1725] town meetings were called and conducted almost identically the same as those of today [1891]."

25. "Records of the Stoneham Co-operative Shoe Company," 62–64.

26. Ibid., 13, 20, 21, 22, 23, 43, 54, 57, 66, 133; "Stoneham Co-operative Shoe Manufactory," *Stoneham Amateur*, January 10, 1874; Coons, "Factories and Workers," 93.

27. Letter from "A Shoemaker," *Stoneham Independent*, December 18, 1875.

28. Stevens, *History of Stoneham*, 304–6. Stevens notes that Best was tax collector for three years. He must have occupied that office before 1875, since he held no public office after that date. See also *Stoneham City Directory*, 1869, 92; United States Ninth Census, 1870, 674; *Valuation of the Town of Stoneham, and State, County and Town Tax for the Year 1873, 4, 64; Valuation of the Town of Stoneham, and State, County and Town Tax for the Year 1872*, Stoneham Historical Society, Stoneham, Mass., 62.

29. "Local," *Stoneham Independent*, July 11, 1874; "Parade of the Fire Department," *Stoneham Independent*, October 17, 1874; Grand Army of the Republic, Post 75, J. P. Gould, List of Officers and Members, January 1875 to January 1876.

30. *Stoneham Amateur*, May 3, 1873 and February 14, 1874; Edwin M. Chamberlin, *The Sovereigns of Industry* (1875; reprint, Westport, Conn.: Hyperion Press, 1976), xix.

31. "Election Notes," *Stoneham Independent*, November 14, 1874; *Manual of the General Court*, 1875, State House Library, Boston, Massachusetts; *Stoneham Independent:* "Local," March 27, 1875; "The Best Bill," February 2, 1875; "Local," March 27, 1875.

32. *Stoneham Independent:* "Larceny Case," May 15, 1875; "Trial of John Best," March 4, 1876. The owner of the grocery, Aaron Hill, accused Best of stealing a total of $1,500 over a period of time. See "Records of the Stone-

ham Co-operative Shoe Company," 49, 66; Grand Army of the Republic, Post 75, J. P. Gould, List of Officers and Members, January 1875 to January 1876; Stevens, *History of Stoneham*, 305–6.

33. *Stoneham Independent:* "The Strike at Mann & Brackett's," July 29, 1876; "Mann & Brackett," August 5, 1876; "Back they Come," November 4, 1876; "Trade Items," March 10, 1877; "Locals," August 11, 1877; "Workingmen's Rally," October 20, 1877. "The Political Quartette," November 3, 1877 (only 790 out of 1,200 possible votes were cast; the winner, Democrat George Cowdrey, received 382 votes); "The Election," November 10, 1877; "Is the Laborer Worthy of his Hire?" November 17, 1877; No title, November 24, 1877.

34. *Stoneham Independent:* August 24, 1878; "Political," September 14, 1878; "The Election," November 9, 1878. The three selectmen were J. W. Osgood, Wm. F. Cowdrey, and Amos Hill; see Stevens, *History of Stoneham*, 104. For Osgood, see "The Strike at Mann & Brackett's," *Stoneham Independent*, July 29, 1876. For Cowdrey, see *Stoneham Independent*, February 9, 1878, September 14, 21, 28, 1878. For Amos Hill, see *Stoneham Amateur*, March 2, 1872; "Local," *Stoneham Independent*, February 3, 1883. See also Jonathan Garlock, *Guide to the Local Assemblies of the Knights of Labor* (Westport, Conn.: Greenwood Press, 1982), 196; "Local," *Stoneham Independent*, March 13, 1886.

35. *Stoneham Amateur*, March 21, 1874; *Stoneham Independent:* "Local" and "People's Column," October 17, 1874; "Local," December 11, 1875. Massachusetts Bureau of the Statistics of Labor, *Annual Report*, 1877, 101; "Death of a Printer," *Stoneham Independent*, May 11, 1878; Stevens, *History of Stoneham*, 174–75; Massachusetts Bureau of the Statistics of Labor, *Annual Report*, 1886, 196–202. L. V. Colahan and John S. Gilmore, both original members of the Stoneham Cooperative, were members of the Middlesex Cooperative; see *Stoneham Independent:* "Base Ball," July 10, 1875; "Cooperative Notes," November 21, 1885; "Over $10,000.00 subscribed for the New Co-operative Currying Company," July 31, 1886; and "Co-operative Bank," January 8, 1887; all but two of the cooperatives lasted at least eight years. No information on the life span of the curriers' association exists. The cooperative bank was created by middle-class reformers and manufacturers as well as workers late in the 1880s and will not be dealt with here. One interesting fact about the bank is that its founders felt compelled to describe it as socialist in order to attract workers' interest.

36. Edward W. Bemis, "Cooperation in New England," in *History of Cooperation in the United States*, ed. Herbert Adams, Johns Hopkins University Studies in Historical and Political Science, vol. 6 (Baltimore: Johns Hopkins University, 1888), 102; Massachusetts Bureau of the Statistics of Labor, *Annual Report*, 1886, 217, 219, 221, 225; William Richardson and George P. Sanger, *Supplement to the General Statutes of the Commonwealth of Massachusetts*, vol. 2, 1873, 231–32. See copy of state law in "Articles of Agreement and By-Laws of the Fall River Workingmen's Association," *Pamphlets in American History*, Cooperative Societies #97 (Sanford, N.C.: Microfilming Corp. of America, 1979–84), microform.

37. The Stoneham Cooperative also paid the Cutters' Union prices in

1886; see "Records of the Stoneham Co-operative Shoe Company," 178, also 25, 27, 30, 31, 36, 44, 45, 55, 67, 89–90, 105–6, esp. 112–13, and for complete list of wages paid, see 108–10. See also *Stoneham Independent:* "Notes of the Shoe Factory. Lasters' Strike!" August 27, 1881; "Lasting Prices," September 3, 1881; "Cooperation in Stoneham," January 2, 1886; "Wages! Lasters Request and Receive an Advance. A Quiet Revolution," March 24, 1883; Massachusetts Bureau of the Statistics of Labor, *Annual Report*, 1886, 218, 220, 226; Coons, "Factories and Workers," 94.

38. Blewett, *Men, Women, and Work*, 148–49; Dawley, *Class and Community*, 139–40; "Records of the Stoneham Co-operative Shoe Company," 42, 44, 95, 96; Coons, "Factories and Workers," 92; "Cooperation in Stoneham," *Stoneham Independent*, January 2, 1886; Massachusetts Bureau of the Statistics of Labor, *Annual Report*, 1886, 216, 225; Federal Census of Manufactures. 1880, Stoneham, Middlesex County, Massachusetts. Special Schedules No. 3 & 4, Boots and Shoes; Coons, "Factories and Workers," 92.

39. "Records of the Stoneham Co-operative Shoe Company," 27, 40–41.

40. Massachusetts Bureau of the Statistics of Labor, *Annual Report*, 1886, 216;"Co-operation in Stoneham," *Stoneham Independent*, January 2, 1886; "Our Industries," *Stoneham Independent*, July 23, 1887; "Records of the Stoneham Co-operative Shoe Company," 103–5, 131, 135, 140, 147, insert between 164 and 165 (Auditor's and Treasurer's Statements, November 2, 1883), insert between 174 and 175 (Auditor Statement, November 2, 1885), insert between 182 and 183 (Auditor's Statement, December 1, 1886), last page (not numbered); Coons, "Factories and Workers," 93.

41. "Cooperation in Stoneham," *Stoneham Independent*, January 2, 1886, reprinted from the *Boston Sunday Globe; Stoneham Independent:* "Our Industries," August 6, 1887; "Annual Meeting," December 21, 1889.

42. Massachusetts Bureau of the Statistics of Labor, *Annual Report*, 1886, 216, 220. The Stoneham and Middlesex cooperatives both had native-born American, Irish, and Canadian members; see the following articles in the *Stoneham Independent:* "Base Ball," July 10, 1875; January 4, 1879; "Factory Warming," February 1, 1879; April 24, 1880; May 29, 1880; "Local News," October 30, 1880; "Social Gatherings," December 18, 1880; "The Stoneham Co-operative Supper," January 8, 1881; "Surprises," January 29, 1881; "Local," March 12, 1881; "Local," July 1, 1881; "Local," June 24, 1882; "Silver Wedding," May 5, 1883; "A Foreman Surprised," February 12, 1887; January 4, 1879; "Obituary," July 18, 1885. See also United States Ninth Census, 1870, 592, 612, 616, 624, 625, 626, 630, 636, 661, 667, 681; United States Tenth Census, 1880, manuscripts, vol. 17, Middlesex County, Massachusetts, 316, 319, 320, 326, 328, 329, 331, 333, 336, 351, 354, 358. (The relative proximity of the various cooperators is a rough estimate; if they appear on the same page of the manuscript census, I consider them neighbors. This probably underestimates the number of cooperators who live in the same "neighborhoods.")

43. "Stoneham Co-operative Shoe Manufactory," *Stoneham Amateur*, January 10, 1874.

44. *Census of Massachusetts: 1885, Population and Social Statistics, Part II*

(Boston: State Printers, 1885), 266–68; Massachusetts Bureau of the Statistics of Labor, *Annual Report*, 1886, 217, 219, 221, 225; Coons, "Factories and Workers," 92. A woman did supervise the stitching room in the Stoneham Co-operative during its early years. See "Stoneham Cooperative Shoe Factory," *Stoneham Amateur*, January 10, 1874. The only unusual development was in 1885, when a cooperative hired a woman to audit its books. See "Records of the Stoneham Co-operative Shoe Company," 174.

45. *Directory of Wakefield, Stoneham, Reading and Saugua*, 1886–87, 151.

46. "Records of the Stoneham Co-operative Shoe Company," 1, 18, 39; Coons, "Factories and Workers," 91. The leaders of the Daughters of St. Crispin (DOSC) in Stoneham, according to Mary Blewett (*Men, Women, and Work*, 169), "represented the self-supporting boarding stitcher and the female-headed family to a greater extent than the constituency of residents living in male-headed families." Martha Wallbridge, a resident of Stoneham who became First Grand Directeress of the DOSC in 1870, supported suffrage for women and "represented a constituency of self-supporting women in the DOSC for whom the meaning of equal rights of women was an open question." (Blewett, *Men, Women, and Work*, 174). Yet the stitchers of Stoneham lived largely within male-headed families in 1870 (Blewett, *Men, Women, and Work*, 394). Wage-earning women probably had conflicting agendas over how far to push their male counterparts toward admitting them into the polity and the cooperatives.

47. "Local News," *Stoneham Independent*, November 1, 1879; "Letter from Fannie Allyn," *Stoneham Independent*, February 12, 1887; United States Ninth Census, 1870, 661; United States Tenth Census, 1880, 349; Geo. C. Kuechler, "Co-operative Fair," *Journal of United Labor*, May 10, 1886, 2065; "Co-operative Fair [Flyer]," February 21, 1886. John Samuel Papers, Box 1, Folder 6, Correspondence, Jan.– May 1886, Wisconsin State Historical Society, Madison (hereafter cited as John Samuel Papers); Coons, "Factories and Workers," 96.

48. "Records of the Stoneham Co-operative Shoe Company," 142; Massachusetts Bureau of the Statistics of Labor, *Annual Report*, 1886, 216–26.

49. Massachusetts Bureau of the Statistics of Labor, *Annual Report*, 1886, 229.

50. "Reports of District Master Workmen," *Journal of United Labor*, October 8, 1884, 760.

51. "Stoneham Shoe Employe[e]s Aroused," *Stoneham Independent*, April 12, 1884; Coons, "Factories and Workers," 96.

52. Knights of Labor, *Record of Proceedings of the Tenth Regular Session of the General Assembly, Held at Richmond, Va., Oct. 4–20, 1886*, Terence Powderly Papers, microfilm (Glen Rock, N. J.: Microfilming Corporation of America, 1979), 14, 314, Reel 67 (hereafter cited as Terence Powderly Papers); "Local," *Stoneham Independent*, February 3, 1883; Coons, "Factories and Workers," 96.

53. "Stoneham Shoe Employe[e]s Aroused," *Stoneham Independent*, April 12, 1884; "Sanborn & Mann," *Stoneham Independent*, May 10, 1884; Coons,

"Factories and Workers," 96.

54. "Sanborn & Mann," *Stoneham Independent*, May 10, 1884.

55. Officers and delegates of the People's Party included C. L. Gill of the American Co-operative; L. V. Colahan, J. Gilmore (Gilmore was a participant only), and George Newhall of the Middlesex Co-operative; E. R. Seaver, Ed Goodness, and A. Harriman of the Stoneham Shoe Co-operative; S. C. Trull and W. F. Cowdrey of the Franklin Co-operative; and Eugene Divitt and Allen Rowe of the Stoneham Co-operative Union; see "The People's Party," *Stoneham Independent*, September 13, 1884 for People's Party members.

56. "Election Day," *Stoneham Independent*, November 8, 1884.

57. "District Assembly, No. 30," *Journal of United Labor*, July 1883, 517–18.

58. "Weekly Payments," *Stoneham Independent*, January 23, 1886; "The Strike [from the *Boston Globe*]," *Stoneham Independent*, January 23, 1886; "Reply to the *Boston Courier* Article," Workman to Editor, *Stoneham Independent*, February 6, 1886; Coons, "Factories and Workers," 94.

59. Massachusetts Bureau of the Statistics of Labor, *Annual Report*, 1886, 222. See also Coons, "Factories and Workers," 94; "The Strike [from the *Boston Globe*]," *Stoneham Independent*, January 23, 1886; "Cooperative Notes," *Stoneham Independent*, November 21, 1885; *Stoneham City Directory*, 1886, 92.

60. *Stoneham Independent:* "The Franklin Co-operative Embarrassment," March 13, 1886; "Franklin Co-operative," April 3, 1886; "Annual Meeting," December 21, 1889. Coons, "Factories and Workers," 92.

61. "Records of the Stoneham Co-operative Shoe Company," 147, 174–75 (insert, Auditor's and Treasurer's Statements, November 2, 1885), 182–83 (insert, Auditor's Statement, December 1, 1886), 190–91 (insert, Treasurer's Statement, November 1, 1887), 196–97 (insert, Treasurer's Statement, November 1, 1888), 197, 202, 205.

62. "Co-operation in Stoneham" (from the *Boston Sunday Globe*) *Stoneham Independent*, January 2, 1886; In the *Valuation of the Town of Stoneham* for 1890 the American dropped the word "co-operative" from its name. The Middlesex still called itself a cooperative.

63. "Co-operation in Stoneham," *Stoneham Independent*, January 2, 1886.

64. Knights of Labor, *Record of the Proceedings of the: Eighth Regular Session of the General Assembly, Held at Philadelphia, Pa., Sept. 1–10, 1884*, 796, Terence Powderly Papers, Reel 67; idem, *Proceedings of the Ninth Regular Session*, 173; idem, *Proceedings of the Tenth Regular Session*, 289, 292, 326; "Report of the General Secretary," in idem, *Record of Proceedings of the General Assembly of the Knights of Labor of America, Twelfth Regular Session, Held at Indianapolis, Indiana, November 13–27, 1888*, 2, Terence Powderly Papers, Reel 67; idem, *Record of the Proceedings of the General Assembly of the Knights of Labor of America, Eleventh Regular Session, Held at Minneapolis, Minnesota, October 4 to 19,1887*, 1595–99, Terence Powderly Papers, Reel 67; L. C. L Schlieber, Chair General Coop Board to John Samuel, March 17, 1887, John Samuel Papers, Box 2, Folder 1, Correspondence, 1887.

65. Massachusetts Bureau of the Statistics of Labor, *Annual Report*, 1886, 216–22.

66. See Knights of Labor, *Proceedings of the Eighth Regular Session*, 805, 806; idem, *Proceedings of the Ninth Regular Session*, 182; Johnathan Garlock, *Guide to the Local Assemblies of the Knights of Labor* (Westport, Conn.: Greenwood Press, 1982), 196.

67. In 1889 the Lasters' Protective Union was still strong in Stoneham and had some former cooperators as supporters. See "The Campfire of the Stoneham Lasters' Protective Union," *Stoneham Independent*, April 13, 1889.

Chapter 5

1. "Knights of Labor Temple," *Minneapolis Tribune*, May 30, 1887.

2. Francis A. Walker, *Ninth Census—Volume 1, The Statistics of the Population of the United States* (Washington, D.C.: Government Printing Office, 1872), 178; United States Tenth Census, *Statistics of the Population of the United States* (Washington, D.C.: Government Printing Office, 1881), 226; Albert Shaw, "Cooperation in the Northwest," in *History of Cooperation in the United States*, ed. Herbert Adams, Johns Hopkins University Studies in Historical and Political Science, vol. 6 (Baltimore: Johns Hopkins University, 1888), 199.

3. Joseph Stipanovich, *City of Lakes: An Illustrated History of Minneapolis* (Woodland Hills, Calif.:Windsor Publications, 1982), 131–58, 214, 224; Lucile M. Kane, *The Waterfall that Built a City* (St Paul: Minnesota Historical Society, 1966), 98–101, 114; Harold Zink, *City Bosses in the United States* (Durham, N.C.: Duke University Press, 1930), 334–49.

4. "Knights of Labor Temple," *Minneapolis Tribune*, May 30, 1887.

5. "Knights of Labor Temple," *Minneapolis Tribune*, May 30, 1887; Shaw, "Cooperation," 203, 207, 219. Curtis was an original member of the first local assembly probably in late 1878 and later a state organizer for the Knights; see George B. Engberg, "The Rise of Organized Labor in Minnesota, 1850–1890" (master's thesis, University of Minnesota, May 1939), 40, 56: Corporation Records of the Minnesota State Archives in the Minnesota Historical Society, St. Paul, Minn., 112-F-14-4(F) 314–17, 366–68.

6. Shaw, "Cooperation," 203–7; G. O. Virtue, "The Co-operative Coopers of Minneapolis," *Quarterly Journal of Economics* 19 (August 1905): 527; "Coopering in Minneapolis," *Northwestern Miller-Holiday Number* 22 (1886), 15.

7. Shaw, "Cooperation," 230–42; Richard Ely, *The Labor Movement in America* (New York: Thomas Y. Crowell and Co., 1886), chapter 7; J. P. McGuaghey, "Land as a Basis for Cooperative Labor," *Journal of United Labor*, February 10, 1886, 1198, John Samuel Papers, Box 5, Newspaper Clippings, Wisconsin State Historical Society, Madison (hereafter cited as John Samuel Papers); *Journal of United Labor:* "Co-operation," September 10, 1886, 2164; "Some Results of Co-operation," May 21, 1887, 2393–94; *Minnesota Mirror:* "Discouraging," August 31, 1883, 2; "Cooperative Freedom," November 9, 1883, 2.

8. Shaw, "Cooperation," 302; Engberg, "Organized Labor," 52–84;

For McGuaghey, see the J. P. McGuaghey Papers, Minnesota Historical Society, St. Paul (hereafter cited as John P. McGuaghey Papers). Brosnan and Cronin are frequently mentioned in relation to the cooperative movement in District Assembly 79 reports and in the press, see Knights of Labor, District Assembly 79, *Record of Proceedings of the Twentieth Regular Meeting of D.A. 79, K. of L. held at St. Paul, Minnesota, July 17, 1887*, John P. McGuaghey Papers; idem, *Record of Proceedings of the Fifth Quarterly Meeting of D.A. 79, K. of l. Held at Mankato, Minnesota, January 16, 1887* (Minneapolis, Minn.: Thos. A. Clark & Co., 1887); idem, *Record of Proceedings of the Twenty-First Regular Meeting of D.A. 79, K. of L. Held at Minneapolis, Minnesota, January 15, 1888* (Minneapolis, Minn.: Thos. A. Clark & Co., 1888), Terence Powderly Papers; Minnesota Bureau of Labor Statistics, *First Biennial Report for the two years ending December 31, 1887–8*, 225; Shaw, "Cooperation," 244. For the tally of cooperatives, see Shaw, "Cooperation," 203–30, 244–45, 263–64, 268, 275, 299–300, 302–5; Corporation Records of the Minnesota State Archives in the Minnesota Historical Society, St. Paul, Minn., 112–F-14–6(F), 242, 255, 596, 112–F-14–7(B), 321, 335, 112–F-14–4(F), 14, 62, 142, 251, 255, 314, 366, 624, 112–F-14–3(B), 188, 112–F-15–1(B), 404; *Minneapolis City Directory. For 1886–87.* (City Directories of the United States, New Haven, Conn.: Research Publications, 1984, microform), see under categories: Cigar Manufacturers, Groceries, Laundries; *Minneapolis City Directory. For 1887–88* (City Directories of the United States, New Haven, Conn.: Research Publications, 1984, microform), see under categories: Shirt Manufacturers, Printers; *Minneapolis City Directory. For 1888–89* (City Directories of the United States [New Haven, Conn.: Research Publications, 1984], microform), see under category: Incorporated Companies; *Minnesota Mirror*: "Discouraging," August 31, 1883, 2; "The Way to Do," November 30, 1883, 1; "Local Items," January 11, 1884, 1; *Northwestern Miller*, December 3, 1886, 574 (all citations of the *Northwestern Miller* are to the weekly column "Coopers' Chips," unless otherwise noted.)

9. See note 7.

10. Shaw, "Cooperation," 199–202; Kane, *The Waterfall that Built a City*, 98–101.

11. Shaw, "Cooperation," 203–5; Engberg, "Organized Labor," 1–5, 16–17, 28, 40, 55–56.

12. Virtue, "Co-operative Coopers," 527–28; Shaw, "Cooperation," 203–5.

13. Shaw, "Cooperation," 207–13. See also "By-laws of the Co-operative Barrel Mfg. Co., Minneapolis, Minn., with the Co-operative Laws of 1870, and Amendments." *Pamphlets in American History*, Cooperative Societies #123 (Sanford, N.C.: Microfilming Corp. of America, 1979–84), microform; "By-Laws of the Hennepin County Barrel Co. with Articles of Incorporation, Co-operative Laws of 1870 & Amendments" (Minneapolis: Book Press of Chas. F. Young & Co., 1886). *Pamphlets in American History*, Cooperative Societies #99 (Sanford, N.C.: Microfilming Corp. of America, 1979–84), microform.

14. United States Ninth Census, 1870, manuscripts, Hennepin County, Minnesota, 558, Roll 715e+f; "House of Representatives," *St. Paul Daily*

Globe, January 1, 1883, 4; *Legislative Manual of the State of Minnesota*, 1883, Minnesota Historical Society, St. Paul, Minn., 488; *Northwestern Miller*, July 2, 1886, 8 and May 31, 1889, 682.

15. Shaw, "Cooperation," 203, 204, 207, 219; *Northwestern Miller*, August 28, 1885, 200.

16. Shaw, "Cooperation," 219–20; *Northwestern Miller:* September 19, 1884, 274; September 26, 1884, 298; November 14, 1884, 466; November 20, 1885, 488; November 26, 1886, 550; November 18, 1887, 542; November 23, 1888, 680; May 24, 1889, 650; *Legislative Manual for the State of Minnesota*, 488.

17. "Cooperation at Home," *Minnesota Mirror*, September 14, 1883; Shaw, "Cooperation," 207.

18. Shaw, "Cooperation," 206; Daniel T. Rodgers, *The Work Ethic in Industrial America, 1850–1920* (Chicago: University of Chicago Press, 1979), 43.

"By Cooperation," *Saint Paul Daily Globe*, January 6, 1889; Wisconsin Bureau of Labor and Industrial Statistics, *Second Biennial Report, 1885–1886* (Madison, Wis.: Democrat Printing Co., State Printers, 1886), 158.

19. Shaw, "Cooperation," 214, 217–18; Virtue, "Co-operative Coopers," 529; *Minnesota Mirror:* "Cooperation at Home," September 14, 1883; "Local Items," November 16, 1883. The coop sold its stave factory in early 1887; *Northwestern Miller*, February 4, 1887, 104.

20. Shaw, "Cooperation," 214–15, 219; "Minneapolis Cooper Shops," *Holiday Northwestern Miller*, 1887, 3.

21. Virtue, "Co-operative Coopers," 529–30; *Northwestern Miller*, December 3, 1886, 574; Shaw, "Cooperation," 199.

22. Virtue, "Co-operative Coopers," 537–38; G. O. Virtue, "The End of the Cooperative Coopers," *Quarterly Journal of Economics* 46, May 1932, 541–42; Herbert G. Gutman, "The Labor Policies of the Large Corporation in the Gilded Age," in *Power and Culture: Essays on the American Working Class* (New York: Pantheon Books, 1987), 213–54.

23. Virtue, "Co-operative Coopers," 537–38; Shaw, "Cooperation," 215. For a description of the barrel-making process, see Franklin E. Coyne, *The Development of the Cooperage Industry in the United States, 1620–1940* (Chicago: Lumber Buyers Publishing Company, 1940).

24. Wisconsin Bureau of Labor and Industrial Statistics, *Second Biennial Report*, 187–88.

25. Shaw, "Cooperation," 203, 207.

26. "By-Laws of the Hennepin County Barrel Co.," 1–12.

27. Shaw, "Cooperation," 214, 221, 226; *Minneapolis Tribune* May 3, 1884, Federal Writers Project, reel 70; "Cooperation at Home," *Minnesota Mirror*, September 21, 1883.

28. Minnesota Bureau of Labor Statistics, *First Biennial Report*, 220–21; *Northwestern Miller*, January 13, 1888, 32.

29. Shaw, "Cooperation," 217–18, 220, 222, 224, 225–26, 228; "Some Results of Co-operation," *Journal of United Labor*, May 21, 1887, 2393–94; *Northwestern Miller*, October 9, 1885, 344.

30. *Northwestern Miller:* July 4, 1884, 6; August 22, 1884, 178; August

29, 1884, 202; November 14, 1884, 466; December 5, 1884, 538; July 17, 1885, 56; December 25, 1885, 612; January 8, 1886, 32; February 26, 1886, 200; July 16, 1886, 56; August 5, 1887, 144; July 19, 1889, 86; *Minneapolis Tribune*, July 30, 1886, Federal Writers' Project, reel 91; *Minnesota Mirror:* "Local Items," November 9, 1883; "Local Items," November 23, 1883.

31. Shaw, "Cooperation," 218, 220, 222, 224–26, 236.

32. Shaw, "Cooperation," 263–67; *St. Paul Daily Globe*, August 15, 1885, Federal Writers' Project, reel 70; untitled and unsigned article, *Minnesota Mirror*, August 31, 1883; *Northwestern Miller:* July 3, 1885, 8; August 14, 1885, 152; September 11, 1885, 248; November 20, 1885, 488; April 1, 1887, 296; January 13, 1888, 32; *Minneapolis City Directory*, 1876, City Directories of the United States: Minneapolis, Minn., Segment 11 (New Haven, Conn.: Research Publications, 1984) microform, 143; *Minneapolis City Directory*, 1877, City Directories of the United States: Minneapolis, Minn., Segment 11 (New Haven, Conn.: Research Publications, 1984) microform, 421.

33. The address was 1424 7th Street South, *St. Paul Daily Globe*, February 7, 1886, Federal Writers' Project, reel 70; Shaw, "Cooperation," 217, 220, 222, 263–67; *Northwestern Miller:* August 14, 1885, 152; August 28, 1885, 200; May 21, 1886, 488.

34. Shaw, "Cooperation," 263–67; *Minneapolis Tribune*, January 13, 1887, Federal Writers' Project, Reel 70; *Saint Paul Daily Globe*, August 15, 1885, Federal Writers' Project, reel 70; *Saint Paul Daily Globe*, February 7, 1886, Federal Writers' Project, reel 70; *Northwestern Miller*, January 4, 1889, 30.

35. Shaw, "Cooperation," 249.

36. Ibid., 238; Coyne, *Cooperage Industry*, 21; *Minnesota Mirror*, August 31, 1883; "By-Laws of the Hennepin County Barrel Co.," 12, 18.

37. Shaw, "Cooperation," 253.

38. *Northwestern Miller*, October 17, 1884, 370.

39. Ibid.; *Northwestern Miller*, October 24, 1884, 394 and October 31, 1884, 418.

40. *Northwestern Miller*, December 4, 1885, 536; *Northwestern Miller*, December 11, 1885, 564.

41. *Northwestern Miller:* December 11, 1885, 564; January 8, 1886, 32; January 22, 1886, 80; January 29, 1886, 104. "Oys Defended," *St. Paul Daily Globe*, January 10, 1886.

42. *Northwestern Miller:* December 18, 1885, 588; January 15, 1886, 56; June 25, 1886, 610.

43. George B. Engberg, "The Knights of Labor in Minnesota," *Minnesota History* 22 (December 1941): 375; Shaw, "Cooperation," 302. See note 8. See also *Minneapolis Tribune*, July 4, 1886, Federal Writers' Project, Reel 91; *Minneapolis Tribune*, April 13, 1887, Federal Writers' Project, Reel 91; John P. McGaughey, "Land as a Basis for Co-operative Labor," *Journal of United Labor*, 1886, 1198, John Samuel Papers, Box 5, Newspaper Clippings; Knights of Labor, District Assembly 79, *Proceedings of the Twentieth Regular Meeting*, 1887, 8, 26, 29, John P. McGaughey Papers; idem, Proceedings of the Twenty-First Regular Meeting, 1888, 12, Terrence Powderly Papers.

44. *Minnesota Mirror:* "Local Items," January 11, 1884; "Topics of the

Day," March 7, 1884; advertisement for North Star Printing Co., June 6, 1884.

45. *Minnesota Mirror*, December 21, 1883, 1.

46. See note 8.

47. Richard Ely, *The Labor Movement in America* (New York: Thomas Y. Crowell & Co., 1886), chapter 7; Shaw, "Cooperation," 242.

48. *Minneapolis Tribune*, May 12, 1875, Federal Writers' Project, Reel 70; *Minneapolis Tribune*, May 22, 1876, Federal Writers' Project, Reel 70.

49. *Minnesota Mirror:* March 14, 1884; "From the Board of Trustees of the *Mirror*," March 28, 1884; May 23, 1884.

50. James S. Rankin, "Hard Times: Their Cause and Cure," *Pamphlets in American History*, Cooperative Series, #290 (Sanford, N.C.: Microfilming Corp. of America, 1979–84), microform; *St. Paul Daily Globe*, January 17 and January 24, 1886; J. S. Rankin, "Cooperation as a Combatant," *Journal of United Labor*, April 1884, 753.

51. Rankin, "Hard Times," 1–3.

52. "Discouraging," *Minnesota Mirror*, August 31, 1883.

53. "Topics of the Day," *Minnesota Mirror*, September 7, 1883.

54. Rankin, "Hard Times," 25–48.

55. Ibid., 45–46.

56. "The Week: Topics of the Day," *Minnesota Mirror*, May 2, 1884; J. S. Rankin, "Co-operation as a Combatant," *Journal of United Labor*, April 1884, 753.

57. Rankin, "Hard Times," 46.

58. Knights of Labor, District Assembly 79, *Proceedings of the Twentieth Regular Meeting*, 1887, 8.

59. Ibid., 26.

60. "Co-operative Freedom," *Minnesota Mirror*, November 9, 1883.

61. Articles of Incorporation of the Cooperative Land Association, Corporation Records held in the Minnesota Historical Society, St. Paul, 112-F-14-6-F; Shaw, "Cooperation," 244–45; Mike Mogan, the first president of the Trades and Labor Assembly, was later a director of the Cooperative Land Association. See *St. Paul Daily Globe*, April 11, 1886; "Fifty Years Ago Today in Local Labor Circles," *Labor Review*, 1916, 1, John P. McGaughey Papers (AM145j).

62. Rankin, "Hard Times," 46.

63. Knights of Labor, District Assembly 79, *Proceedings of the Twentieth Regular Meeting*, 1887, 9.

64. Shaw, "Cooperation," 245.

65. Ibid., 244–48.

66. *Minneapolis Tribune:* April 1, 1886; "Knights of Labor Forum," May 16, 1886; May 1, 1887, Federal Writers Project, reel 70; *Minneapolis Tribune*, May 3, 1887, 5; "A Step Forward. A Cooperative Land Association Formed at Minneapolis," *St. Paul Daily Globe*, March 21, 1886, April 11, May 30, August 1, 1886 and the *Cooperative News*, printed in *Journal of United Labor*, May 25, 1886, 2078. See also Steve Keillor, "The Farm that Wouldn't Cooperate," *Lake Country Journal* 2 (January/February 1998): 46–47.

67. Knights of Labor, District Assembly 79, *Proceedings of the Twentieth*

Regular Meeting, 1887, 59–64, 70; idem, *Proceedings of the Twenty-First Regular Meeting*, 1888, 5–11, 23; idem, *Record of Proceedings of the Twenty-Third Regular Meeting of D.A. 79, K. of L. held at Minneapolis, Minnesota, January 20, 1889* (Minneapolis: Thos. A. Clark & Co.), 14–19, Terence Powderly Papers.

68. See note 3; Shaw, "Cooperation," 238; *St. Paul and Minneapolis Pioneer Press:* February 2, 1883, 2; "Twenty-fourth Legislature," January 26, 1885, 5; "House of Representatives," *St. Paul Daily Globe*, January 1, 1883, 4.

69. Engberg, "Organized Labor," 103–12.

70. Knights of Labor, District Assembly 79, *Proceedings of the Twentieth Regular Meeting*, 1887, 26.

71. Ibid.

72. Minnesota Bureau of Labor Statistics, *First Biennial Report*, 225.

73. Virtue, "Co-operative Coopers," 537–38; Minnesota Bureau of Labor Statistics, *First Biennial Report*, 222–23.

74. *Minnesota Mirror:* "The Week. Topics of the Day," May 2, 1884; May 9, 1884; May 16, 1884. *Minneapolis Tribune:* May 3, 1884, Federal Writers Project, reel 70; July 19, 1884, reel 91.

75. *Northwestern Miller*, August 15, 1884, 154.

76. *Northwestern Miller*: July 18, 1884, 58; August 1, 1884, 107; August 15, 1884, 154.

77. *Northwestern Miller:* August 29, 1884, 202; September 5, 1884, 226; September 12, 1884, 250.

78. Shaw comments on the sale of shares in the cooperatives ("Cooperatives," 236–37), and the *Northwestern Miller*'s *Coopers' Chips* column during the mid-1880s mentions the sale of shares frequently.

79. *Northwestern Miller*, December 19, 1884, 586; December 26, 1884, 610.

80. "Coopering in Minneapolis," *Northwestern Miller, Holiday Number*, 1885, 18; Virtue, "Co-operative Coopers," 538–39; Shaw, "Cooperation," 215–16, 219–20. The Hennepin Cooperative had introduced machinery a year or two before the other cooperative shops. See Shaw, "Cooperation," 221.

81. "Coopering in Minneapolis," 18; Kane, *The Waterfall That Built a City*, 42, 119.

82. "Coopering in Minneapolis", 18; *Minneapolis Tribune*, September 24, 1885, Federal Writers' Project, Reel 91.

83. *Northwestern Miller*, February 26, 1886, 200; "Coopering in Minneapolis," *Northwestern Miller, Holiday Number*, 1886, 15.

84. *Northwestern Miller* (1886): February 26, 200; March 5, 224; March 26, 296; April 2, 320; April 23, 392; April 30, 416. *Minneapolis Tribune*, April 30, 1886, Federal Writers' Project, Reel 91.

85. *Northwestern Miller* (1886): June 18, 586; June 25, 610; July 2, p. 8; August 20, 178; September 10, 260; September 17, 288; September 24, 320; October 1, 352; October 8, 378. *Minneapolis Tribune*, September 12, 1886, Federal Writers' Project, Reel 91.

86. *Minneapolis Tribune*, October 13, 1886, Federal Writers' Project, Reel 91; *Northwestern Miller*, October 15, 1886, 404.

87. *Minneapolis Tribune*, October 14, 15, 19, 24, and 27, 1886, Federal Writers' Project, Reel 91; *Northwestern Miller* (1886): October 22, 430; Octo-

ber 29, 454. "Partly Over," *St. Paul Daily Globe*, October 24, 1886.

88. Knights of Labor, District Assembly 79, *Proceedings of the Fifth Quarterly Meeting*, 1887, 17–24, 26, 34–35; *Northwestern Miller*, January 14, 1887, 32.

89. *Northwestern Miller*, April 1, 1887, 296.

90. Knights of Labor, District Assembly 79, *Proceedings of the Fifth Quarterly Meeting*, 1887, 17–24, 26, 34–35; *Northwestern Miller*, January 14, 1887, 32; Knights of Labor, District Assembly 79, *Proceedings of the Twentieth Regular Meeting*, 1887, 36–37, 42–44; *Northwestern Miller*, February 4, 1887, 104; *Northwestern Miller*, August 12, 1887, 168.

91. *Northwestern Miller*, April 29, 1887, 406.

92. Minnesota Bureau of Labor Statistics, *First Biennial Report*, 225; Knights of Labor, District Assembly 79, *Proceedings of the Fifth Quarterly Meeting*, 1887, 17, 18, 20, 26, 34–35, 36, 40, 42–43; *Northwestern Miller*, June 3, 1887, 546.

93. John F. Cronin, Secretary of District Assembly 79 to John Lamb, State Commissioner of Labor Statistics, see Minnesota Bureau of Labor Statistics, *First Biennial Report*, 225–26.

94. Ibid.

95. "Still Apart," *Minneapolis Tribune*, May 21, 1887.

96. *Northwestern Miller* (1887): April 29, 406; May 6, 434; May 20, 490; June 3, 546; June 10, 578; June 17, 602; July 1, 8; July 8, 40. Knights of Labor, District Assembly 79, *Proceedings of the Twentieth Regular Meeting*, 1887, 46–47.

97. Knights of Labor, District Assembly 79, *Proceedings of the Twentieth Regular Meeting*, 1887, 47; *Northwestern Miller* (1887): April 29, 406; May 27, 522; June 3, 546.

98. *Northwestern Miller* (1887): May 6, 434; May 20, 490; July 1, p. 8; July 22, 92; August 12, 168; October 14, 412.

99. The North Star would remain obstructionist even after W. H. Bailey, a member of the national executive board of the Knights of Labor and president of the Cannelburg cooperative mine, came to negotiate a solution to the crisis. *Northwestern Miller* (1887): July 15, 64; July 22, 92; August 12, 168; August 19, 200; August 26, 224; September 9, 276; September 16, 304. Knights of Labor, District Assembly 79, *Proceedings of the Twenty-First Regular Meeting*, 1888, 30.

100. *Northwestern Miller* (1887): October 21, 436; November 4, 490. Knights of Labor, District Assembly 79, *Proceedings of the Twenty-First Regular Meeting*, 1888, 32.

101. *Northwestern Miller* (1887): December 2, 594; December 9, 622.

102. "Still Apart," *Minneapolis Tribune*, May 21, 1887.

103. *Northwestern Miller* (1887): June 24, 634; December 9, 622. The ruling of the court judge, a member of the Sixth Street Shop, is not known.

104. William Argus to E. W. Bemis, August 25, 1896 and September 15, 1896, Wisconsin State Historical Society Labor Collection, Misc. Biographies and Papers, Box 2, Bemis Papers, Folder Bemis Papers, Wisconsin State Historical Society, Madison.

105. *Northwestern Miller* (1888) January 20, 60; March 2, 218.

106. *Northwestern Miller* (1887): June 3, 546; June 10, 578; June 17, 602; July 8, 40; July 15, 64; July 22, 92; August 12, 168; August 19, 200; August 26, 224; September 2, 252; September 9, 276; September 16, 304; September 23, 328; September 30, 356; January 20, 60; March 2, 218. Knights of Labor, District Assembly 79, *Proceedings of the Twentieth Regular Meeting*, 1887, 44, 46–47; idem, *Proceedings of the Twenty-First Regular Meeting*, 1888, 29–30, 32.

107. *Northwestern Miller* (1887) August 12, 168; September 16, 304.

108. Knights of Labor, District Assembly 79, *Proceedings of the Twentieth Regular Meeting*, 1887, 15; idem, *Proceedings of the Twenty-Third Regular Meeting*, 1889, 13; *Northwestern Miller* (1888): June 22, 698; Aug. 3, 156; Sept. 14, 356; Sept. 28, 424; Oct. 5, 456.

109. Virtue, "The End," 541–45.

110. *Northwestern Miller*, Jan. 4, 1889, 30; Virtue, "Co-operative Coopers," 539–40, 544; idem, "The End," 541–45. I found no mention of the cooperative colony after 1887 in the Minneapolis newspapers or in the Knights of Labor publications.

111. *Northwestern Miller*, August 28, 1885, 200; April 30, 1886, 416; Aug. 19, 1887, 200; Oct. 7, 1887, 384; *Minneapolis City Directory. For 1884–85.* City Directories of the United States. New Haven, Conn.: Research Publications, 1984, microform; *Minneapolis City Directory. For 1888–1889.* City Directories of the United States. New Haven, Conn.: Research Publications, 1984, microform.

Conclusion

1. Thomas Phillips, "Biography of Thomas Phillips," Cooperative Associations Papers, Box 1, Folder 4a, Wisconsin State Historical Society, Madison, 4.

2. Ibid.; Clifton K. Yearley Jr., "Thomas Phillips, A Yorkshire Shoemaker in Philadelphia," *Pennsylvania Magazine of History and Biography* 79 (1955): 167–96.

3. "The Industrial Republic," *Pamphlets in American History*, Cooperative Societies #107 (Sanford, N.C.: Microfilming Corp. of America, 1979–84), microform; "The Industrial Republic," *Pamphlets in American History*, Cooperative Societies #117 (Sanford, N.C.: Microfilming Corp. of America, 1979–84), microform; "Ritual of the Industrial Republic," *Pamphlets in American History*, Cooperative Societies #115 (Sanford, N.C.: Microfilming Corp. of America, 1979–84), microform; "The Industrial Republic: Homes for All," *Pamphlets in American History*, Cooperative Societies #254 (Sanford, N.C.: Microfilming Corp. of America, 1979–84), microform; "Constitution and Laws of the Industrial Republic," *I. R.*, August 1, 1891, vol. 1, no. 1, Microfilm of Labor Newspapers, Temple University Library, Philadelphia, Pa.

4. John Samuel to Mr. J. C. Gray, Gen. Sec. C. U. Manchester, England, December 2, 1891, John Samuel Papers, Box 2, Folder 3, Correspondence, 1889–92, Wisconsin State Historical Society, Madison (hereafter cited as John Samuel Papers).

5. Ibid.

6. Joseph G. Knapp, *The Rise of American Cooperative Enterprise, 1620–1920* (Danville, Ill.: Interstate Printers and Publishers, 1969), 40; "Co-operative Congress," reprinted from the *Seneca Falls Reveille*, December 6, 1889, John Samuel Papers, Box 2, Folder 3, Correspondence, 1889–92; Mrs. Imogene C. Fales, Newspaper clipping, John Samuel Papers, Box 2, Folder 3, Correspondence, 1889–92; I. C. Fales to John Samuel, December 26, [189?], John Samuel Papers, Box 2, Folder 3, Correspondence, 1889–92.

7. Norman Ware, *The Labor Movement in the United States* (New York: Vintage Books, 1929), 115–16, 221; "Address to the Independent Order of Knights of Labor," Official Historical Handbook Independent Order Knights of Labor, Knights of Labor Papers, Box 1, Wisconsin State Historical Society, Madison; Nick Salvatore, *Eugene V. Debs: Citizen and Socialist* (Urbana: University of Illinois Press, 1982), 162–64; Chester McArthur Destler, *American Radicalism, 1865–1901* (Chicago: Quadrangle Books, 1966), 21; Timothy Messer-Kruse, *The Yankee International: Marxism and the American Reform Tradition* (Chapel Hill: University of North Carolina Press, 1998), 251.

8. Phillip Foner, *History of Labor*, vol. 2, 174–77; Dana Frank, *Purchasing Power: Consumer Organizing, Gender, and the Seattle Labor Movement, 1919–1929* (Cambridge: Cambridge University Press, 1994).

Bibliography

Primary Sources, Unpublished

Bemis Papers. Misc. Biographies and Papers. Wisconsin State Historical Society, Madison.

"Chinese Sampson's Imports." A one-page typed account from the vertical file of the North Adams Public Library, North Adams, Massachusetts.

Commons, John. Papers. Wisconsin State Historical Society, Madison.

Cooperative Associations Papers. Wisconsin State Historical Society, Madison.

Corporation Records of the Minnesota State Archives in the Minnesota Historical Society, St. Paul.

Ely, Richard. Papers. Wisconsin State Historical Society, Madison.

Grand Army of the Republic. Post 75. J. P. Gould. List of Officers and Members. Stoneham Historical Society, Stoneham, Massachusetts.

International Workingmen's Association. Minutes of Meetings of the Philadelphia Section. October 9, 1871 to March 10, 1873. International Workingmen's Association Papers, Microfilm Edition. Wisconsin State Historical Society, Madison.

Knights of Labor Papers. Wisconsin State Historical Society, Madison.

Knights of St. Crispin Papers. Miscellaneous Holdings. Wisconsin State Historical Society, Madison.

Labor Collection: Miscellaneous Biographies and Papers. Wisconsin State Historical Society, Madison.

McGaughey, John P. Papers. Minnesota Historical Society, St. Paul.

Missouri Co-operative Coal Association Membership List and Minutes. 1883. John Samuel Papers. Microfilm Edition. Wisconsin State Historical Society, Madison.

Phillips, Thomas. Papers. Wisconsin State Historical Society, Madison.

Powderly, Terence. Papers. Microfilm Edition. Glen Rock, N.J.: Microfilming Corporation of America, 1974.

Records of the Stoneham Co-operative Shoe Company from 1872 to 1889. Stoneham Historical Society, Stoneham, Massachusetts.

Samuel, John. Papers. Wisconsin State Historical Society, Madison.

Samuel, John. Papers. Microfilm Edition. Wisconsin State Historical Society, Madison.

Sovereigns of Industry Papers. Wisconsin State Historical Society, Madison.

Union Cooperative Association Account Book. Vols. 1–3. Cooperative Associations Papers. Wisconsin State Historical Society, Madison.

Union Cooperative Association—Committee of Management Minutes. Cooperative Associations Papers. Wisconsin State Historical Society, Madison.

Union Cooperative Printing Co. Minutes. Cooperative Associations Papers. Wisconsin State Historical Society, Madison.

United States Ninth Census. 1870. Manuscripts, vol 21, Middlesex County, Massachusetts.

United States Ninth Census. 1870. Manuscripts, Roll no. 715e, Microfilm. Hennepin County, Minnesota.

United States Tenth Census. 1880. Manuscripts, vol 17, Middlesex County, Massachusetts.

United States Census of Manufactures, 1880. Manuscripts, Stoneham, Middlesex County, Massachusetts. Special Schedules no. 3 & 4, Boots and Shoes. John F. Kennedy Presidential Library, Boston, Massachusetts.

Primary Sources, Published

Adams, Herbert B., ed. *History of Cooperation in the United States.* Johns Hopkins University Studies in Historical and Political Science, vol. 6. Baltimore: Johns Hopkins University Press, 1888.

The Attractions of North Adams and Vicinity, Its Drives, Rambles, Views, Places of Interest, Hotels, Manufactories, Business Houses, &c., By a Visitor. North Adams, Mass.: Jas. C. Angell, Publisher, 1871.

Bemis, Edward W. "Cooperation in New England." In *History of Cooperation in the United States,* edited by Herbert Adams, 17–140. Johns Hopkins University Studies in Historical and Political Science, vol. 6. Baltimore: Johns Hopkins University, 1888.

———. "Cooperation in the Middle States." In *History of Cooperation in the United States,* edited by Herbert Adams, 141–98. Johns Hopkins University Studies in Historical and Political Science, vol. 6. Baltimore: Johns Hopkins University, 1888.

Census of Massachusetts: Population and Social Statistics, Part 2. Boston: State Printer, 1885.

Census of Massachusetts: Population and Social Statistics, Part 2. Boston: State Printers, 1887.

Chamberlin, Edwin M. *The Sovereigns of Industry.* Boston: Lee & Shepard, 1875. Reprint, Westport, Conn.: Hyperion Press, 1976.

City Directories of the United States—Minneapolis, Minn. Segment II, III. New Haven, Conn.: Research Publications, 1984. Microform.

Commons, John R., ed. *A Documentary History of American Industrial Society.* 11 vols. Cleveland: A. H. Clark Co., 1910–11.

"Constitution and Laws of the Industrial Republic." *I. R.,* 1 August 1891, vol. 1, no. 1. Microfilm of Labor Newspapers, Temple University Library, Philadelphia.

Directory of North and South Adams, 1872. New Haven, Conn.: Ridley and Co., Publishers, 1872.

Directory of North Adams, 1874. New Haven, Conn.: Ridley and Co., Publishers, 1874.

Directory of North Adams, for 1875–76. New Haven, Conn.: Price Lee & Co., 1875.

District Assembly Forty-Nine, Knights of Labor. New York and Vicinity. New York: Concord Co-operative Printing Company, 1888. Knights of Labor. Miscellaneous. Catherwood Library Cornell Labor Documentation Center, Ithaca, N.Y.

Du Bois, W. E. Burghardt, ed. *Economic Co-operation among Negro Americans.* Atlanta University Publications, no. 12. Atlanta: Atlanta University Press, 1907.

Ely, Richard. *The Labor Movement in America.* New York: Thomas Y. Crowell & Co., 1886.

Excerpts from Books, Magazines and Newspapers Concerning Labor Unions, 1827–1879. Wisconsin State Historical Society, Madison.

Ford, James. *Co-operation in New England: Urban and Rural.* Philadelphia: Press of Wm. F. Fell Co., 1913.

Giddings, Franklin Henry. "Co-operation." In *The Labor Movement: The Problem of Today,* edited by George E. McNeill, 508–31. New York: M. W. Hazen, 1886.

Holyoake, George Jacob. *Self-help by the People. History of Co-operation in Rochdale.* London: Holyoake & Co., 1858.

Iron Molders' Union. *Synopsis of the Proceedings of the Seventh Session of the Iron Molders' Union.* 1866. Research Collections in Labor Studies, Labor Union Periodicals, Part 1, Metal Trades. Bethesda, Maryland: University Publications of America, 1990, microform, reel 1.

Iron Molders' Union. *Synopsis of the Proceedings of the Eighth Session of the Iron Molders' Union.* 1867. Research Collections in Labor Studies, Labor Union Periodicals, Part 1, Metal Trades. Bethesda, Maryland: University Publications of America, 1990, microform, reel 1.

Iron Molders' Union. *Synopsis of the Proceedings of the 13th Session of the Iron Molders' International Union.* July 1876. Research Collections in Labor Studies, Labor Union Periodicals, Part 1, Metal Trades. Bethesda, Maryland: University Publications of America, 1990, microform, reel 1.

Iron Molders' Union. *Synopsis of the Proceedings of the International Iron Molders' Union Convention of 1868.* Research Collections in labor Studies, Labor Union Periodicals. Part 1, Metal Trades. Bethesda, Maryland: University Publications of America, 1990, microform.

Journal of the House of Representatives of the Commonwealth of Massachusetts, 1866. State Library of Massachusetts, Boston.

Journal of the House of Representatives of Massachusetts. Boston: Wright & Potter, State Printers, 1866.

Knights of Labor. *Record of the Proceedings of the Second Regular Session of the General Assembly of the ***** Held at St. Louis, Mo., January 14–17, 1879.* Terence Powderly Papers, microfilm edition. Glen Rock, N.J.: Microfilming Corporation of America, 1974.

Knights of Labor. *Record of the Proceedings of the Third Regular Session of the General Assembly Held at Chicago, Ill. Sept. 2–6, 1879.* Terence Powderly Papers, microfilm edition. Glen Rock, N.J.: Microfilming Corporation of America, 1974.

Knights of Labor. *Record of the Proceedings of the Fourth Regular Session of the General Assembly Held at Pittsburgh, Pa., Sept. 7–11, 1880,* Terence Powderly Papers, microfilm edition. Glen Rock, N.J.: Microfilming Corporation of America, 1974.

Knights of Labor. *Record of the Proceedings of the Sixth Regular Session of the General Assembly, Held at New York City, N.Y., Sept 5–12, 1882.* Terence Powderly Papers, microfilm edition. Glen Rock, N.J.: Microfilming Corporation of America, 1974.

Knights of Labor. *Record of the Proceedings of the Seventh Regular Session of the General Assembly, Held at Cincinnati, Ohio, Sept. 4–11, 1883.* Terence Powderly Papers, microfilm edition. Glen Rock, N.J.: Microfilming Corporation of America, 1974.

Knights of Labor. *Record of the Proceedings of the Eighth Regular Session of the General Assembly, Held at Philadelphia, PA, Sept. 1–10, 1884.* Terence Powderly Papers, microfilm edition. Glen Rock, N.J.: Microfilming Corporation of America, 1974.

Knights of Labor. *Record of the Proceedings of the Ninth Regular Session of the General Assembly, Held at Hamilton, Ontario, Oct. 5–13, 1885.* Terence Powderly Papers, microfilm editon. Glen Rock, N.J.: Microfilming Corporation of America, 1974.

Knights of Labor. *Record of the Proceedings of the Special Session of the General Assembly, Held at Cleveland, O., May 25 to June 3, 1886.* Terence Powderly Papers, microfilm editon. Glen Rock, N.J.: Microfilming Corporation of America, 1974.

Knights of Labor. *Record of the Proceedings of the Tenth Regular Session of the General Assembly, Held at Richmond, Va., Oct 4–20, 1886.* Terence Powderly Papers, microfilm edition. Glen Rock, N.J.: Microfilming Corporation of America, 1974.

Knights of Labor. *Record of the Proceedings of the General Assembly of the Knights of Labor of America. Eleventh Regular Session, Held at Minneapolis, Minnesota, October 4 to 19, 1887.* Terrence Powderly Papers, microfilm edition. Glen Rock, N.J.: Microfilming Corporation of America, 1974.

Knights of Labor. *Record of the Proceedings of the General Assembly of the Knights of Labor of America. Twelfth Regular Session. Held at Indianapolis, Indiana. November 13 to 27, 1888.* Terence Powderly Papers, microfilm edition. Glen Rock, N.J.: Microfilming Corporation of America, 1974.

Knights of Labor. *Record of the Proceedings of the Thirteenth Regular Session of the General Assembly Held at Atlanta, Ga., 1889.* Terence Powderly Papers, microfilm edition. Glen Rock, N.J.: Microfilming Corporation of America, 1974.

Knights of Labor, District Assembly 79. *Record of Proceedings of the Fifth Quarterly Meeting of D.A. 79, K. of L. Held At Mankato, Minnesota, January 16, 1887.* Minneapolis, Minn.: Thos. A. Clark & Co., 1887. Terence

Powderly Papers, microfilm editon. Glen Rock, N.J.: Microfilming Corporation of America, 1974.

Knights of Labor, District Assembly 79. *Record of Proceedings of the Twentieth Regular Meeting of D.A. 79, K. of L. Held at St. Paul, Minnesota. July 17, 1887.* John P. McGaughey Papers. Minnesota Historical Society, Madison.

Knights of Labor, District Assembly 79. *Record of Proceedings of the Twenty-First Regular Meeting of D.A. 79, K. of L. Held at Minneapolis, Minnesota, January 15, 1888.* Minneapolis, Minn.: Thos. A. Clark & Co. Terence Powderly Papers, microfilm edition. Glen Rock, N.J.: Microfilming Corporation of America, 1974.

Knights of Labor, District Assembly 79. *Record of Proceedings of the Twenty-Third Regular Meeting of D.A. 79, K. of L. Held at Minneapolis, Minnesota, January 20, 1889.* Minneapolis, Minn.: Thomas A. Clark & Co. Terence Powderly Papers, microfilm edition. Glen Rock, N.J.: Microfilming Corporation of America, 1974.

Knights of St. Crispin. *Proceedings of Third Annual Meeting of the International Grand Lodge of the Order of Knights of St. Crispin, Held in Boston, Massachusetts.* Milwaukee: Evening Wisconsin Book and Job Printing House, 1870. Wisconsin State Historical Society, Madison.

Knights of St. Crispin. *Report of the Special Committee on Co-operation to the International Grand Lodge, K.O.S.C., Adopted April 26th, 1871.* Lowell, Mass.: Stone & Huse Book Printers, 1871. Wisconsin State Historical Society, Madison.

Legislative Manual of the State of Minnesota. 1883. Minnesota Historical Society, St. Paul.

Manual of the General Court. 1875. Massachusetts. State House Library, Boston.

Massachusetts Bureau of the Statistics of Labor. *Annual Report.* 1870. In *State Labor Reports: from the first reports to 1900.* Westport, Conn.: Greenwood Press, 1976. Microfiche.

Massachusetts Bureau of the Statistics of Labor. *Annual Report.* 1871. In *State Labor Reports: from the first reports to 1900.* Westport, Conn.: Greenwood Press, 1976. Microfiche.

Massachusetts Bureau of the Statistics of Labor. *Annual Report.* 1875. In *State Labor Reports: from the first reports to 1900.* Westport, Conn.: Greenwood Press, 1976. Microfiche.

Massachusetts Bureau of the Statistics of Labor. *Annual Report.* 1877. In *State Labor Reports: from the first reports to 1900.* Westport, Conn.: Greenwood Press, 1976. Microfiche.

Massachusetts Bureau of the Statistics of Labor. *Annual Report.* 1886. In *State Labor Reports: from the first reports to 1900.* Westport, Conn.: Greenwood Press, 1976. Microfiche.

McNeill, George, ed. *The Labor Movement: The Problem of To-day.* New York: M. W. Hazen Co., 1887.

Minnesota Bureau of Labor Statistics. *First Biennial Report for the two years ending December 31, 1887–8.* In *State Labor Reports: from the first reports to 1900.* Westport, Conn.: Greenwood Press, 1976. Microfiche.

Official Historical Hand-Book Independent Order Knights of Labor. Jersey City, N.J.: Press of A. Datz, 1898. Knights of Labor Papers. Wisconsin State Historical Society, Madison.

Pennsylvania Bureau of Labor Statistics. *First Annual Report.* 1873. In *State Labor Reports: from the first reports to 1900.* Westport, Conn.: Greenwood Press, 1976. Microfiche.

"The Pioneers of North Adams." In *North Adams, Mass.* Troy, N.Y.: Troy Daily Times, 1890.

Powderly, Terence V. *The Path I Trod: An Autobiography.* New York: Columbia University Press, 1940.

———. *Thirty Years of Labor, 1859–1889.* New York: Augustus M. Kelley Publishers, 1967.

Record of Service of Stoneham Soldiers in the Civil War, 1861–1865. Stoneham, Mass.: Press of F. L. & W. E. Whittier, 1891.

Rhen, Isaac. "Defects of the Wages System." *Second Annual Report of the Bureau of Statistics of Pennsylvania, for the Years 1873–74.* Harrisburg, Penn.: B. F. Myers, State Printer, 1875.

Richardson, William, and George P. Sanger. *Supplement to the General Statutes of the Commonwealth of Massachusetts,* vol. 2, 1873–.

Shaw, Albert. "Cooperation in the Northwest." In *History of Cooperation in the United States,* edited by Herbert Adams, 199–366. Johns Hopkins University Studies in Historical and Political Science, vol. 6. Baltimore: Johns Hopkins University, 1888.

Spear, W. F. *History of North Adams, Mass., 1749–1885.* North Adams, Mass.: Hoosac Valley News Printing House, 1885.

Stevens, William B. *History of Stoneham Massachusetts with Biographical Sketches of Many of Its Pioneers and Prominent Men.* Stoneham, Mass.: F. L. & W. E. Whittier, 1891.

Stoneham City Directory. 1869, 1886–87, 1888–89. State Library of Massachusetts, Boston.

United States Tenth Census. *Statistics of the Population of the United States.* Washington, D.C.: Government Printing Office, 1881.

Valuation of the Town of Stoneham, and State, County, and Town Tax. 1867–89. Stoneham Historical Society, Stoneham, Mass.

Walker, Francis *A. Ninth Census-Volume 1. The Statistics of the Population of the United States.* Washington, D.C.: Government Printing Office, 1872.

Warner, Amos. "Three Phases of Co-operation in the West." In *History of Cooperation in the United States,* edited by Herbert Adams, 367–446. Johns Hopkins University Studies in Historical and Political Science, vol. 6. Baltimore: Johns Hopkins University, 1888

Wisconsin Bureau of Labor and Industrial Statistics. *Second Biennial Report, 1885–1886.* Madison, Wis.: Democrat Printing Co., State Printers, 1886.

Wright, Carroll D. *Compendium of the Census of Massachusetts: 1875.* Boston: Albert J. Wright, State Printer, 1877.

From: *Pamphlets in American History.* Microform Edition. Sanford, N.C.: Microfilming Corp. of America, 1979–84.

"Articles of Agreement and By-Laws of the Fall River Workingmen's Association. *Pamphlets in American History*. Cooperative Societies #97.

"By-Laws of M.W.C.A." *Pamphlets in American History*. Cooperative Societies #140.

"By-Laws of the Hennepin County Barrel Co. with Articles of Incorporation, Co-operative Laws of 1870 & Amendments." Minneapolis: Book Press of Chas. F. Young & Co., 1886. *Pamphlets in American History*. Co-operative Societies #99.

"Charter: Cooperative Store of Philadelphia." *Pamphlets in American History*. Cooperative Societies #122.

"Constitution and By-Laws of the Painesville Co-operative Boot and Shoe Manufacturing Association." 1869. *Pamphlets in American History*. Cooperative Societies #155.

"Constitution and By-Laws of the Trenton Cooperative Benefit Society, No. 1." *Pamphlets in American History*. Cooperative Societies #214.

"Constitution and By-Laws of the Troy Workingmen's Co-operative Association." *Pamphlets in American History*. Cooperative Societies #213.

"Co-operative Tract, No. 1." *Pamphlets in American History*. Cooperative Societies #20.

Giddings, Franklin Henry. "Twelve Principles of Cooperation." 1887. *Pamphlets in American History*. Cooperative Societies #35.

"The Industrial Co-operator." October 1880, vol 1, no. 1. *Pamphlets in American History*. Cooperative Societies #242.

"The Industrial Republic." *Pamphlets in American History*. Cooperative Societies #107.

"The Industrial Republic." *Pamphlets in American History*. Cooperative Societies #117.

"The Industrial Republic: Homes for All." *Pamphlets in American History*. Cooperative Societies #254.

"Journeymen Shoemakers' Co-operative Shoe Company Circular." *Pamphlets in American History*. Cooperative Societies #252.

"Laws of the Pennsylvania Co-operative General Trading and Manufacturing Association, Incorporated March 1st, 1876." *Pamphlets in American History*. Cooperative Societies #168.

"Our Girls' Co-operative Clothing Mfg. Co. of Chicago Illinois." *Pamphlets in American History*. Cooperative Societies #161.

Phillips, Thomas. "Grumblers." 1865. *Pamphlets in American History*. Cooperative Societies #31.

Rankin, James S. "Hard Times: Their Cause and Cure." *Pamphlets in American History*. Cooperative Societies #290.

"Ritual of the Industrial Republic." *Pamphlets in American History*. Cooperative Societies #115.

"Rules and Regulations of the Jewel Co-operative Knitting Co. of St. Louis, Mo." *Pamphlets in American History*. Cooperative Societies #111.

"Statements of Co-operative Associations, Certified to Secretary of Commonwealth as Organized under Chapter 290, Acts of 1866." Boston: Wright & Potter, State Printers, 1868. *Pamphlets in American History*. Cooperative Societies #134.

Dissertations, Papers, etc.

Abernathy Jr., John H. "The Knights of Labor in Alabama." Master's thesis, University of Alabama-Tuscaloosa, 1960.

Aldrich, Howard, and Robert N. Stern. "Resource Mobilization and the Creation of U.S. Producer's Cooperatives, 1835–1935." Unpublished paper. New York State School of Industrial and Labor Relations, Cornell University, January 1982.

Bennett, Richard B. "Crispins, Calvin and the Chinese." Master's thesis, Wesleyan University, 1986.

Cale, Edgar Barclay. "The Organization of Labor in Philadelphia, 1850–1870." Ph.D. diss., University of Pennsylvania, 1940.

Chung, Bowen. "Chinese in North Adams." Unpublished paper in possession of author.

Engberg, George. "The Rise of Organized Labor in Minnesota, 1850–1890." Master's thesis, University of Minnesota, May 1939.

Frank, Dana. "Labor's 'Cooperative Moment': Working-Class Cooperatives in Seattle, Washington, 1918–1922." Paper presented at International Conference on Consumer Cooperation in the Western World, 1840–1950: An Alternative to Capitalist Consumerism? University of Kansas, Lawrence, April 7, 1990.

Furlough, Ellen. "French Consumer Cooperation 1885–1930: From the 'Third Pillar' of Socialism to 'A Movement for All Consumers.'" Paper presented at the International Conference on Consumer Cooperation in the Western World, 1840–1950: An Alternative to Capitalist Consumerism? University of Kansas, Lawrence, April 7, 1990.

Goldberg, Judith Lazarus. "Strikes, Organizing, and Change: The Knights of Labor in Philadelphia, 1869–1890." Ph.D. diss., New York University, 1985.

Horner, Clare. "Producers' Co-operatives in the United States, 1865–1890." Ph.D. diss., University of Pittsburgh, 1978.

Leikin, Steven. "The Practical Utopians: Cooperation and the American Labor Movement, 1860–1890." Ph.D. diss., University of California, Berkeley, 1992.

Rozwenc, Edwin Charles. "Cooperatives Come to America: The History of the Protective Union Store Movement, 1845–1867." Ph.D. diss., Columbia University, 1941.

Turbin, Carol. "Women's Work and Woman's Rights: A Comparative Study of the Woman's Trade Union Movement and the Woman Suffrage Movement in the Mid-Nineteenth Century." Ph.D. diss., New School for Social Research, 1978.

Newspapers

American Workman.

Chicago Tribune.

Daily Evening Voice.

Fincher's Trades' Review.

Hoosac Valley News.
The Iron Molders' International Journal.
Journal of United Labor.
K.O.S.C. Monthly Journal.
Minneapolis Tribune.
Minnesota Mirror.
New York Tribune.
The North Adams Transcript.
The Northwestern Miller.
The Revolution.
St. Paul and Minneapolis Pioneer Press.
St. Paul Daily Globe.
Sovereigns of Industry. Bulletin!
Stoneham Amateur.
Stoneham Independent.
Workingman's Advocate.

Secondary Sources

Baron, Ava. "Gender and Labor History: Learning from the Past, Looking to the Future." In *Work Engendered: Toward a New History of American Labor,* edited by Ava Baron. Ithaca, N.Y.: Cornell University Press, 1991.

———. "Women and the Making of the American Working Class: A Study of the Proletarianization of Printers." *Review of Radical Political Economics* 14, no. 3 (1982): 23–42.

Baron, Ava. editor. *Work Engendered: Toward a New History of American Labor.* Ithaca, N.Y.: Cornell University Press, 1991.

Bender, Thomas. *Community and Social Change in America.* Baltimore: Johns Hopkins University Press, 1978.

Bestor, Arthur. *Backwoods Utopias: The Sectarian Origins and the Owenite Phase of Communitarian Socialism in America: 1663–1829.* Philadelphia: University of Pennsylvania Press, 1970.

Birchall, Johnston. *Co-op: The People's Business.* Manchester, UK: Manchester University Press, 1994.

Blaszak, Barbara. *George Jacob Holyoake (1817–1906) and the Development of the British Cooperative Movement.* Lewiston, N.Y.: Edwin Mellen Press, 1988.

Blewett, Mary. *Men, Women, and Work: Class, Gender, and Protest in the New England Shoe Industry, 1780–1910.* Urbana: University of Illinois Press, 1988.

———. "The Sexual Division of Labor and the Artisan Tradition in Early Industrial Capitalism: The Case of New England Shoemaking, 1780-1860." In *"To Toil the Livelong Day": America's Women at Work, 1780–1980,* edited by Carol Groneman and Mary Beth Norton. Ithaca, N.Y.: Cornell University Press, 1987.

Boston, Ray. *British Chartists in America.* Totowa, N.J.: Rowman and Littlefield, 1971.

Cassity, Michael. *Defending a Way of Life: An American Community in the*

Nineteenth Century. Albany: State University of New York Press, 1989.

Cebula, James E. *The Glory and Despair of Challenge and Change: A History of the Iron Molders' Union*. Cincinnati, Ohio: International Molders' and Allied Workers' Union, 1976.

Clark, Victor. *History of Manufactures in the United States*. Vol. 2. New York: McGraw-Hill Book Company, 1929.

Cole, G. D. H. *A Short History of the British Working Class Movement, 1789–1947*. London: George Allen & Unwin, 1948.

Commons, John R., David Saposs, Helen L. Sumner, E. B. Mittleman, H. E. Hoagland, John B. Andrews, and Selig Perlman. *History of Labor in the United States*. Vols. 1 and 2. New York: Macmillan Company, 1918.

Coons, Martha. "Section Two: Factories and Workers in the Nineteenth Century." In *Stoneham Massachusetts: A Shoe Town*. Stoneham, Mass.: Stoneham Historical Commission, 1981.

Cooper, Patricia. "Women Workers, Work Culture, and Collective Action in the American Cigar Industry, 1900–1919." In *Life and Labor: Dimensions of American Working-Class History*, edited by Charles Stephenson and Robert Asher. Albany: State University of New York Press, 1986.

Cornford, Daniel A. *Workers and Dissent in the Redwood Empire*. Philadelphia: Temple University Press, 1987.

Couvares, Franis G. *The Remaking of Pittsburgh: Class and Culture in an Industrializing City, 1877–1919*. Albany: State University of New York Press, 1984.

Cowling, Ellis. *Co-operatives in America: Their Past, Present and Future*. New York: Coward-McCann, 1943.

Coyne, Franklin E. *The Development of the Cooperage Industry in the United States, 1620–1940*. Chicago: Lumber Buyers Publishing Company, 1940.

Cross, Ira. *Twelfth Biennial Report of the Bureau of Labor and Industrial Statistics. Part 1, Cooperative Stores, State of Wisconsin, 1905–1906*. Madison, Wisc.: Democrat Printing Co., 1906.

Cumbler, John T. *Working-Class Community in Industrial America: Work, Leisure, and Struggle in Two Industrial Cities, 1880–1930*. Westport, Conn.: Greenwood Press, 1979.

Cummings, Scott, ed. *Self-Help in Urban America: Patterns of Minority Business Enterprise*. Port Washington, N.Y.: Kennikat Press, 1980.

Davis, Susan. *Parades and Power: Street Theatre in Nineteenth-Century Philadelphia*. Philadelphia: Temple University Press, 1986.

Dawley, Alan. *Class and Community: The Industrial Revolution in Lynn*. Cambridge: Harvard University Press, 2000.

Destler, Chester McArthur. *American Radicalism, 1865–1901*. Chicago: Quadrangle Books, 1966.

Dublin, Thomas. "Rural-Urban Migrants in Industrial New England: The Case of Lynn, Massachusetts, in the Mid-Nineteenth Century." *Journal of American History* 73, no. 3 (1986): 623–44.

Dubois, Ellen Carol. *Feminism and Suffrage: The Emergence of an Independent Women's Movement in America, 1848–1869*. Ithaca, N.Y.: Cornell Uni-

versity Press, 1978.
Dubofsky, Melvyn. *Industrialism and the American Worker, 1865–1920.* Arlington Heights, Illinois: Harlan Davidson, 1985.
Dubofsky, Melvyn, and Warren Van Tine, eds. *Labor Leaders in America.* Urbana: University of Illinois Press, 1987.
Dudden, Faye. "Small Town Knights: The Knights of Labor in Homer, New York." *Labor History* 28 (summer 1987): 307–27.
Engberg, George B. "The Knights of Labor in Minnesota." *Minnesota History* 22 (December 1941): 367–90.
Filson, Brent. "Calvin Sampson's Chinese Experiment." *Yankee Magazine*, February 1985, 93–137.
Fink, Leon. *In Search of the Working Class: Essays in American Labor History and Political Culture.* Urbana: University of Illinois Press, 1994.
———. "Looking Backward: Reflections on Workers' Culture and Certain Conceptual Dilemmas within Labor History." In *Perspectives on American Labor History: The Problems of Synthesis*, edited by J. Carroll Moody and Alice Kessler-Harris, 5–29. DeKalb: Northern Illinois University Press, 1989.
———. "The New Labor History and the Powers of Historical Pessimism: Consensus, Hegemony, and the Case of the Knights of Labor." *Journal of American History* 75, no. 1 (1988): 115–36.
———. *Workingmen's Democracy: The Knights of Labor and American Politics.* Urbana: University of Illinois Press, 1983.
Fite, Emerson. *Social and Industrial Conditions in the North during the Civil War.* New York: Frederick Unger Publishing Co., 1963.
Foner, Eric. *Politics and Ideology in the Age of the Civil War.* New York: Oxford University Press, 1980.
Foner, Philip. *History of the Labor Movement in the United States.* Vol. 1. New York: International Publishers, 1978.
———. *The History of the Labor Movement in the United States.* Vol. 2. New York: International Publishers, 1955.
Fones-Wolf, Ken. *Trade Union Gospel: Christianity and Labor in Industrial Philadelphia, 1865–1915.* Philadelphia: Temple University Press, 1989.
Forbath, William E. "The Ambiguities of Free Labor: Labor and the Law in the Gilded Age." *Wisconsin Law Review*, July/August (1985): 767–817.
Frank, Dana. "Gender, Consumer Organizing, and the Seattle labor Movement, 1919–1929." In *Work Endangered: Toward a New History of American Labor*, edited by Ava Baron, 273–96. Ithaca, N.Y.: Cornell University Press, 1991.
———. *Purchasing Power: Consumer Organizing, Gender, and the Seattle Labor Movement, 1919–1929.* Cambridge: Cambridge University Press, 1994.
Furlough, Ellen, and Carl Strikwerda, eds. *Consumers against Capitalism? Consumer Cooperation in Europe, North America, and Japan, 1840–1990.* New York: Rowman and Littlefield, 1999.
Galster, Augusta E. *The Labor Movement in the Shoe Industry; With Special Reference to Philadelphia.* New York: Ronald Press Company, 1924.

Garlock, Jonathan. *Guide to the Local Assemblies of the Knights of Labor.* Westport, Conn.: Greenwood Press, 1982.

Gerstle, Gary. "Ideas of the American Labor Movement, 1880–1950." In *Ideas, Ideologies, and Social Movements: The United States Experience since 1800,* edited by Peter A. Coclanis and Stuart Bruchey. Columbia: University of South Carolina Press, 1999.

Glickman, Lawrence. *A Living Wage: American Workers and the Making of Consumer Society.* Ithaca, N.Y.: Cornell University Press, 1997.

Gordon, David M., Richard Edwards, and Michael Reich. *Segmented Work, Divided Workers: The Historical Transformation of Labor in the United States.* New York: Cambridge University Press, 1982.

Grant, H. Roger. *Self-Help in the 1890s Depression.* Ames: Iowa State University Press, 1983.

Greenberg, Brian. *Worker and Community: Response to Industrialization in a Nineteenth-Century American City, Albany, New York, 1850–1884.* Albany: State University of New York Press, 1985.

Greenberg, Edward. *Workplace Democracy: The Political Effects of Participation.* Ithaca, N.Y.: Cornell University Press, 1986.

Grob, Gerald. *Workers and Utopia.* New York: Quadrangle/New York Times Book Company, 1969.

Groneman, Carol, and Mary Beth Norton, eds. *"To Toil the Livelong Day": America's Women at Work, 1780–1980.* Ithaca, N.Y.: Cornell University Press, 1987.

Grossman, Jonathan. "Co-operative Foundries." *New York History* April 1943. 196–210.

———. *William Sylvis: Pioneer of American Labor.* Columbia University Studies in History, Economics, and Public Law, no. 516. New York: Columbia University Press, 1945.

Guarneri, Carl J. *The Utopian Alternative: Fourierism in Nineteenth-Century America.* Ithaca, N.Y.: Cornell University Press, 1991.

Gurney, Peter. "George Jacob Holyoake: Socialism, Association and Cooperation in Nineteenth-Century England." In *New Views of Co-operation,* edited by Stephen Yeo, 52–72. London: Routledge, 1988.

———. "Labor's Great Arch: Cooperation and Cultural Revolution in Britain, 1795–1926." In *Consumers against Capitalism,* edited by Ellen Furlough and Carl Strikwerda, 135–72. New York: Rowman and Littlefield, 1999.

Gutman, Herbert G. "Class, Status, and Community Power in Nineteenth-Century American Industrial Cities, Paterson, New Jersey: A Case Study." In *Work, Culture, and Society in Industrializing America,* 234–60. London: Basil Blackwell, Oxford, 1976.

———. "Labor in the Land of Lincoln: Coal Miners on the Prairie." In *Power and Culture: Essays on the American Working Class,* 117–212. New York: Pantheon Books, 1987.

———. "The Labor Policies of the Large Corporation in the Gilded Age." In *Power and Culture: Essays on the American Working Class,* 213–54. New York: Pantheon Books, 1987.

———. "Protestantism and the American Labor Movement: The Christian

Spirit in the Gilded Age." In *Work, Culture and Society in Industrializing America*, 79–117. Oxford: Basil Blackwell, 1966.

———. "The Workers' Search for Power: Labor in the Gilded Age." In *Power and Culture: Essays on the American Working Class*, 70–92. New York: Pantheon Books, 1987.

Hanagan, Michael P., Leslie Page Moch, Wayne te Brake, eds. *Challenging Authority: The Historical Study of Contentious Politics*. Minneapolis: University of Minnesota Press, 1998.

Hayden, Dolores. *The Grand Domestic Revolution: A History of Feminist Designs for American Homes, Neighborhoods, and Cities*. Cambridge, Mass.: MIT Press, 1981.

Haydu, Jeffrey. *Between Craft and Class: Skilled Workers and Factory Politics in the United States and Britain, 1890–1922*. Berkeley: University of California Press, 1988.

Hoagland, H. E. "The Rise of the Iron Molders' International Union." *American Economic Review* 3 (June 1913): 296–313.

Ignatiev, Noel. *How the Irish Became White*. New York: Routledge, 1995.

Jackall, Robert, and Henry M. Levin. *Worker Cooperatives in America*. Berkeley: University of California Press, 1984.

Jacob, Margaret, and John Jacob. *The Origins of Anglo-American Radicalism*. London: George Allen & Unwin, 1984.

Jacobson, Matthew Frye. *Whiteness of a Different Color: European Immigrants and the Alchemy of Race*. Cambridge: Harvard University Press, 1998.

Jones, Derek C. "American Producer Cooperatives and Employee-Owned Firms: A Historical Perspective." In *Worker Cooperatives in America*, edited by Robert Jackall and Henry M. Levin, 37–56. Berkeley: University of California Press, 1984.

———. "The Economics and Industrial Relations of Producer Cooperatives in the United States, 1791–1939." *Economic Analysis and Workers' Management* 11, no. 3/4 (1977): 295–317.

Kane, Lucile M. *The Waterfall that Built a City*. St. Paul. Minn.: Minnesota Historical Society, 1966.

Kealey, Gregory, and Bryan Palmer. *Dreaming of What Might Be: The Knights of Labor in Ontario*. Cambridge: Cambridge University Press, 1982.

Keillor, Steve. "The Farm that Wouldn't Cooperate." *Lake County Journal* 2 (January 1998): 47.

Kessler-Harris, Alice. "Independence and Virtue in the Lives of Wage-Earning Women, The United States, 1870–1930." In *Women in Culture and Politics: A Century of Change*, edited by Judith Friedlander, Blanche Weisen Cook, Alice Kessler-Harris, and Carroll Smith-Rosenberg, 3–17. Bloomington: Indiana University Press, 1986.

———. *Out to Work: A History of Wage-Earning Women in the United States*. Oxford: Oxford University Press, 1982.

———. *A Woman's Wage: Historical Meanings and Social Consequences*. Lexington: University of Kentucky Press, 1990.

Keyssar, Alexander. *Out of Work: The First Century of Unemployment in Massachusetts*. Cambridge: Cambridge University Press, 1986.

Knapp, Joseph G. *The Rise of American Cooperative Enterprise: 1620–1920*.

Danville, Ill.: Interstate Printers and Publishers, 1969.

Kramnick, Isaac, "Republican Revisionism Revisited." *American Historical Review* 87, no. 3 (1982): 629–64.

Lancaster, Bill. *Radicalism, Cooperation and Socialism: Leicester Working-Class Politics 1860–1906.* Leicester, UK: Leicester University Press, 1987.

Laslette, John H. M. "Samuel Gompers and the Rise of American Business Unionism." In *Labor Leaders in America,* edited by Melvyn Dubofsky and Warren Van Tine, 62–88. Urbana: University of Illinois Press, 1987.

Laurie, Bruce. *Artisans into Workers: Labor in Nineteenth-Century America.* New York: Noonday Press, 1989.

———. *Working People of Philadelphia, 1800–1850.* Philadelphia: Temple University Press, 1980.

Laurie, Bruce, and Mark Schmitz. "Manufacture and Productivity: The Making of an Industrial Base, Philadelphia, 1850–1880." In *Philadelphia: Work, Space, Family, and Group Experience in the 19th Century,* edited by Theodore Hershberg, 43–92. Oxford: Oxford University Press, 1981.

Lazerow, Jama. "Religion and Labor Reform in Antebellum America: The World of William Field Young." *American Quarterly* 38 (1986): 265–86.

Leikin, Steven. "The Citizen Producer: The Rise and Fall of Working-Class Cooperatives in the United States." In *Consumers against Capitalism? Consumer Cooperation in Europe, North America, and Japan, 1840–1990,* edited by Ellen Furlough and Carl Strikwerda, 93–113. New York: Rowman and Littlefield Publishers, 1999.

Lescohier, Don D. *The Knights of St. Crispin, 1867–1874: A Study in the Industrial Causes of Trade Unionism.* Bulletin of the University of Wisconsin, no. 355, Economics and Political Science Series, vol. 7, no. 1, 1910. Madison: University of Wisconsin, 1910.

Levine, Susan. *Labor's True Woman: Carpet Weavers, Industrialization, and Labor Reform in the Gilded Age.* Philadelphia: Temple University Press, 1984.

———. "Labor's True Woman: Domesticity and Equal Rights in the Knights of Labor." *Journal of American History* 70 (September 1983): 323–39.

LeWarne, Charles Pierce. *Utopias on Puget Sound, 1885–1915.* Seattle: University of Washington Press, 1975.

McBride, John. "Coal Miners." In *The Labor Movement: The Problem of Today,* edited by George McNeill, 241–67. Boston: A. M. Bridgman & Co., 1886.

McDougall, Harold. *Black Baltimore: A New Theory of Community.* Philadelphia: Temple University Press, 1993.

McLaurin, Melton. *The Knights of Labor in the South.* Westport, Conn.: Greenwood Press, 1978.

McPherson, James. *Battle Cry of Freedom: The Civil War Era.* New York: Oxford University Press, 1988. Balantine Books Edition.

Merril, Marion. "The Startling Tale of C. T. Sampson." *North Adams Transcript Supplement.* August 4, 1978.

Messer-Kruse, Timothy. *The Yankee International: Marxism and the American Reform Tradition, 1848–1876.* Chapel Hill: University of North Carolina Press, 1998.

Montgomery, David. *Beyond Equality: Labor and the Radical Republicans, 1862–1872.* Urbana: University of Illinois Press, 1981.

———. *Citizen Worker: The Experience of Workers in the United States with Democracy and the Free Market during the Nineteenth Century.* Cambridge: Cambridge University Press, 1993.

———. *Fall of the House of Labor: The Workplace, the State, and American Labor Activism, 1865–1925.* Cambridge: Cambridge University Press, 1987.

———. "Strikes in Nineteenth-Century America." *Social Science History* 4 (February 1980): 81–104.

———. "William H. Sylvis and the Search for Working-Class Citizenship." In *Labor Leaders in America,* edited by Melvyn Dubofsky and Warren Van Tine, 3–29. Urbana: University of Illinois Press, 1987.

———. *Workers' Control in America: Studies in the History of Work, Technology, and Labor Struggles.* Cambridge: Cambridge University Press, 1979.

Moody, J. Carroll, and Alice Kessler-Harris, eds. *Perspectives on American Labor History: The Problems of Synthesis.* Dekalb: Northern Illinois University Press, 1989.

Nelson, Bruce. *Divided We Stand: American Workers and the Struggle for Black Equality.* Princeton, N.J.: Princeton University Press, 2001.

Nourse, Edwin G. *The Legal Status of Agricultural Co-operation.* New York: MacMillan Company, 1927.

Oestreicher, Richard. *Solidarity and Fragmentation: Working People and Class Consciousness in Detroit, 1875–1900.* Urbana: University of Illinois Press, 1986.

———. "Terence V. Powderly, the Knights of Labor, and Artisanal Republicanism." In *Labor Leaders in America,* edited by Melvyn Dubofsky and Warren Van Tine, 30–61. Urbana: University of Illinois Press, 1987.

Parker, Florence E. *The First 125 Years: A History of Distributive and Service Cooperation in the United States, 1829–1954.* Superior, Wisconsin: Cooperative Publishing Association, 1956.

Phelan, Craig. *Grand Master Workman: Terence Powderly and the Knights of Labor.* Westport, Conn.: Greenwood Press, 2000.

Pollard, Sidney. "Nineteenth-Century Co-operation: From Community Building to Shopkeeping." In *Essays in Labour History,* edited by Asa Briggs and John Saville, 74–112. London: MacMillan & Co. Ltd., 1960.

Rachleff, Peter. *Black Labor in Richmond, 1865–1890.* Urbana: University of Illinois Press, 1989.

Rodgers, Daniel T. *The Work Ethic in Industrial America, 1850–1920.* Chicago: University of Chicago Press, 1979.

Roediger, David. *The Wages of Whiteness: Race and the Making of the American Working Class.* New York: Verso, 1991.

Rorabaugh, W. J. "Who Fought for the North in the Civil War? Concord, Massachusetts, Enlistments." *Journal of American History* 73, no. 3

(1986): 695–701.
Ross, Steven J. *Workers on the Edge: Work, Leisure, and Politics in Industrializing Cincinnati, 1788–1890.* New York: Columbia University Press, 1985.
Rudolph, Frederick. "Chinamen in Yankeedom: Anti-Unionism in Massachusetts in 1870." *American Historical Review* 51 (October 1947): 1–29.
Salvatore, Nick. *Eugene V. Debs: Citizen and Socialist.* Urbana: University of Illinois Press, 1982.
Schneirov, Richard. *Labor and Urban Politics: Class Conflict and the Origins of Modern Liberalism in Chicago, 1864–97.* Urbana: University of Illinois Press, 1998.
Schneirov, Richard, and Thomas J. Suhrbur. *Union Brotherhood, Union Town: The History of the Carpenters' Union of Chicago, 1863–1987.* Carbondale: Southern Illinois University Press, 1988.
Scott, Joan. *Gender and the Politics of History.* New York: Columbia University Press, 1988.
Shefter, Martin. "Trade Unions and Political Machines: The Organization and Disorganization of the American Working Class in the Late Nineteenth Century." In *Working-Class Formation: Nineteenth-Century Patterns in Western Europe and the United States,* edited by Ira Katznelson and Aristide R. Zolberg, 197–276. Princeton, N.J.: Princeton University Press, 1986.
Spann, Edward K. *Brotherly Tomorrows: Movements for a Cooperative Society in America, 1820–1920.* New York: Columbia University Press, 1989.
Stipanovich, Joseph. *City of Lakes: An Illustrated History of Minneapolis.* Woodland Hills, Calif.:Windsor Publications, 1982.
Stockton, Frank. "Productive Cooperation in the Molders' Union." *American Economic Review* 21, no. 2 (1931): 260–74.
Stromquist, Shelton. *A Generation of Boomers: The Pattern of Railroad Labor Conflict in Nineteenth-Century America.* Urbana: University of Illinois, 1987.
Takaki, Ron. *Strangers from a Different Shore: A History of Asian Americans.* New York: Penguin Books, 1989.
Turbin, Carole. *Working Women of Collar City: Gender, Class and Community in Troy, New York, 1864–1886.* Urbana: University of Illinois Press, 1992.
Vinovskis, Maris A., ed. *Toward a Social History of the American Civil War: Exploratory Essays.* Cambridge: Cambridge University Press, 1990.
Virtue, G. O. "The Co-operative Coopers of Minneapolis." *Quarterly Journal of Economics* 19 (August 1905): 527–44.
———. "The End of the Cooperative Coopers." *Quarterly Journal of Economics* 46 (May 1932): 541–45.
Voss, Kim. "Claim Making and the Framing of Defeats: The Interpretation of Losses by American and British Labor Activists, 1886–1895." In *Challenging Authority: The Historical Study of Contentious Politics,* edited by Michael P. Hanagan, Leslie Page Moch, and Wayne te Brake, 136–48. Minneapolis: University of Minnesota Press, 1998.
———. "Labor Organization and Class Alliance: Industries, Communities, and the Knights of Labor." *Theory and Society* 17 (1988): 329–64.

———. *The Making of American Exceptionalism: The Knights of Labor and Class Formation in the Nineteenth Century*. Ithaca, N.Y.: Cornell University Press, 1993.

Walker, Juliet E. K. *The History of Black Business in America: Capitalism, Race, Entrepreneurship*. New York: Simon & Schuster Macmillan, 1998.

Walkowitz, Daniel. *Worker City, Company Town: Iron and Cotton-Worker Protest in Troy and Cohoes, New York, 1855–1884*. Urbana: University of Illinois Press, 1981.

Wallace, Anthony F. C. *St. Clair: A Nineteenth-Century Coal Town's Experience with a Disaster-Prone Industry*. Ithaca, N.Y.: Cornell University Press, 1987.

Ware, Norman. *The Industrial Worker, 1840–1860: The Reaction of American Industrial Society to the Advance of the Industrial Revolution*. New York: Quadrangle/New York Times Book Co., 1964.

———. *The Labor Movement in the United States, 1860–1895*. New York: Vintage Books, 1929.

Webb, Sidney, and Beatrice Webb. *The Consumers' Cooperative Movement*. London: Longmans, Green and Co., 1921.

Weinstein, Gregory. *The Ardent Eighties: Reminiscences of an Interesting Decade*. New York: International Press, 1929.

Weir, Robert. *Beyond Labor's Veil: The Culture of the Knights of Labor*. University Park: Pennsylvania State University Press, 1996.

———. *Knights Unhorsed: Internal Conflict in a Gilded Age Social Movement*. Detroit: Wayne State University Press, 2000.

Wilentz, Sean. *Chants Democratic: New York City and the Rise of the American Working Class, 1788–1850*. New York: Oxford University Press, 1984.

Yearley, Clifton K., Jr. *Britons in American Labor: A History of the Influence of the United Kingdom Immigrants on American Labor, 1820–1914*. Johns Hopkins University Studies in Historical and Political Science, series 75, no. 1. Baltimore: Johns Hopkins University Press, 1957.

———. "Thomas Phillips: A Yorkshire Shoemaker in Philadelphia." *Pennsylvania Magazine of History and Biography* 79 (April 1955).

Yellowitz, Irwin. *Industrialization and the American Labor Movement, 1850–1900*. Port Washington, N.Y.: Kennikat Press, 1977.

Yeo, Stephen, ed. *New Views of Co-operation*. London: Routledge, 1988.

Zink, Harold. *City Bosses in the United States*. Durham, N.C.: Duke University Press, 1930.

Index

www.ingramcontent.com/pod-product-compliance
Lightning Source LLC
LaVergne TN
LVHW010355080826
844660LV00016B/975/J

* 9 7 8 0 8 1 4 3 3 1 2 8 6 *